About Wolters Kluwer Law & Business

Wolters Kluwer Law & Business is a leading provider of research information and workflow solutions in key specialty areas. The strengths of the individual brands of Aspen Publishers, CCH, Kluwer Law International and Loislaw are aligned within Wolters Kluwer Law & Business to provide comprehensive, in-depth solutions and expert-authored content for the legal, professional and education markets.

CCH was founded in 1913 and has served more than four generations of business professionals and their clients. The CCH products in the Wolters Kluwer Law & Business group are highly regarded electronic and print resources for legal, securities, antitrust and trade regulation, government contracting, banking, pension, payroll, employment and labor, and healthcare reimbursement and compliance professionals.

Aspen Publishers is a leading information provider for attorneys, business professionals and law students. Written by preeminent authorities, Aspen products offer analytical and practical information in a range of specialty practice areas from securities law and intellectual property to mergers and acquisitions and pension/benefits. Aspen's trusted legal education resources provide professors and students with high-quality, up-to-date and effective resources for successful instruction and study in all areas of the law.

Kluwer Law International supplies the global business community with comprehensive English-language international legal information. Legal practitioners, corporate counsel and business executives around the world rely on the Kluwer Law International journals, loose-leafs, books and electronic products for authoritative information in many areas of international legal practice.

Loislaw is a premier provider of digitized legal content to small law firm practitioners of various specializations. Loislaw provides attorneys with the ability to quickly and efficiently find the necessary legal information they need, when and where they need it, by facilitating access to primary law as well as state-specific law, records, forms and treatises.

Wolters Kluwer Law & Business, a unit of Wolters Kluwer, is headquartered in New York and Riverwoods, Illinois. Wolters Kluwer is a leading multinational publisher and information services company.

CHECK OUT THESE OTHER GREAT TITLES

Friedman's Practice Series

Outlining Is Important But PRACTICE MAKES PERFECT!

All Content Written By *Top Professors* • 100 Multiple Choice Questions • Comprehensive *Professor* Answers and Analysis for Multiple Choice Questions • *Real Law School* Essay Exams • Comprehensive *Professor* Answers for Essay Exams

Available titles in this series include:

Friedman's Administrative Law

Friedman's Bankruptcy

Friedman's Civil Procedure

Friedman's Constitutional Law

Friedman's Contracts

Friedman's Criminal Law

Friedman's Criminal Procedure

Friedman's Property

Friedman's Torts

Friedman's Wills, Trusts, and Estates

ASK FOR THEM AT YOUR LOCAL BOOKSTORE
IF UNAVAILABLE, PURCHASE ONLINE AT *www.AspenLaw.com*

About the Editor

Joel Wm. Friedman
Tulane Law School
Jack M. Gordon Professor of Procedural Law & Jurisdiction,
   Director of Technology
BS, 1972, Cornell University; JD, 1975, Yale University

Professor Joel Wm. Friedman, the Jack M. Gordon Professor of Procedural Law & Jurisdiction at Tulane Law School, is the lead author of two highly regarded casebooks — "The Law of Civil Procedure: Cases and Materials" (published by Thomson/West) and "The Law of Employment Discrimination" (published by Foundation Press). His many law review articles have been published in, among others, the Cornell, Texas, Iowa, Tulane, Vanderbilt, and Washington & Lee Law Reviews.

Professor Friedman is an expert in computer assisted legal instruction who has lectured throughout the country on how law schools can integrate developing technologies into legal education. He is a past recipient of the Felix Frankfurter Teaching Award and the Sumpter Marks Award for Scholarly Achievement.

TABLE OF CONTENTS

BANKRUPTCY
ESSAY EXAMINATION
QUESTIONS

BANKRUPTCY ESSAY EXAM #1 [CHAPTER 7]

Joel and Vivian Manfried are married and live in Ohio. They own a home there and a beach house in North Carolina where they often vacation. The Ohio home is held by them as joint tenants with no provision for right of survivorship and is encumbered. They own the North Carolina beach house, which Vivian inherited years ago, "free and clear" as joint tenants by the entirety.

During the last 18 months or so, the couple has spent considerably more time at the beach because Joel has been caring for his uncle, Steve Hummel, who lives in North Carolina. Uncle Steve has been very ill and depends on Joel to support and care for him.

Joel feels a special responsibility for Uncle Steve, whose illness stems from injuries suffered in a car wreck. He was riding with Joel who was texting while driving. Their car collided with another vehicle. Uncle Steve and the other driver were hurt. They both had causes of action against Joel, which Uncle Steve never pursued. The other driver sued Joel for malicious negligence and won a judgment for $50,000 in compensatory damages and $50,000 in punitive damages.

Uncle Steve's care has been very expensive. Hospital and doctors' bills are high and keep climbing. Joel and Vivian have financed some of the cost using their 12 credit cards, most of which the couple obtained for this very purpose. Now, as they expected, the cards have "maxed out." The available credit on every card has been exhausted.

So, Joel decided to withdraw money from his tax-qualified, 401K retirement account, which contains about $375,000. However, the size of the withdrawal penalty convinced Joel to look elsewhere for financial help.

Therefore, Joel and Vivian took out a second mortgage for $100,000 on their Ohio home. The market value of the property (unencumbered) at the time was $300,000. The balance owed on the first mortgage was $200,000. They used the loan proceeds partly for Uncle Steve's care; to pay tuition for their children to attend Agnon, a private, religious school; and about $20,000 to refurbish the basement of the Ohio home just in case Uncle Steve's health deteriorates and he moves in with them. Refurbishing the basement increased the market value of the home to $320,000.

Just when this money was exhausted, Vivian lost her job, seriously reducing the couple's cash flow. They could not fully pay monthly house and car payments, installment payments to the judgment creditor, student loans, credit card bills, the children's educational expenses, and everything else.

Finally, just a few months later, Joel and Vivian sought advice from a bankruptcy lawyer, Erick Burnett. He advised them to file a Chapter 7 case but only after taking $21,900 from Joel's 401K and using the proceeds to pay Mr. Burnett's fee of $1500 and the balance to pay down the debt on the first mortgage, which at the time was $200,000.

Burnett also advised the Manfrieds to trade in their old car, buy a new vehicle, and finance the purchase price and any negative equity on the trade-in. The lawyer explained that increasing secured debt can help prevent converting the case to Chapter 13; and, in any event, the direct and indirect costs of the old car made it very expensive to operate.

The Manfrieds took Burnett's advice:

- They withdrew $21,900 from the 401K, leaving a balance (after penalty and taxes) of around $300,000. They used the $21,900 to pay Burnett's $1500 fee and applied the remaining $20,400 on the first mortgage, which reduced the first mortgage debt to $179,600.
- They also traded in their stretch Hummer for a hybrid Ford, which Ford Credit financed. The financing was backed by a perfected, Article 9 security interest in the vehicle. The value of the vehicle equaled the secured debt. The monthly car payments increased, but immediate and long-term operating costs decreased.

Burnett filed the Manfrieds' joint Chapter 7 bankruptcy case in the federal district of Ohio where the debtors lived.

The principal exemptions under Ohio law (Ohio Rev. Code tit. 23, §2329.66) include a debtor's interest in a homestead not to exceed $20,200 in value; the person's interest, not to exceed $3225, in one motor vehicle; and the person's right in the assets held in, or to receive any payment under, any individual retirement account, individual retirement annuity, "Roth IRA," or education individual retirement account that provides benefits by reason of illness, disability, death, or age. Ohio law also provides: "Pursuant to the 'Bankruptcy Reform Act of 1978,' 92 Stat. 2549, 522, this state specifically does not authorize debtors who are domiciled in this state to exempt the property specified in the 'Bankruptcy Reform Act of 1978,' 92 Stat. 2549, 522." *Id.* §2329.662.

QUESTION #1 (20%)

Estate Property and Avoidance

a) What property will initially fill the bankruptcy estate?
b) Can the trustee recover and keep for the estate any property transferred before bankruptcy was filed?

QUESTION #2 (30%)

Exemptions and Choice of Law

a) What source of law governs the debtors' choice of exemptions?
b) Without considering the North Carolina house, what property can the debtors exempt?
c) Can the debtors exempt the North Carolina house?

QUESTION #3 (25%)

Debts and Discharge

a) To whom and in what order will the trustee distribute the proceeds of the property?
b) Which debts will be discharged?

QUESTION #4 (25%)

Dismissal and Accountability

a) Are there substantial grounds for arguing, in good faith, to dismiss the Manfrieds' Chapter 7 case?
b) Did lawyer Burnett make any serious mistakes in planning the Manfrieds' bankruptcy and handling the case?

BANKRUPTCY ESSAY EXAM #2 [CHAPTER 7]

Max Murphy operates a wrecker service. He specializes in towing heavy-duty vehicles, such as over-the-road tractors and trailers and road construction equipment. These days, however, he'll tow anything. Recently, he towed a wrecked car from North Carolina to Ohio. The owner of the car, Joel Manfried, still owes Max $1000 for the work.

Max's two children and brother work for him in the business, which operates as an unincorporated sole proprietorship.

Business has been slow. A bad economy means fewer goods to distribute by truck and less money to spend on road projects, which means fewer trucks on the road and fewer construction vehicles on the job. As a result, there are fewer breakdowns and less work for Max.

Max laid off all of his non-family employees and still owes them earned wages. He sold two of his trucks (001 and 002) for much less than he wanted and expected. Both of these trucks were separately encumbered by Article 9 security interests held by Bank. Max did not ask Bank's permission to sell the collateral and thereby violated the terms of the security agreements, and he didn't remit the proceeds to Bank. He kept and spent the money for personal and business uses.

Max's other three trucks (003, 004, and 005) were also subject to security interests held by another secured party, Lender. Lender repossessed two of these trucks (003 and 004); sold one of the trucks (003) for half its value at a public auction; and still held the other truck (004), which it was preparing to sell.

The building where Max operated his business was rented under a month-to-month lease. He had defaulted, owed back rent, and, by its own terms, the lease had terminated.

Max's terrible financial situation had broken his marriage. He and his wife had split. They had not yet divorced, but she was living elsewhere and working on her master's degree. Max had unilaterally promised her monthly payments of $1000 to supplement her earnings from various part-time jobs.

Max was desperate. The value of the car he used for every purpose, including personal, family, and household purposes, is far less than the amount of the GMAC loan that the car secures. The house that he and his wife jointly owned was in an up-and-coming neighborhood, but the first and second mortgages left no equity in the property.

In a final effort to keep things going, Max got an unsecured loan from Third Bank by convincing his brother to cosign the note. Using this money, he tried to operate the business by himself, driving his last remaining truck (005). Finally, just before the economy and the wrecking business picked up, Max ran out of money.

And, Max's wife, Mary, filed for divorce.

Max properly filed Chapter 7 bankruptcy and in doing so filed everything the law requires, but he didn't expect to go through with the case. He imagined that staying creditor action would give his business the few more months needed to "turn the corner." He reasoned that by this point, business would have returned, and he would have worked out his financial problems with creditors. Then, he could dismiss the bankruptcy case.

Immediately, Lender filed a motion to lift stay with respect to Max's last, remaining truck (005).

QUESTION #1 (10%)

Property of the Estate and Avoidance

a) What property initially filled the bankruptcy estate?
b) Is any property Max owned before bankruptcy included in the estate?

QUESTION #2 (25%)

Automatic Stay

a) Does the stay prevent Third Bank from suing or otherwise acting to collect from Max the loan on which the brother was liable with Max as surety?
b) Can Lender sell truck 004, which Lender had already repossessed before Max filed bankruptcy?
c) How should the court decide Lender's motion to lift the stay to enforce its security interest in truck 005?
d) Is Mary's divorce action against Max stayed?

QUESTION #3 (15%)

Claims Against the Estate

Describe the nature of these persons' claims against the bankruptcy estate.

a) Bank's claims
b) Lender's claims
c) Landlord's claim
d) GMAC's claim
e) Mortgagees' claims
f) Brother's claim
g) Wife's claims
h) Employees' claims

QUESTION #4 (25%)

Scope and Effect of the Discharge

How does the bankruptcy discharge in Max's case affect these claims?

a) Secured claims (over and under)

b) Bank's claim for conversion (basis for "objecting" to discharge or "excepting" the debt)

c) Third Bank's claim against Max's brother as a surety on the loan to Max (a/k/a effect of discharge on third-party nondebtors)

QUESTION #5 (25%)

Dismissal of the Case

a) Can Max freely dismiss the bankruptcy case?

b) Could the court dismiss the case *sua sponte* or on motion of a party in interest?

BANKRUPTCY ESSAY EXAM #3 [CHAPTER 13]

Steve Hummel lived in Wilmington, North Carolina, right on the beach. His house is a converted lighthouse. The location is perfect. The market value of the house is high, but the property is subject to a mortgage owned by Bank of America (BofA). There is substantial equity, which Steve wants to keep, but the mortgage payments are nevertheless burdensome for Steve, which is a problem heightened by his medical history.

Steve has not worked very much during the last year because of injuries and illness resulting from an accident. He was riding in a car driven by his nephew, Joel Manfried, who lost control while text messaging. Their car collided with another vehicle. Steve and the other driver were injured.

The other driver sued for malicious negligence and won a judgment for $50,000 in compensatory damages and $50,000 in punitive damages. Despite being a guest in Joel's car, Steve has a possible cause of action himself against Joel but has not pursued it.

Ever since the accident, Joel had provided considerable care and support for Steve. Recently, however, the money from Joel stopped because Joel and his wife filed Chapter 7 bankruptcy.

Unfortunately, despite Joel's aid, Steve had accumulated a crushing amount of medical and other debt. Also, Steve is behind on his mortgage and had purchased a new truck and travel trailer, an Airstream. Ford Credit financed the total purchase price of the new truck and trailer and associated costs, including the negative equity on the vehicle Steve traded in. Almost from the start, the amount of the secured debt exceeded the value of the collateral, and the gap will almost surely continue to widen even as Steve makes the required payments.

Buying the truck and trailer was part of Steve's plan to better his financial situation. He had decided to turn the beach house into income property; hire a real estate management company to rent the place to vacationers; buy a cheap, inland lot; and live there most of the time in the new Airstream, which Steve would also use as his moving vacation home pulled behind the new truck.

The plan was good. The timing was bad. It was late September, the beginning of the off season for vacation rentals on the North Carolina beach. Steve can expect no substantial net income until next spring and summer. He could possibly rent the place for several weeks in the fall and winter but this would not bring in enough to cover costs.

Fortunately, Steve's health had sufficiently recovered so that he could return to work as a systems engineer making $55,000 a year. He also makes some money from a few investments in regional companies, such as Midwest Medical Widgets, Inc. (MMW), from which Steve historically receives from $1500 to $2500 in dividends every quarter.

This income alone, however, is doubtfully or, at best, barely sufficient to pay all his actual expenses and live comfortably. And, at this point, Steve is living in the trailer but it is parked in his brother-in-law's backyard. With a secured purchase money loan from local Bank, supplemented by a second mortgage from Coastal Finance that covered the down payment, Steve had purchased an inland lot where he will eventually permanently park his little home, but he hasn't moved there because utilities have not been connected to the property.

Steve visited a local bankruptcy lawyer, Chloe Burnett, in Wilmington. (Her father, Erick Burnett, practices bankruptcy in Ohio.) Ms. Burnett thinks bankruptcy is a good idea for Steve but not Chapter 7. She thinks Chapter 13 is the better and perhaps the only choice for Steve. She's filing one or the other kind of case today.

QUESTION #1 (25%)

Choosing Between Chapter 7 and Chapter 13

a) Why does Ms. Burnett believe Chapter 13 is better for Steve than Chapter 7?
b) Why does Ms. Burnett believe Chapter 13 may be Steve's only choice?

QUESTION #2 (50%)

Aspects of the Chapter 13 Plan

a) Outline the overall structure and likely main components of Steve's Chapter 13 plan.
b) Can the plan "strip down" Ford Credit's security interest to the value of the collateral (the new car and trailer)?
c) How much, if any, interest is paid on Ford Credit's secured claim?
d) Explain (i) how the circumstances in Steve's case could possibly result in Ms. Burnett proposing a "zero percent" plan for her client and (ii) whether or not the court will likely confirm such a plan over the creditors' objections.

QUESTION #3 (25%)

Post-Confirmation Issues

a) Before payments under the plan are completed, can Steve obtain credit to finance the acquisition or improvement of property or services?
b) Is there any effect on the Chapter 13 case if after a year or so, the lighthouse becomes a successful investment and creates a source of substantial income for Steve?
c) Is there any effect on the Chapter 13 case if after a year or so, a hurricane washes away the lighthouse and all vacation rentals, the MMW dividends drop to zero, or Steve loses his job?

BANKRUPTCY ESSAY EXAM #4 [CHAPTER 13]

Midwest Medical Widgets, Inc. (MMW) is a Delaware corporation doing business mainly in the southeastern United States. A bad economy and uncertainty about new federal laws "reforming" health care have suddenly slowed business and caused layoffs.

One victim is Elizabeth Jack, who had worked 10 years for MMW as a corporate communications specialist and was abruptly "let go" by the company several months ago. She lost her $80,000 a year salary and benefits and was left with a severance package that included a cash allowance equaling two months of salary and a six-month contract for the services of a third-party, professional career coach.

She suspects that her termination was discriminatory, based on her gender and religion.

Ms. Jack owns a home and two vehicles: a Lexus and a Jeep. The home is subject to three mortgages. The value of the house supports fully only the first mortgage. The second mortgage is undersecured, and the third mortgage is completely unsecured. She has missed several payments on the first mortgage, which is the biggest debt with the largest payments.

The Jeep is unencumbered, but the Lexus is subject to a perfected security interest favoring Bank.

Ms. Jack's three credit cards are loaded. She has other, unpaid bills for utilities, medical costs, and some back taxes. She owes a sizeable student loan and is liable on a recent, unsecured note to her parents.

Fortunately, three months after leaving MMW, Ms. Jack found another, somewhat comparable job. However, because of oversupply in the labor market, the new salary is only $50,000 a year, which is $30,000 a year less than she earned at MMW. Plus, the new job has no benefits.

A friend, Kate Epstein, who is also a lawyer, advised Ms. Jack to file Chapter 13 bankruptcy and agreed to represent her in the case.

Elements of the proposed Chapter 13 plan include:

— preserving the first mortgage (which has 20 years to run) and continuing to pay the first mortgage, as usual, in monthly installments according to the unmodified terms of the mortgage; and stripping away completely the second and third mortgages so that both debts are totally unsecured;

— eliminating or substantially reducing the principal of the student loan;

— separately classifying the reduced student loan and the note to her parents and paying these claims fully while paying as little as possible toward other unsecured claims;

— reducing the disposable income paid to satisfy unsecured claims by deducting ownership and operating expenses for the Jeep, even though Ms. Jack owns the vehicle; and

— doing the same with respect to the Lexus, even though Ms. Jack plans to surrender it.

QUESTION #1 (20%)

Providing for the Three Mortgage Debts in the Chapter 13 Plan

a) How does the plan deal with the default on the first mortgage?

b) How does the plan deal with the term of the first mortgage that is much longer than the term of the Chapter 13 plan?

c) Can the plan strip down the second mortgage and entirely strip off the third mortgage?

QUESTION #2 (10%)

Providing for Any Unsecured, Priority Claims

Are there any unsecured, priority claims that must be paid in full?

QUESTION #3 (15%)

The Effect of Bankruptcy on the Student Loan

a) Is the student loan discharged along with other general, unsecured claims?

b) Can the plan reduce the student loan?

QUESTION #4 (15%)

Classifying and Treating Some Debts Differently (Paying Them More)

a) Can the plan provide for paying the student loan fully or more completely than other unsecured claims?

b) Can the plan treat the debt owed Ms. Jack's parents more favorably?

QUESTION #5 (15%)

Maximizing Expenses Associated with the Two Vehicles in Calculating Disposable Income

a) Is the debtor allowed vehicle expenses for the Jeep that she owns?

b) Is the debtor allowed vehicle expenses for the Lexus if she surrenders it?

QUESTION #6 (25%)

Post-Discharge

a) What is the effect of Ms. Jack winning a discrimination action against MMW after she completes all the payments under the plan and is discharged?

b) What happens if a creditor sues Ms. Jack after she is discharged, for personal liability on a prepetition debt that the plan provided for and that was paid according to the plan, though not paid fully according to the terms of the contract between the parties?

c) What happens if she defaults on the mortgages after discharge, the mortgages are foreclosed, and the property is more valuable now than at the time Ms. Jack filed her Chapter 13 case?

BANKRUPTCY ESSAY EXAM #5 [CHAPTER 11 (PART 1)]

After Ms. Jack's firing and bankruptcy filing in Essay Exam #4, her former employer, Midwest Medical Widgets, Inc. (MMW), continued to decline. Layoffs and other standard cost-cutting strategies had not worked.

Suppliers were not being regularly paid. Inventories were shrinking. MMW's principal lender, Florida National Bank (FNB), had capped the company's credit line.

The company's founding family, the Richardson clan, which collectively remains a principal owner, poured in $3.5 million to keep operations going. Much of the money, about $2.5 million, was in the form of an unsecured loan from Regional Finance Bank (RFB) guaranteed by the Richardson's investment firm, Anna Vision, Inc. (AVI), which managed the family's personal assets and investments.

The Richardson matriarch, Kathryn, had stepped in as ACEO (associate chief executive officer). The reason, said the press release, was to "restore MMW's traditional values, brand integrity, and fiscal responsibility." Really, and not unexpectedly, Ms. Richardson's aims were to protect the family's investment and, if possible, enlarge its position in the company.

The company's decline continued. Cash flow and stock value further dwindled. MMW and AVI executives, led by Ms. Richardson, began secretly meeting with the law firm of Hewes & Shayes to plot a bankruptcy strategy.

All the while, MMW remained publicly optimistic through the always cheerful face of Kathryn Richardson. Together with FNB, MMW announced a "partnership for profitability," which was really a marketing campaign dreamed up by Ms. Richardson to reassure and calm investors, suppliers, and workers. The company and the bank committed themselves to work more closely together and unselfishly to save MMW, make the company profitable again, and keep stakeholders economically healthy and secure. The marketing materials proclaimed the birth of:

> an innovative, strategic alliance with all shareholders — the community, labor, and vendors — so that everyone participates equally in rebuilding the company and participating in future prosperity for the common good.

The mood among workers improved. Productivity surged. Suppliers noticed the change. They increased credit sales and extended payment terms. Several local governments where MMW operated suspended tax obligations. Overall, after prices were modestly reduced, corresponding sales more than modestly increased.

FNB, however, did not extend more credit. Instead, pursuant to the comprehensive security arrangement between the bank and MMW, which gave FNB a perfected security interest in all of MMW's property present and after-acquired, the stream of the company's gross revenue flowing to FNB was enlarged.

MMW also disproportionately paid accounts of certain critical suppliers who would be most important to the success of any reorganization plan should the company file Chapter 11 bankruptcy. The loan from RFB was also repaid (which was very good for the bank and also the surety, AVI, because MMW would end up filing bankruptcy a little more than three months later).

Behind the scenes, the Hewes & Shayes lawyers have crafted a plan of reorganization that includes these elements:

- The balance of prepetition debts to critical suppliers will quickly be paid in full, and these suppliers would continue business with MMW and fill the gaps left by discontinuing business with the other, legacy suppliers.
- All employees' wages will be paid without interruption.
- RFB would provide DIP financing by purchasing most of MMW's debt to FNB and making new advances to MMW. Most of the debt RFB purchased was secured, but some of the debt was unsecured. FNB retained a substantially reduced secured claim.
- A subsidiary owned by MMW, Fresh Air Oxygen (FAO), would be sold as soon as possible and, to the extent possible, eliminate the looming threat of liability for employment discrimination and products liability claims against FAO.
- The operations and functions of one plant would be merged with other facilities having excess capacity; the plant would be closed; and MMW would either reject or sell the commercial real estate lease under which the company, as lessee, is committed for three more years to the lessor, Land Development, Inc. (LDI), at the rate of $15,000 per month.

The family, banks, AVI, and the MMW board agreed in general principle on these and other elements of the draft proposed plan, and the MMW board voted to file Chapter 11 bankruptcy to pursue the plan.

QUESTION #1 (10%)

Managing the Process

a) Explain the role and importance of the debtor-in-possession (DIP) in the Chapter 11 process.
b) Identify critical counterweights to the DIP's control of the process.

QUESTION #2 (20%)

Continuing Operations

a) What property of the estate can the DIP use to continue MMW's business?
b) Explain why paying the prepetition debts of critical vendors and suppliers is more likely objectionable than paying employees' wages, including accrued prepetition wages.

QUESTION #3 (15%)

Staying Unsecured Creditors

a) Can critical suppliers simply refuse to do further business with the debtor?

b) In terms of statutory language and underlying policy, explain whether or not critical suppliers can likely convince the court to lift the automatic stay so they can prosecute their claims in state court.

QUESTION #4 (10%)

Lifting the Stay for Secured Creditor FNB

Discuss whether or not the court will likely grant or deny an early motion by FNB to lift the stay in order to enforce its security interest in the collateral.

QUESTION #5 (25%)

DIP Financing

a) What collateral is available to secure the DIP financing?

b) To what extent can the DIP financing provide for securing any of the prepetition debt that RFB is buying from FNB?

QUESTION #6 (20%)

Rejecting or Assuming the Commercial Real Estate Leases

a) Explain (i) why and how MMW would reject the commercial real estate lease between MMW, as lessee, and the lessor, LDI and (ii) how LDI's damages would be limited (which is why the ability to reject a lease is a powerful reason in itself for many companies to file Chapter 11).

b) Explain (i) why and how MMW would assume and keep the lease or assume and assign it, and (ii) the principal limitations on assumption and assignment that protect the lessor, LDI.

BANKRUPTCY ESSAY EXAM #6 [CHAPTER 11 (PART 2)]

The Chapter 11 bankruptcy of Midwest Medical Widgets, Inc. (MMW), begun in Essay Exam #5, was not an easy or happy affair. The Committee of Unsecured Creditors (the Committee) became very distrustful of management, the Richardson family (especially Kathryn Richardson), and the DIP financer, which was Regional Finance Bank (RFB). The Committee suspected that the whole process was being too closely orchestrated and controlled by Kathryn and the Richardsons' investment firm, Anna Vision, Inc. (AVI), which managed the family's personal assets and investments.

It was clear to the Committee that the strategy was to bring MMW out of bankruptcy still owned by the Richardson family and under a reorganization plan that promised to pay unsecured creditors only a few cents on every dollar owed them. The Committee therefore closely scrutinized every step of the plan process, vigorously challenged key aspects of the DIP's final plan of reorganization as illegal and unenforceable, and sought to hold personally accountable some of the nondebtor parties.

At the start, the Committee asked the court to replace the DIP with a trustee or, alternatively, to appoint an examiner to investigate the "incestuous, unnatural, and possibly unlawful relationship" between the debtor and the Richardson family investment firm AVI.

The Committee also asked the court for permission to assert avoidance actions that the DIP had declined to pursue. The Committee was especially eager to go after the loan repayment to RFB on which AVI was the surety. It was a large amount, and the Committee believed the DIP was trying unfairly to protect RFB and AVI.

Suspecting further unfair protection, the Committee contested a provision in the DIP's plan of reorganization that released the debtor's officers, directors, banks, accountants, and lawyers and held them harmless for any harm caused in any way to third parties, including creditors. There were allegations that the conduct of the released persons in dealing with creditors had breached duties owned directly to the creditors and thus the released persons were personally liable for the resulting damages to creditors.

The Committee next attacked the claims filed against the estate by the Richardson family and the secured claim of FNB. The Committee argued that the putative debts MMW owed the family were really equity investments and should be recharacterized as such. And, in any event, the claims of the family and FNB should be subordinated to all unsecured claims because of the misleading, harmful conduct toward creditors in the months leading up to the bankruptcy.

Finally, the Committee argued that the plan violated the absolute priority rule and could not be confirmed. This argument is based on the plan paying almost nothing to unsecured creditors but leaving unimpaired the interests of the Richardson family, which proposed to add such value to the Chapter 11 plan (for the benefit of creditors and other existing equity interests) as would allow the family to acquire full ownership of the reorganized company.

As a result of this contentiousness, the bankruptcy court is required to rule on numerous motions and other requests for judicial action spawned by the Committee's many and varied challenges to the MMW bankruptcy.

QUESTION #1 (25%)

Getting the Plan Confirmed

Identify the key steps and requirements in getting the Chapter 11 plan confirmed.

QUESTION #2 (5%)

Displacing the Debtor in Possession

a) Explain the grounds for the Committee asking the court to replace the DIP with a trustee.
b) What is different about an examiner?

QUESTION #3 (20%)

Avoidance Action and Other Extraordinary Litigation by the Committee

a) Does an individual creditor or the Committee have standing to pursue an avoidance action with respect to the debtor's prepetition repayment of the loan to RFB?
b) Is the repayment of the loan avoidable?
c) What possible liability worries the officers, directors, banks, accountants, and lawyers?

QUESTION #4 (15%)

Third-Party Releases of Officers, Directors, and Professionals

Will the Committee likely win or lose in its attack against the provision in the plan releasing officers and directors and the company's banks, accountants, and lawyers from liability to creditors?

QUESTION #5 (20%)

Challenging Claims of the Family and FNB

a) Explain the meaning and significance of subordinating the family's claims and FNB's secured claim.
b) Explain the meaning and the significance of recharacterizing the family's claims against the estate.

QUESTION #6 (15%)

Cramming Down the Plan and Absolute Priority

Explain how the court is likely to rule on the Committee's argument that the plan cannot be confirmed because of the provision giving the Richardson family full ownership of the reorganized company.

BANKRUPTCY
ESSAY EXAMINATION
ANSWERS

BANKRUPTCY ESSAY EXAM #1 [CHAPTER 7]

QUESTION #1

Estate Property and Avoidance

a) What property will initially fill the bankruptcy estate?   The commencement of a case creates an estate that is comprised, as a general rule, of all legal or equitable interests of the debtor in property as of the commencement of the case. 11 U.S.C. §541(a)(1). The Manfrieds filed a joint case, but each of them is independently a debtor with a separate bankruptcy estate. Their estates are not automatically consolidated simply because they filed a joint case. *Id.* §302(b).

Each debtor's estate includes all of the debtor's interests in property when the bankruptcy petition was filed, including the debtor's interest in the Ohio home and the Ford. The North Carolina beach house is also included because section 541(a) of the Code includes property held by the entirety, though the debtor may later exempt such property from the estate. See 11 U.S.C. §522(b)(3)(B).

However, the 401K retirement account is not part of the estate. It is inalienable under nonbankruptcy, federal law, which means Joel's interest cannot be voluntarily or involuntarily transferred. The Bankruptcy Code honors this nonbankruptcy inalienability. *Id.* §541(c)(2). As a result, Joel's interest in the retirement account is excluded from his bankruptcy estate without relying on any otherwise applicable exemption law and with no effect of such a law on the exclusion.

Importantly, the property that fills the estate is only *the debtor's interest* in the property at the time the petition was filed. As a general rule, the Bankruptcy Code honors the interests of other people in the property, including creditors' liens. These interests do not pass to the estate and are *substantively* unaffected by the bankruptcy filing, the stay, and the creation of the estate. The stay temporarily prevents the creditor from enforcing the interest but does not otherwise reduce it. So, the property to be distributed in a Chapter 7 case is really the value of the property less the value of these other interests, that is, the property distributed is the debtor's equity.

b) Can the trustee recover and keep for the estate any property transferred before bankruptcy was filed?   The estate is comprised of the debtor's interests in property *at the time bankruptcy is filed*. 11 U.S.C. §541(a). Therefore, property interests a debtor effectively transferred before filing bankruptcy are not part of the estate.

However, the trustee is empowered, in limited circumstances, to avoid certain prepetition transfers of the debtor's property, including liens. The *principal* avoiding powers allow the trustee to avoid secret liens and other unrecorded transfers, fraudulent transfers, and preferences. 11 U.S.C. §§544(a), 544(b), 548 & 547.

Any transfer or lien avoided is preserved for the benefit of the estate, *id.* §551, except that the debtor may claim exemptions from property that the trustee recovers. *Id.* §522(g).

The mortgages on the Ohio home and the security interest in the new Ford are liens that must be perfected under state law to be effective against judicial lien creditors and bona fide purchasers. Therefore, if a mortgage is not recorded or the security interest is not perfected, the trustee can avoid the lien. *Id.* §544(a). The effect would be to increase the debtor's equity in the property and thus the value of the bankruptcy estate the trustee would distribute to creditors. In real life, however, mortgages and security interests of professional creditors are almost always recorded and perfected.

These liens are not likely vulnerable under bankruptcy's fraudulent conveyance law, section 548, *id.* §548(a) (which has a two-year reach-back period), or state fraudulent conveyance law, which the trustee can exercise through section 544(b). *Id.* §544(b) (and state law usually has a longer reach-back period). There is no evidence of actual fraud in creating any of these liens, see *id.* §548(a)(1)(A); and there is no constructive fraud because each lien was given in exchange for reasonably equivalent value. See *id.* §548(a)(1)(B). Creating a lien to secure a debt is perfectly equivalent value.

A lien is possibly a preference if the lien is deemed to have been created within 90 days before bankruptcy was filed. See *id.* §547(b) & (e). However, in the typical case involving a professional creditor, there is no gap between creating the debt and creating the lien so that the transfer is not for an antecedent debt and is not a preference under section 547(b) or was substantially contemporaneous and therefore is excepted and protected under section 547(c)(1).

Money paid, spent, or otherwise transferred for less than reasonably equivalent value can be recovered for constructive fraud if the debtor was insolvent when the transfer was made or the debtor became insolvent because of the transfer. Reasonably equivalent value is received, however, if the money is paid in exchange for equivalent goods or services or to satisfy a preexisting debt that is not itself avoidable for fraud or other reason. Therefore, the Manfrieds' mortgage and car payments, purchase of the new Ford, installment payments to the judgment creditor, payments on student loans and credit cards, money spent on home improvements, and lawyer's fee are not constructively fraudulent.

If the Manfrieds are contractually obligated for the children's tuition, payment of the tuition is for a preexisting debt and is not constructively fraudulent. However, incurring the obligation itself is arguably constructively fraudulent. The Manfrieds themselves received no value within the meaning of fraudulent transfer law. The tuition payments that were made within the applicable reach-back period of fraudulent transfer law could be avoided as constructively fraudulent if the debtors were insolvent when the payments were made or if they were rendered insolvent as a result of the payments. *Id.* §548(a)(1)(B).

Payments made on preexisting debts within 90 days before bankruptcy are avoidable as preferences under section 547(b), *id.* §547(b), unless the payments are excepted transfers and protected under section 547(c), as in the case of paying debts in the ordinary course, 11 U.S.C. §547(c)(2), or the debts paid were fully secured. In the latter event, the payment has no preferential effect, which is necessary for a preference under section 547(b). *Id.* §547(b)(5).

To the extent a transfer is avoided as a fraudulent transfer, preference, or for any other reason, the trustee may generally recover, for the benefit of the estate, the property transferred or the value of the property. Persons liable are (1) the initial transferee of such transfer or the entity for whose benefit such transfer was made or (2) any immediate or mediate transferee of such initial transferee. *Id.* §550(a).

QUESTION #2

Exemptions and Choice of Law

a) What source of law governs the debtors' choice of exemptions?   The starting place is this provision of the Bankruptcy Code: "an individual debtor may exempt from property of the estate the property listed in either *paragraph (2)* or, in the alternative, *paragraph (3)* of this subsection." 11 U.S.C. §522(b)(1) (emphasis added).

Paragraph (2) incorporates a list of property that the Bankruptcy Code allows a debtor to exempt as a matter of federal law in bankruptcy cases. This property, comprising the federal bankruptcy exemptions, is listed in section 522(d). *Id.* §§522(b)(2); 522(d).

Paragraph (3) allows a bankruptcy debtor to exempt:

- any property that is exempt under federal, nonbankruptcy law;
- any property that is exempt under applicable state or local law;
- any interest in property in which the debtor had, immediately before the commencement of the case, an interest as a tenant by the entirety or joint tenant to the extent that such interest as a tenant by the entirety or joint tenant is exempt from process under applicable nonbankruptcy law; and
- retirement funds to the extent that those funds are in a fund or account that is tax exempt under certain provisions of the Internal Revenue Code.

Id. §522(b)(3). This collection of property is sometimes called the "state bankruptcy exemptions," even though the collection includes some property that is exempt under federal, nonbankruptcy law and property held by the entirety that is not exempt but is inalienable in some states.

So, as written, the Code allows an individual debtor to choose between the federal exemptions of section 522(b)(2) & (d) and the state law and other exemptions described in section 522(b)(3). However, a debtor cannot choose the federal exemptions of section 522(b)(2) & (d) if "the State law that is applicable to the debtor . . . specifically does not so authorize." 11 U.S.C. §522(b)(2). The law of most states does not "so authorize," that is, the law in most states specifically prohibits debtors from choosing the federal bankruptcy exemptions. See, e.g., Ohio Rev. Code tit. 23, §2329.662. These states are said to have "opted out" of the federal exemptions. When the law of any of these states is the applicable law with respect to exemptions, the debtor has no choice between paragraphs (2) and (3) and is limited to the state and other exemptions described in section 522(b)(3).

Some states have not only opted out of the federal bankruptcy exemptions, they have also enacted state law exemptions specifically designed for debtors in bankruptcy. So, when the law of such a state is the applicable law with respect to a debtor's exemptions, the debtor's exemptions of state or local law, as allowed under section 522(b)(3)(A), are these special, state-law bankruptcy exemptions, not the usual state-law exemptions that would be available to the debtor against judicial creditors in a nonbankruptcy case.

In a joint case of debtors who are husband and wife, each debtor is entitled to his or her own set of exemptions. 11 U.S.C. §522(m). However, in such a case "one debtor may not elect to exempt property listed in paragraph (2) and the other debtor elect to exempt property listed in paragraph (3) of this subsection. If the parties cannot agree on the alternative to be elected, they shall be deemed to elect paragraph (2), where such election is permitted under the law of the jurisdiction where the case is filed." 11 U.S.C. §522(b)(1). The problems of different elections do not arise in most cases because most states have opted out and the debtor cannot elect between sets of exemptions.

The state law that is applicable is not necessarily the law of the state where the bankruptcy case is filed. The applicable law is the law of the state "on the date of the filing of the petition at the place in which the debtor's domicile has been located for the 730 days immediately preceding the date of the filing of the petition or if the debtor's domicile has not been located at a single State for such 730-day period, the place in which the debtor's domicile was located for 180 days immediately preceding the 730-day period or for a longer portion of such 180-day period than in any other place. . . ." *Id.* §522(b)(3)(A).

For the entire 730-day period, even though the Manfrieds have frequently visited or even resided in North Carolina during the time, they have been domiciled in Ohio. Therefore, Ohio law is the applicable state law with respect to their exemptions.

Ohio has opted out of the federal bankruptcy exemptions. Ohio Rev. Code tit. 23, §2329.662. ("Pursuant to the 'Bankruptcy Reform Act of 1978,' 92 Stat. 2549, 522, this state specifically does not authorize debtors who are domiciled in this state to exempt the property specified in the 'Bankruptcy Reform Act of 1978,' 92 Stat. 2549, 522."). The debtors' exemptions are therefore limited to Ohio state-law exemptions and the other property listed in section 522(b)(3).

b) Without considering the North Carolina house, what property can the debtors exempt? Ohio law allows a debtor to exempt his or her interest, not to exceed $3225, in one motor vehicle. The Manfrieds own the new Ford, but their interest is fully encumbered by a consensual lien. Exemptions are not effective against consensual liens, and there is no equity. So, even though Ohio law allows a debtor to "hold property exempt from execution, garnishment, attachment, or sale to satisfy a judgment or order . . . ," Ohio Rev. Code tit. 23, §2329.66(A), the vehicle exemption is useless in the Manfried's bankruptcy case.

Ohio law allows a debtor to exempt his or her interest in a homestead not to exceed $20,200 in value. The Ohio home is the Manfrieds' homestead. Its value is $320,000. The mortgages total $279,600. The equity is $40,400. Together, the Manfrieds can exempt all of the equity.

Half of this exempt equity was acquired by withdrawing funds from Joel's retirement account and paying down the first mortgage. The trustee or a party in interest may argue that this action was purposeful and therefore fraudulent because the debtor acted with the actual intent to hinder, delay, or defraud creditors. However, the retirement account was excluded from the estate (11 U.S.C. §541(c)(2)), exempt under Ohio law, Ohio Rev. Code tit. 23, §2329.66, and exempt under bankruptcy law (11 U.S.C. §522(3)(c) & (n)). Generally, converting exempt property into another form of exempt property is not fraudulent. Also, converting even nonexempt property to exempt property is not itself fraudulent absent fraud extrinsic to the conversion.

In In re Addison, 540 F.3d 805 (8th Cir. 2008), Addison, a part-owner of a cable company, had personally guaranteed some of his company's debt. In early 2005 the business was unable to pay its debts, and JP Morgan Chase ("Chase"), a company creditor, began to pursue Addison on a $1.3 million personal guarantee. Around June 2005, Addison first sought the advice of bankruptcy counsel in an effort to protect himself from Chase's attempts to enforce the guarantee. On or about July 21, 2005, Addison used $4000 of his nonexempt funds to establish a Roth IRA for himself and used another $4000 of the nonexempt funds to establish a Roth IRA for his wife. The funds came from a brokerage account that contained $45,476.71 in nonexempt funds prior to these transfers. On October 14, 2005, Addison instructed his wife to use $11,500 in nonexempt funds to make a voluntary principal payment on their home mortgage. Addison's wife transferred $9,000 of this payment from the brokerage account mentioned above, and $2,500 came from a bank account at U.S. Bank. Later that same day, Addison filed an individual Chapter 7 bankruptcy petition. He chose the Minnesota state exemptions and claimed his Roth IRA and the equity in the house as exempt.

The Trustee objected to Addison's homestead and Roth IRA exemptions, and asserted that the accounts were property of the estate not subject to any exemption. The bankruptcy court held an evidentiary hearing on the Trustee's objection and subsequently ruled in favor of the Trustee on all three issues. The court found that Addison made the $11,500 house payment and the $4000 Roth IRA payment with the intent to hinder, delay, or defraud his creditors, and thus denied, in full, Addison's claimed exemption in the Roth IRA and ordered that the homestead exemption be reduced by $11,500. The bankruptcy court also ruled that the IRA plans were property of Addison's bankruptcy estate and that they were not subject to any applicable exemption.

The BAP affirmed, ruling that the bankruptcy court's finding that Addison had the intent to hinder, delay, or defraud his creditors when he converted the non-exempt assets into exempt assets was not clearly erroneous. The BAP also affirmed the bankruptcy court's determination that the accounts were property of the estate and not subject to exemption. Addison appealed to the Eighth Circuit.

After the bankruptcy court found that Addison intended to hinder, delay, or defraud a creditor when he converted his nonexempt assets into his homestead and Roth IRA, the Trustee initiated an additional proceeding to deny Addison's discharge under 11 U.S.C. §727(a)(2). Because a debtor's discharge can be denied under section 727(a)(2) if "the debtor, with intent to hinder, delay, or defraud a creditor . . . has transferred . . . property of the debtor, within one year before" his bankruptcy filing, and the bankruptcy court had already concluded that Addison transferred nonexempt property to exempt property with the intent to hinder, delay, or defraud a creditor within a year before his bankruptcy filing, the court denied Addison's discharge under section 727(a)(2) on collateral estoppel grounds. Addison also appealed this ruling to the BAP, which certified the appeal directly to the Eighth Circuit Court of Appeals.

The Court of Appeals reversed for the debtor:

> Under §522(b) of the Bankruptcy Code, "a debtor can choose to exempt from property of the bankruptcy estate that property which is exempt under the applicable state or federal law." Here, Addison elected to use the Minnesota state exemptions, and claimed a homestead exemption of $91,250 under Minn. Stat. Ann. §510.02 and claimed his $4,000 Roth IRA as exempt under Minn. Stat. Ann. §550.37(24). These claimed exemptions were within the permissible amounts as provided by Minnesota law.
>
> However, under Minnesota's enactment of the Uniform Fraudulent Transfers Act (UFTA), a debtor may not claim an exemption in property obtained through a transfer made by the debtor "with actual intent to hinder, delay, or defraud any creditor of the debtor." Minn. Stat. Ann. §513.44. Section 513.44(b) "contains a lengthy list of factors or 'badges of fraud' which a court may look to for help in determining actual intent." Thus, Addison's claimed exemptions in his homestead and Roth IRA are not permitted if those assets were obtained by transfers made "with actual intent to hinder, delay, or defraud any creditor." Minn. Stat. Ann. §513.44(a).
>
> "The question of whether an individual acted with intent to defraud in converting non-exempt property into exempt property is a question of fact, on which the bankruptcy court's finding will not be reversed unless clearly erroneous." "It is well settled that the mere conversion of non-exempt assets to exempt assets is not in itself fraudulent." Nevertheless, "[w]here the debtor acts with actual intent to defraud creditors, his exemptions will be denied."
>
> *"Before actual fraudulent intent can be found 'there must appear in evidence some facts or circumstances which are extrinsic to the mere facts of conversion of non-exempt assets into exempt and which are indicative of such fraudulent purpose.' "*
>
> In finding that Addison had the requisite intent to defraud, the bankruptcy court . . . found four badges of fraud resulting from Addison's day-of-filing mortgage payment: (1) the transfer was to an insider; (2) Addison retained control of the property after the transfer; (3) the transfer was made after Addison had been sued on his personal guarantee; and (4) Addison was insolvent at the time he transferred the funds to his homestead. Additionally, the bankruptcy court noted that Addison already had significant equity in his home before he made the transfer and that the payment only increased Addison's equity in the home, but did not reduce his monthly mortgage payment. . . . [I]t found that the homestead transfer was made with the intent to hinder, delay, or defraud Addison's creditors, as his intent was "to keep value away from creditors." . . .
>
> The bankruptcy court's underlying factual findings are themselves not clearly erroneous; however, they do not identify any "extrinsic evidence of fraud." In the absence of extrinsic evidence of fraud, we find clear error in the bankruptcy court's ultimate determination of intent to defraud. As discussed above, "[i]t is well established that . . . a debtor's conversion of non-exempt property to exempt property on the eve of bankruptcy for the express purpose of placing that

property beyond the reach of creditors, without more, will not deprive the debtor of the exemption to which he otherwise would be entitled." Rather, for fraudulent intent to be found "there must appear in evidence some facts or circumstances which are extrinsic to the mere facts of conversion of non-exempt assets into exempt and which are indicative of such fraudulent purpose."

Here, only the fact that Addison had been sued or threatened with suit prior to making the mortgage payment was extrinsic to the fact of conversion — all of the other facts cited relate to a debtor's simple conversion of nonexempt property to exempt property on the eve of bankruptcy, which we have long held to be permissible. . . . [T]hese facts alone [do not] constitute extrinsic evidence of intent to defraud. . . . Moreover, the bankruptcy court's finding that Addison converted his nonexempt property to exempt property with the intent "to keep value away from creditors" does not provide extrinsic evidence of fraud as such an intent is not automatically impermissible. . . .

"The sort of indicia of fraud necessary to find fraudulent use on an exemption would be, *inter alia*, conduct intentionally designed to materially mislead or deceive creditors about the debtor's position or use of credit to buy exempt property." Additionally, "[c]onverting a very great amount of property could also be an indication of fraud," as could "[t]he existence of conveyances for less than adequate consideration." In the present case, the record contains no extrinsic evidence of any of these indicia of fraud. The record only indicates that Addison's intent was to convert some of his nonexempt property to exempt property on the eve of bankruptcy, something that is "well established" in this circuit that he is allowed to do. Accordingly, we conclude that it was clear error for the bankruptcy court to find that Addison had the requisite intent to hinder, delay, or defraud a creditor when he converted some nonexempt property into his homestead on the day he filed bankruptcy. . . .

The bankruptcy court also denied Addison's claimed exemption in his $4,000 Roth IRA, finding that Addison had transferred nonexempt funds into the Roth IRA with the intent to hinder, delay, or defraud a creditor. Again, the determination of intent is a finding of fact reviewed for clear error. The bankruptcy court found Addison acted with intent to hinder, delay, or defraud regarding the transfer of funds to the Roth IRA "for the same reasons" as it found intent to hinder, delay, or defraud regarding the payment on the home mortgage. As discussed above, that finding of intent was clearly erroneous, and thus the disallowance of the Roth IRA exemption must be reversed as well. Likewise, the bankruptcy court's additional finding that Addison's real reason for converting nonexempt assets into the Roth IRA was "just [to] keep the money out of the hands of creditors," will not suffice to establish intent to hinder, delay, or defraud as a debtor may intentionally convert nonexempt assets to exempt assets for the express purpose of keeping the money out of the hands of creditors, unless there is extrinsic evidence of fraud.

Id. at 809–18 (emphasis added).

c) Can the debtors exempt the North Carolina house? Section 522(b)(3) separately exempts "any interest in property in which the debtor had, immediately before the commencement of the case, an interest as a tenant by the entirety or joint tenant to the extent that such interest as a tenant by the entirety or joint tenant is exempt from process *under applicable nonbankruptcy law*." 11 U.S.C. §522(b)(3)(B).

Here is an explanation of the interrelation between state and bankruptcy law with respect to entireties property:

[A] tenancy by the entireties is a form of co-ownership of real or personal property by husband and wife. It is a venerable common law doctrine of ancient vintage, based on the legal fiction that husband and wife are one person. The essential characteristic is that "each spouse is seised per tout et non per my, i.e., of the whole of the entirety and not of a share, moiety or divisible part." *In re Gallagher's Estate*, 352 Pa. 476, 43 A.2d 132, 133 (1945) (citations omitted). As the author of a respected treatise explains,

> "[H]usband and wife are looked upon, together, as a single entity, like a corporation. The single entity is the owner of the whole estate. When the husband or wife dies, the entity continues, although it is now composed of only one natural person rather than two."

Ladner on Conveyancing in Pennsylvania, §1.08 at 16 (John Makdisi, ed., rev. 4th ed. 1979). Further, "neither tenant by the entirety owns any undivided share at all; both together, as a single entity, own the whole, or entire, estate."

Entireties property may not be accessed by the creditors of only one spouse. As the Pennsylvania Supreme Court explained in *Madden v. Gosztonyi Savings & Trust Co.*, 331 Pa. 476, 200 A. 624 (1938), with respect to property owned by the entireties, neither spouse "has any individual portion which can be alienated or separated, or which can be reached by the creditors of either spouse." . . .

[With respect to] the effect that filing for bankruptcy has on the interest a spouse has in entireties holdings . . . [the starting place is] 11 U.S.C. §541(a)(1), [providing that] "all legal and equitable interests that a debtor holds in property at the commencement of a bankruptcy case" are included in the bankruptcy estate.

We have held that §541(a) is "certainly broad enough to include an individual debtor's interest in property held as a tenant by the entirety." *Napotnik v. Equibank & Parkvale Savings Ass'n*, 679 F.2d 316, 318 (3d Cir. 1982).

Although entireties property may be initially included in a bankruptcy estate, the process does not end there because a debtor may exempt certain holdings pursuant to §522.

The Bankruptcy Code provides two alternative plans of exemption. Under §522(b)(2), a debtor may elect the specific federal exemptions listed in §522(d) ("federal exemptions") or, under §522(b)(3), may choose the exemptions permitted, inter alia, under state law and general (nonbankruptcy) federal law ("general exemptions"). . . .

A debtor who chooses to use the general exemptions may claim an exemption in "any interest in property in which the debtor had, immediately before the commencement of the case, an interest as a tenant by the entirety . . . to the extent that such interest . . . is exempt from process under applicable nonbankruptcy law." 11 U.S.C. §522(b)(3)(B).

Where spouses are *joint* debtors [which means they are obligated on a debt they both, jointly owe] they may not claim the general exemption in §522(b)(3)(B) for property they hold by the entireties. In *Napotnik*, we held that where a creditor had claims against both husband and wife jointly one spouse could not exempt the entire value of property held by the entireties because "in Pennsylvania entirety property may be reached by creditors to satisfy the joint debts of husband and wife." We thus concluded, "In this respect at least, such property is not exempt from process in Pennsylvania."

Nevertheless, filing a bankruptcy petition does not sever a tenancy by the entirety and thus an individual spouse may be able to exempt the whole of entireties property from the bankruptcy estate in some circumstances. *Bonanno v. Peyton [In re Bunker]*, 312 F.3d 145 (4th Cir. 2002) presented a situation in which husband and wife filed joint bankruptcy petitions and, under the general entireties exemption of §522(b)(3)(B), sought to exempt the home that they owned as tenants by the entirety. The Court held that the benefits of entireties property survived bankruptcy filings and that the debtors' home could not be reached by creditors of only one of the spouses.

Bunker makes it clear that a joint filing in bankruptcy does not sever a tenancy by the entireties so as to make the property available to creditors of either husband or wife individually. That holding is different from, but consistent with, *Napotnik*.

Likewise, in a companion opinion to this case, *O'Lexa v. Zebley*, No. 06-2254, we concluded that the wife's home which she held as a tenant by the entirety was exempt under the general entireties exemption of §522(b)(3)(B) from creditor's claims against her individually.

In that case, we rejected the trustee's argument that entireties property could be accessed under a Pennsylvania statute that made both spouses liable for debts contracted for necessaries by one spouse. Because the statute as we read it did not create joint liability, but rather made the spouse contracting for the necessaries primarily liable and the other only secondarily liable, we held that the entireties property was not subject to execution for the primary debtor's obligations.

O'Lexa makes clear that the presence of joint liability is necessary for a creditor to access property in a bankruptcy estate held as tenants by the entireties.

In re Brannon, 476 F.3d 170, 173 (3d Cir. 2007) (emphasis added).

Returning to the question whether or not the Manfrieds' interests in the North Carolina beach house can be exempted, first, look at state law. Suppose that Ohio law does not exempt or likewise protect property held by the entirety as an incidental right of such an estate. Suppose Ohio law does not even recognize the pure, common law form of such an estate in property. On the other hand, North Carolina recognizes a tenancy by the entirety with respect to real property, and under North Carolina law neither joint tenant owns an interest that can be reached by creditors of only one of them.

The beginning question of bankruptcy law is which state's law is the "applicable nonbankruptcy law" within the meaning of section 522(b)(3)(B). Is Ohio law the applicable law for purposes of section 522(b)(3)(A), or is it North Carolina law where the property is located? As of now, the preferred answer is that the situs of the real property applies, In re Holland, 366 B.R. 825 (N.D. Ill. 2007), appeal dismissed, 539 F.3d 563 (7th Cir. 2008), on remand, 2009 WL 2971087 (Bankr. N.D. Ill. 2009), which in this case means North Carolina.

However, even under North Carolina law, entirety property is not immune from the claims of creditors to whom the husband and wife are jointly liable. But, this exception does not apply in bankruptcy to completely destroy the exemption of entirety property simply because the debtors have filed a joint bankruptcy case. In re Payne, 2004 WL 2757907 (Bankr. M.D.N.C. 2004). Rather, the entirety property is exempted to the "extent that such interest . . . is exempt . . . under applicable non-bankruptcy law." 11 U.S.C. §522(b)(2)(B). So, according to the heaviest authorities, the entirety property is exempt in bankruptcy from the claims of creditors to whom only one of the spouses is liable, but the property is not exempt from the claim of a joint creditor who, in the bankruptcy case, can satisfy claims against the entire undivided interest of the husband and wife. Therefore, the debtor's interest in entirety property is generally exempt but not from any joint claims. The trustee can dispose of the debtor's interest in entirety property (see 11 U.S.C. §363(h)) and satisfy the claims of joint creditors while individual creditors get nothing. The excess proceeds beyond the amount of joint claims are exempt for the debtor. Sumy v. Schlossberg, 777 F.2d 921 (4th Cir.1985); 5 Collier on Bankruptcy ¶541.05[6][a] ("When entireties property is sold, the proceeds are entireties property, and are distributable to joint creditors of the husband and wife. Any surplus is claimable as an exception under Code section 522(b)(2)(B)."). Only the creditors, if any, to whom the Manfrieds are jointly liable on debts can reach the North Carolina property.

QUESTION #3

Debts and Discharge

a) To whom and in what order will the trustee distribute the proceeds of the property of the estate? Nothing will be distributed to anybody if the Manfrieds' case is a "no assets" case, which means there is no property of the estate. Put another way, the value of each debtor's interest in property, which the trustee can liquidate and give to creditors, is zero.

Assuming there is property of the estate to distribute, claims paid first are priority claims described in section 507, beginning with domestic support obligations and administrative expenses. 11 U.S.C. §§726(a)(1); 507(a). The balance of the estate is paid pro rata to general unsecured creditors, except that secured or unsecured claims for exemplary or punitive damages and claims for interest are paid last. *Id.* §726(a) & (b).

None of the Manfrieds' prepetition creditors has a priority claim. Claims for personal injury are given priority but only if resulting from operating a motor vehicle or vessel while intoxicated.11 U.S.C. §507(a)(10). So, after satisfying any administrative expenses, the balance of the estate, if any, will be shared pro rata by the creditors holding claims for the compensatory judgment debt, the medical bills, and the credit card debts.

In the highly unlikely event that all of the general unsecured claims are paid in full, the claim for punitive damages is satisfied and any residual balance is paid to the debtor.

It appears, however, that the Manfrieds' joint bankruptcy case is a "no assets" case, which means they have no equity in any property that is property of the estate. As a result, none of the unsecured claims will be paid anything.

b) Which debts will be discharged?   Unless there is a valid objection to discharge, and save debts excepted from discharge, the court will grant the debtor a discharge which "discharges the debtor from all debts that arose before the date of the order for relief [i.e., before the petition was filed]." 11 U.S.C. §727(b). The major effects of the discharge are that it:

- voids any judgment at any time obtained, to the extent that such judgment is a determination of the personal liability of the debtor with respect to any debt discharged . . . whether or not discharge of such debt is waived; [and]
- operates as an injunction against the commencement or continuation of an action, the employment of process, or an act, to collect, recover or offset any such debt as a *personal liability* of the debtor, whether or not discharge of such debt is waived. . . .

Section 727(a) lists 12 reasons for *objecting* to and denying a discharge, which means none of the debtor's obligations are discharged. The facts of the Manfrieds' bankruptcy do not realistically support any objection to discharge, not even subsection (a)(2), which denies a discharge if "the debtor, with intent to hinder, delay, or defraud a creditor . . . has transferred, removed, destroyed, mutilated, or concealed, or has permitted to be transferred, removed, destroyed, mutilated, or concealed — property of the debtor, within one year before the date of the filing of the petition. . . ." 11 U.S.C. §727(a)(2)(A). The earlier determination that paying down the mortgage was not a fraudulent transfer the trustee can avoid also means there is no intent to defraud for purposes of denying the debtor a discharge. In re Addison, 540 F.3d 805 (8th Cir. 2008).

The debts listed in section 523(a) are *excepted* from discharge even though the court grants the debtor a general discharge under section 727. See 11 U.S.C. §523(a). Included in these excepted debts is a debt "for willful and malicious injury by the debtor to another entity or to the property of another entity." *Id.* §523(a)(6). Does this exception cover the judgment against Joel for malicious negligence that awarded the plaintiff $50,000 in compensatory damages and $50,000 in punitive damages? No.

The Supreme Court in Kawaauhau v. Geiger (In re Geiger), 523 U.S. 57 (1998), made clear that for section 523(a)(6) to apply, the actor must intend the consequences of the act, not simply the act itself. Both willfulness and maliciousness must be proven to block discharge of the debt under section 523(a)(6). "[T]he Supreme Court clarified that the §523(a)(6) exception 'is confined to debts based on what the law has for generations called an intentional tort.' Drawing on the Second Restatement of Torts, the Supreme Court noted that '[i]ntentional torts generally require that the actor intend "the *consequences* of an act," not simply "the act itself,"' stated definitively that 'debts arising from recklessly or negligently inflicted injuries do not fall within the compass of §523(a)(6).'" Ditto v. McCurdy, 510 F.3d 1070, 1075 (9th Cir. 2007). "[E]ven gross negligence or reckless disregard of the rights of others is not sufficient as a basis upon which to fasten the label of nondischargeability." In re Iberg, 395 B.R. 83, 91 (Bankr. E.D. Ark. 2008).

Also excepted from discharge is a debt:

for money, property, services, or an extension, renewal, or refinancing of credit, to the extent obtained by —

(A) false pretenses, a false representation, or actual fraud, other than a
statement respecting the debtor's or an insider's financial condition;
(B) use of a statement in writing —
　　(i) that is materially false;
　　(ii) respecting the debtor's or an insider's financial condition;
　　(iii) on which the creditor to whom the debtor is liable for such money,
property, services, or credit reasonably relied; and
　　(iv) that the debtor caused to be made or published with intent to
deceive.

11 U.S.C. §523(a)(2). Does this exception cover the Manfrieds' debts for their many
credit cards that they knowingly, even deliberately "maxed out"? Probably not.

A common argument is that with each use of her credit card, a debtor who ends
up in bankruptcy knowingly, impliedly, falsely represented her ability and intent to
pay; and, therefore, the credit card debts are nondischargeable under section
523(a)(2)(A). "The operative terms in §523(a)(2)(A), . . . 'false pretenses, a false representation, or actual fraud,' carry the acquired meaning of terms of art . . . [and] are
common-law terms." Field v. Mans, 516 U.S. 59 (1995). So, in order to prevail
under §523(a)(2)(A), the creditor must prove that the debtor acted intentionally,
subjectively in bad faith with knowledge that she could not and would not repay the
debts. "Creditors must show fraudulent intent, which requires an actual intent to
mislead, more than mere negligence." In re Finnerty, 418 B.R. 1, 8 (Bankr. D.N.H.
2009). Credit card issuers pursuing section 523(a) nondischargeability claims can
rarely show with direct evidence that a debtor did not intend to repay the debt.
Therefore, courts often say that a debtor's intent may be inferred from the totality of
the circumstances. However, the necessary wrongful intent is not inferred from card
use itself or even from the fact of the debtor's insolvency at the time of use. And, the
creditor must additionally prove reliance on any implicit misrepresentations by the
debtor and also that the reliance was justified. The circumstances known about
the Manfrieds' use of their credit cards are simply not sufficient to satisfy the requirements of section 523(a)(2)(A).

Some credit card debts incurred for luxury goods or services and excessive cash
advances shortly before bankruptcy are presumed nondischargeable. 11 U.S.C.
§523(a)(2)(C). Based on the known circumstances, none of these presumptions
seems clearly applicable to the Manfrieds' use of their credit cards.

QUESTION #4

Dismissal and Accountability

*a) Are there substantial grounds for arguing, in good faith, to dismiss the
Manfrieds' Chapter 7 case?*　To begin with, the facts don't say whether or not the
debtors had a credit counseling briefing before they filed bankruptcy.

> [A]n individual may not be a debtor under this title unless such individual has,
> during the 180-day period preceding the date of filing of the petition by such
> individual, received from an approved nonprofit budget and credit counseling
> agency described in section 111(a) an individual or group briefing (including a

briefing conducted by telephone or on the Internet) that outlined the opportunities for available credit counseling and assisted such individual in performing a related budget analysis.

11 U.S.C. §109(h). This requirement applies to any individual, not just an individual with primarily consumer debts.

And, section 521 requires an individual debtor to file with the bankruptcy petition "a certificate from the approved nonprofit budget and credit counseling agency that provided the debtor services under section 109(h) describing the services provided to the debtor. . . ." 11 U.S.C. §521(b)(1). "[T]he certification is supposed to describe the services that were provided to the debtor and must be provided by the agency that provided the counseling. [T]he time for filing these documents was with the Petition, or within a court approved extended period." In re Manalad, 360 B.R. 288, 292-93 (Bankr. C.D. Cal. 2007).

Timely filing the certification is excused if the debtor alternatively files a certification that:

(i)   describes exigent circumstances that merit a waiver of the requirements [to file a certification of having had the credit counseling briefing] . . . ;

(ii) states that the debtor requested credit counseling services from an approved nonprofit budget and credit counseling agency, but was unable to obtain the services referred to in paragraph (1) during the 5-day period beginning on the date on which the debtor made that request; and

(iii) is satisfactory to the court.

11 U.S.C. §109(h)(3)(A).

A majority of courts have concluded that dismissal is mandated when a debtor has failed to comply with the credit counseling requirements, and in virtually all of these cases, the issue has been whether a debtor has timely provided a satisfactory explanation of exigent circumstances. Absent these exigent circumstances, some courts will dismiss the case or, alternatively, strike the debtor's bankruptcy petition. Other courts have decided that dismissal or striking is not the only remedy, as in the *Manalad* case, and the bankruptcy judge in her discretion can allow the case to continue and impose a less drastic remedy.

Abuse of Chapter 7 is another reason for dismissing a bankruptcy case.

After notice and a hearing, the court, on its own motion or on a motion by the United States trustee, trustee (or bankruptcy administrator, if any), or any party in interest, may dismiss a case filed by an individual debtor under this chapter whose debts are primarily consumer debts, or, with the debtor's consent, convert such a case to a case under chapter 11 or 13 of this title, if it finds that the granting of relief would be an abuse of the provisions of this chapter.

11 U.S.C. §707(b)(1).

The best known reason for finding abuse is that the debtor's statutorily calculated disposable income is sufficient to fund a Chapter 13 case. In this event, the case is dismissed or, with the debtor's concurrence, is converted to Chapter 13. *Id.*

The case can also be dismissed, alternatively, if:

- the debtor filed the petition in bad faith; or
- the totality of the circumstances (including whether the debtor seeks to reject a personal services contract and the financial need for such rejection as sought by the debtor) of the debtor's financial situation demonstrates abuse.

Id. §707(b)(3). Generally, "the courts tend to apply the bad faith standard along with a consideration of a totality of the circumstances standard . . . , and as a practical matter, in most cases, a consideration of the totality of circumstances, rather than a single factor or circumstance, would be needed to reach a conclusion of bad faith. Additionally, it would seem that most motions to dismiss for bad faith would also be considered under the totality of the circumstances, but not necessarily vice versa. To date, it appears that there is only one reported decision in which the dismissal was based solely on bad faith and not on bad faith coupled with the totality of the circumstances test." Robert J. Landry, *The Means Test: Finding a Safe Harbor, Passing the Means Test, or Rebutting the Presumption of Abuse May Not Be Enough*, 29 N. Ill. U. L. Rev. 245, 262 (2009).

In the Manfrieds' bankruptcy, a possible good faith argument is that the totality of the debtors' financial situation demonstrates abuse because of the large amount of property the debtors will retain. Plus, increasing secured debt to avoid Chapter 13 was bad faith that adds to the totality of circumstances arguing for dismissal.

In a few cases, the courts have implied that even though an individual debtor commits the statutorily required future income to a Chapter 11 or 13 plan, keeping too much other property, including too much exempt property, may be a reason for dismissal. Susan M. Freeman, *Are DIP and Committee Counsel Fiduciaries for Their Clients' Constituents or the Bankruptcy Estate? What Is a Fiduciary, Anyway?*, 17 Am. Bankr. Inst. L. Rev. 291, 310 (2009). And, in extreme cases, the courts may define bad faith conduct to include the debtor spending freely and irresponsibly before bankruptcy or loading up on secured debt so as to help avoid Chapter 13 or reduce disposable income in a Chapter 13 case. See In re Hageney, 422 B.R. 254 (Bankr. E.D. Wash. 2009) (debtors' purchase, a bare 10 weeks prior to their Chapter 7 filing, of a $20,000 motorcycle for Chapter 7 debtor–husband was indicative of bad faith); In re Oot, 368 B.R. 662 (Bankr. N.D. Ohio 2007); In re James, 345 B.R. 664, 667 (Bankr. N.D. Iowa 2006); In re Mitchell, 357 B.R. 142 (Bankr. C.D. Cal. 2006); In re McKeag, 77 Bankr. 716 (Bankr. D. Neb. 1987).

However, the courts are very, very slow to find that such circumstances amount to abuse justifying dismissal. Two factors count heavily the other way. First, there is no abuse if the property was acquired for a legitimate, extraneous reason and in ordinary course, not recklessly or frivolously. In re Hageney, 422 B.R. 254 (Bankr. E.D. Wash. 2009) (debtors' purchase of $63,995 pick-up truck roughly 10 months prepetition, as replacement vehicle for debtor–husband whose job required him to travel thousands of miles per year in various western states, did not warrant finding of "bad faith"); In re Vansickel, 309 B.R. 189, 200 (Bankr. E.D. Va. 2004) (Debtor's purchase of new car was not evidence of substantial abuse because "the new car was not purchased with the intent to artificially inflate their monthly expenses. It was purchased in the ordinary course of the debtors' financial affairs when the lease on their old car expired. There is no indication that they financed it for an unusually short period of time to force their monthly payments up and to make it appear that they had no disposable income.").

Second, a finding of abuse is not likely based on the debtor acquiring or keeping property that is exempt.

> [U]nder totality [of circumstances], the court may not consider the debtor's exempt property. In the 1978 Bankruptcy Reform Act, Congress expressly provided for debtors' exemptions in §522, thereby implementing a policy in favor of allowing debtors, under the Bankruptcy Code or under applicable state law (or federal nonbankruptcy law), to shield property that Congress or the state legislatures deemed to be unreachable by creditors in general. This is in accord with the primary goal of bankruptcy law, which is to give the honest debtor a fresh start.
>
> The legislative history of §727(a)(2) provides a good analogy. This subsection provides a ground for denial of a Chapter 7 discharge because the debtor has transferred property "with intent to hinder, delay, or defraud a creditor." A frequently litigated issue under §727(a)(2) is whether the debtor's conversion of nonexempt property to exempt property shortly before bankruptcy was permissible, or was a basis for dismissal under §727(a)(2). The legislative history concerning this issue clearly states: "As under current law, the debtor will be permitted to convert nonexempt property into exempt property before filing a bankruptcy petition. The practice is not fraudulent as to creditors, and permits the debtor to make full use of the exemptions to which he is entitled under the law."
>
> Case law has construed this legislative history to mean that "the conversion of non-exempt to exempt property for the purpose of placing the property out of the reach of creditors, without more [i.e., conduct evidencing indicia of fraud], will not deprive the debtor of the exemption to which he otherwise would be entitled." Logic dictates that if the policy in favor of allowing the debtor to make full use of his exemptions will not prevent the granting of Chapter 7 relief under §727(a)(2), then analogously that same policy should not allow the debtor's ownership of exempt property to be deemed an abuse that would be cause for dismissal under the totality of the circumstances. More specifically, if converting nonexempt property to exempt property shortly before bankruptcy "without more" is permissible, then, a fortiori, merely owning exempt property at the time of the filing of a Chapter 7 petition should not be considered abusive under the congressional policy in favor of allowing the debtor's exemptions. In both instances, the issue at hand is the granting or denial of relief under Chapter 7; and in both instances, the policy in favor of treating the debtor's exemptions as sacrosanct should be applied as Congress intended. Therefore, the court may not consider the debtor's exempt property under totality, thereby encroaching on the debtor's fresh start.

Ned W. Waxman & Justin H. Rucki, *Chapter 7 Bankruptcy Abuse: Means Testing Is Presumptive, But "Totality" Is Determinative*, 45 Hous. L. Rev. 901, 922-24 (2008).

The totality of circumstances in the Manfrieds' case is mixed. Much of the property was exempt. However, they acted deliberately and by design to enlarge exemptions and acquire secured debt, but such intent was lacking with respect to the North Carolina property. On the other hand, the value of the North Carolina property is very large, and the property is unencumbered, which is itself a factor in evaluating the totality of circumstances.

Nevertheless, because the courts are slow to find abuse for these reasons, the odds on dismissing the Manfrieds' case favor them. Still, it's not a certainty, and there seems to a good faith argument for dismissing their Chapter 7 case.

b) Did lawyer Burnett make any serious mistakes in planning the Manfrieds' bankruptcy and handling the case? The Manfrieds could allege malpractice if their case is dismissed or if the case is not dismissed but they lose their arguments with respect to exemptions. Realistically, however, Burnett's handling of the case seems within the usually wide range of conduct that is professionally reasonable. A lawyer losing arguments in a case or losing the whole case is an unhappy result for her and the client but is not itself negligent if the lawyer's decisions, arguments, and other conduct are professionally reasonable. Plus, winning a malpractice action requires proving proximate cause and loss and, in some states, the collectability of damages.

Based on bankruptcy rules, the court's inherent powers, or section 105(a) (11 U.S.C. §105(a)), the bankruptcy judge can sanction a lawyer for acting in bad faith or unprofessionally, but Burnett's handling of the case is not suspect under the applicable standards for judicial discipline or contempt.

Some of Mr. Burnett's advice to the Manfrieds may violate section 526, which prohibits a "debt relief agency" from advising a client or prospective client

> to incur more debt in contemplation of such person filing a case under this title or to pay an attorney or bankruptcy petition preparer fee or charge for services performed as part of preparing for or representing a debtor in a case under this title.

11 U.S.C. §526(a)(4). Mr. Burnett, whether he practices by himself or in a firm, is a "debt relief agency" because he is a "person who provides any bankruptcy assistance to . . . [a client] in return for the payment of money or other valuable consideration. . . ." 11 U.S.C. §101(12A). And, if Burnett violated the section 526 prohibitions, the Bankruptcy Code invites the state to take action against him and explicitly authorizes the bankruptcy court to impose a civil penalty against him. *Id.* §526(3) & (4). In addition, Burnett would be liable to his clients

> in the amount of any fees or charges in connection with providing bankruptcy assistance to such person that such debt relief agency has received, for actual damages, and for reasonable attorneys' fees and costs if such agency is found, after notice and a hearing, to have — intentionally or negligently failed to comply with any provision of this section. . . .

Id. §526(c)(3).

However, the section 526 prohibitions against advising a client to incur more debt in contemplation of bankruptcy are not literal and, properly, are somewhat narrowly interpreted and applied. The Supreme Court has said that section 526 does not prohibit an attorney from providing "'beneficial advice [that] could help the assisted person avoid filing for bankruptcy altogether.'" Milavetz, Gallop & Milavetz, P.A. v. United States, 130 S. Ct. 1324, 1334 (2010). Rather,

> we think the phrase refers to a specific type of misconduct designed to manipulate the protections of the bankruptcy system. . . . [W]e conclude that §526(a)(4) prohibits a debt relief agency only from advising a debtor to incur more debt because the debtor is filing for bankruptcy, rather than for a valid purpose. . . .
>
> [A]dvice to incur more debt because of bankruptcy presents a substantial risk of injury to both debtors and creditors. Specifically, the incurrence of such debt stands to harm a debtor if his prepetition conduct leads a court to hold his debts nondischargable, see §523(a)(2), convert his case to another chapter, or dismiss it altogether, see §707(b), thereby defeating his effort to obtain bankruptcy relief. If a debt, although manipulatively incurred, is not timely identified as abusive and therefore is discharged, creditors will suffer harm as a result of the discharge and the consequent dilution of the bankruptcy estate. . . . For all of these reasons, we conclude that §526(a)(4) prohibits a debt relief agency only from advising an assisted person to incur more debt when the impelling reason for the advice is the anticipation of bankruptcy. . . .
>
> Under our reading of the statute, of course, the prohibited advice is not defined in terms of abusive prefiling conduct but rather the incurrence of additional debt when the impelling reason is the anticipation of bankruptcy . . . only when the impetus of the advice to incur more debt is the expectation of filing for bankruptcy and obtaining the attendant relief.

Id. at 1336-39. By express admission, the Court did not decide if the statute, as narrowly construed, withstands First Amendment scrutiny. *Id.* at 1339.

Burnett advised financing the purchase of a new car, and, depending on how the Manfrieds tapped the 401K account, Burnett may have advised incurring debt to pay him. The anticipation of bankruptcy was an impelling reason but not "the" impelling reason, at least not with respect to advising the new car purchase. Is there a difference? Burnett may well be accountable under section 526, though the First Amendment may protect him.

BANKRUPTCY ESSAY EXAM #2 [CHAPTER 7]

QUESTION #1

Property of the Estate and Avoidance

a) What property initially filled the bankruptcy estate? Filing bankruptcy "creates an estate" that "is comprised of" all of the debtor's property, i.e., "all legal and equitable interests of the debtor in property as of the commencement of the case. . . ." 11 U.S.C. §541(a)(1). The nature of the interest is irrelevant. The size of the interest is irrelevant. The location of the property is irrelevant. The estate is everything, everywhere in which the debtor has some interest, any interest at the time bankruptcy is filed.

Of course, only the debtor's interests in property become part of the bankruptcy estate. Another person's interest in the same property is not part of the estate. Although bankruptcy may affect the other person's interest in various ways, bankruptcy of the debtor who also owns an interest in the property does not itself cut off the other person's interest for the benefit of the estate or anyone else.

Therefore, only Max's interest in the house that he and Mary owned is part of the estate. Mary keeps her interest despite Max's bankruptcy.

Max's car is fully encumbered by GMAC's security interest (i.e., consensual lien). Nevertheless, GMAC's lien did not displace Max's interest. Rather, the lien attached to Max's interest, and he retains it despite the lien. So, Max has an interest in the car that is part of the estate, but GMAC's property interest, i.e., the lien, is not part of the estate. GMAC's lien is substantively unaffected by Max filing bankruptcy. The automatic stay stops GMAC from enforcing the lien but does not cut off the lien.

Max also retained an interest in truck 004, which Lender had repossessed but had not sold. A secured party repossessing its collateral under UCC Article 9 does not end the debtor's interest. The debtor's interest continues until a proper disposition under Article 9. And, the debtor's interest in property passes to the estate even though the debtor lacks possession or other means of control. As a result, Max's interest in truck 004 is part of the estate.

Max now has no interest in the building where he operated his business. The only interest Max ever owned with respect to the building was maybe some kind of leasehold interest. But, when the lease ended, so did Max's interest in the property, unless state law provides otherwise.

The debtor's property that comprises the estate is not limited to real property and goods but also includes every other kind of property, including intangible personal property. Therefore, any right or liability that somebody else owes Max is part of the estate, including Max's contract cause of action against Joel Manfried, which Max's trustee would pursue as a claim in Joel's bankruptcy.

b) Is any property Max owned before bankruptcy included in the estate? Ordinarily, the estate includes only the debtor's interests in property owned at the time bankruptcy is filed. 11 U.S.C. §541(a)(1) ("all legal and equitable interests of the debtor in property as of the commencement of the case"). There are a few exceptions to this general rule that add to the estate some property the debtor acquires *after* having filed the case. *Id.* §541(b).

Interests in property the debtor owned but effectively transferred *before* bankruptcy (so that the debtor retained no interest whatsoever) is generally not part of the estate. However, the Bankruptcy Code gives the trustee certain powers to unwind certain prepetition transfers. These avoidance powers are limited but potent as far as they go.

For example, the trustee can avoid a prepetition fraudulent transfer of property by the debtor. The trustee can rely on state law to do so, 11 U.S.C. §544(a), or on the Code's own fraudulent transfer provision. *Id.* §548. Usually, with one big exception, there are no significant differences between state law and section 548. As a result it usually makes no meaningful difference whether the trustee relies on state fraudulent transfer law or section 548 to avoid the transfer.

The big exception is the length of the "reach-back" period. Section 548 allows the trustee to avoid fraudulent transfers "made or incurred on or within 2 years before the date of the filing of the petition." 11 U.S.C. §548(a)(1). Reach-back periods under state law are often longer and sometimes much longer.

If a transfer is avoided under either law, the trustee's remedies are varied. The trustee can recover the property itself or the value of the property from the initial transfer or a subsequent transferee, subject to limited defenses. 11 U.S.C. §550.

Under either state law or section 548, the trustee can avoid prepetition transfers of the debtor's property made with actual intent to hinder, delay, or defraud creditors, even if the debtor received perfect value in exchange. On this basis, the trustee could try to avoid Max's sales of trucks 001 and 002. The problem, of course, is proving actual fraud. It is true that Max sold the trucks in violation of the security agreement with Bank, but breaking a contract is not itself actually fraudulent. And, some of the money—maybe most of it—was used to pay other creditors, which is not a bad thing in itself. It is not clear that the sales were actually fraudulent.

More often, transfers are avoided because they are "constructively" fraudulent, that is, for a reason described in the fraudulent transfer law that requires no actual, fraudulent, or otherwise tacky intent. If a transfer is constructively fraudulent, the trustee can avoid it even though the debtor and transferee acted in good faith, with a pure, honest interest, and acted for a good cause.

The broadest constructively fraudulent transfer is one made by the debtor without a reasonably equivalent value (sometimes called "fair consideration") if the debtor was already insolvent at the time of the transfer or was rendered insolvent by the transfer. On this basis, if Max was insolvent throughout the facts, the trustee can argue that these transfers were constructively fraudulent:

- Max's sale of trucks 001 and 002, maybe because what he received in exchange ("much less than he wanted and expected") was less than reasonably equivalent value.

- The $1000 payments to Max's wife, Mary. Max received nothing of value as value is defined for purposes of fraudulent transfer law, i.e., economic equivalent to the value of the property transferred so that the net effect on the debtor's financial status is zero.

Also, Lender's sale of truck 003 for half its value is suspect. It's true that the transfer was by Lender and not Max. However, the law requires only a transfer of a debtor's interest in property, not that the debtor herself effected the transfer. But, a forced sale by a secured creditor to enforce a lien is typically immune from attack as a fraudulent transfer (even if less than reasonably equivalent value was received) if the sale complied with applicable state law governing the creditor's disposition of the property. See BFP v. Resolution Trust Corp., 511 U.S. 531 (1994).

QUESTION #2

Automatic Stay

a) Does the stay prevent Third Bank from suing or otherwise acting to collect from Max the loan on which the brother was liable with Max as surety? The automatic stay stops, among other things, "the commencement or continuation, including the issuance or employment of process, of a judicial, administrative, or other action or proceeding against the debtor that was or could have been commenced before the commencement of the case under this title, or to recover a claim against the debtor that arose before the commencement of the case under this title." 11 U.S.C. §362(a). So, Third Bank cannot take any action to collect the loan from Max, except filing a claim in the bankruptcy case.

The stay does not protect third parties or their property. So, efforts by Third Bank to collect from Max's brother are not stayed.

Sometimes, the court will supplement the stay by enjoining conduct now covered by the stay. See 11 U.S.C. §105(a) ("The court may issue any order, process, or judgment that is necessary or appropriate to carry out the provisions of this title."). On this basis, courts can enjoin actions against third-party nondebtors, such as the brother, but usually only if the action threatens to affect property of the estate. Third Bank's action against the brother does not threaten estate property, and winning a section 105 injunction is therefore very unlikely.

b) Can Lender sell truck 004, which Lender had already repossessed before Max filed bankruptcy? Among other things, the automatic stay stops:

(3) any act to obtain possession of property of the estate or of property from the estate or to exercise control over property of the estate;

(4) any act to create, perfect, or enforce any lien against property of the estate;

(5) any act to create, perfect, or enforce against property of the debtor any lien to the extent that such lien secures a claim that arose before the commencement of the case under this title;

(6) any act to collect, assess, or recover a claim against the debtor that arose before the commencement of the case under this title. . . .

11 U.S.C. §362(a). Even though Lender had repossessed truck 004 before Max filed bankruptcy, Max still retained his interest in the property. Lender's security interest attached to this interest and did not displace it. And, repossession did not terminate Max's interest. When Max filed bankruptcy, this interest in truck 004 passed to the bankruptcy estate. Therefore, Lender's state-law rights to sell or otherwise dispose of truck 004 are stayed under section 362(a)(3)-(6).

On the other hand, the court will surely lift the stay for Lender to dispose of the truck if the truck is not worth more than the secured debt. *Id.* §362(d)(2)(A).

However, if there is equity in the property, Lender can be required to return the property so the trustee can sell the debtor's interest and keep the net equity, 11 U.S.C. §542(a) ("[A]n entity . . . in possession, custody, or control, during the case, of property that the trustee may use, sell, or lease . . . or that the debtor may exempt . . . shall deliver to the trustee, and account for, such property or the value of such property, unless such property is of inconsequential value or benefit to the estate."). Or, the court can lift the stay to allow Lender to dispose of the property and remit the net equity to the trustee.

c) How should the court decide Lender's motion to lift the stay to enforce its security interest in truck 005?   In a Chapter 7 case, the court will grant relief from the stay, "such as by terminating, annulling, modifying, or conditioning the stay," with respect to property of the estate and other property protected by the stay, if "the debtor does not have an equity in such property. . . ." 11 U.S.C. §362(d)(1)(2)(A). The creditor must also show, in addition to the debtor's lack of equity, that the creditor lien is fully perfected under state law.

The explanation is simple. It is the debtor's equity in collateral that the trustee will collect and distribute to unsecured creditors in a Chapter 7 case. If the debtor lacks any equity, there is nothing in the property for the trustee and creditors. There is no reason to continue to prevent the creditor from enforcing its state-law rights with respect to the collateral.

Proof of perfection of the creditor's lien is required because if the lien is not perfected, the trustee can almost certainly avoid the lien under section 544(a). 11 U.S.C. §544(a). As a result, the lien would be stripped away, the creditor's claim would be entirely unsecured, and the full value of the property (save any third party's interests) would be property of the estate. Then, there is nothing in the property for the creditor, and the stay will not be lifted.

d) Is Mary's divorce action against Max stayed?   The automatic stay stops most types of litigation against the debtor and most actions against property of the estate. Certain types of suits, however, are excluded from the stay. These include a suit "for the dissolution of a marriage, *except to the extent that such proceeding seeks to determine the division of property that is property of the estate.*" 11 U.S.C. §362(b)(2)(a)(iv) (emphasis added).

When Max filed bankruptcy, all of his interests in property passed to the bankruptcy estate, including any property interests that could be awarded to Mary in the divorce case. See In re Taub, 2010 WL 1443889, *8 (E.D.N.Y. 2010) ("The Debtor's real property constitutes property of the estate protected by the automatic stay even though the Debtor's legal interests may be modified by legal actions presently pending in this Court, the matrimonial court, and elsewhere" and "even where 'the debtor's claimed interest in property may turn out to be groundless.' "). To the extent that Mary's divorce action can possibly affect property of the estate, her action is stayed.

On the other hand, the bankruptcy court can modify the stay to allow the parties' divorce action to proceed even to determine a division of the marital debts and property, including property of the estate. Such modifications are common because state courts have so much more expertise in the applicable law. As explained by the court in In re Takacs, 2008 WL 4401395 (Bankr. E.D. Va. 2008):

> There can be no doubt that equitable distribution is governed solely by state law and is a subject area, not only in which state courts have a special expertise, but in which federal courts owe special deference to state courts. Almost by definition, judicial economy would be promoted, since this court — while it has jurisdiction to determine traditional property interests in assets of the bankruptcy estate — has no domestic relations jurisdiction, and there would thus be no overlapping proceedings with respect to the specific issues affecting equitable distribution.

Id. at *2.

QUESTION #3

Claims Against the Estate

In a Chapter 7 case, property of the estate is liquidated and distributed to unsecured creditors with allowed claims against the estate that have been filed with the court. A "claim" is any "right to payment, whether or not such right is reduced to judgment, liquidated, unliquidated, fixed, contingent, matured, unmatured, disputed, undisputed, legal, equitable, secured, or unsecured. . . ." 11 U.S.C. §101(5)(A). To the extent that a claim is secured, the secured creditor is not paid from the estate and, instead, looks to its collateral.

Describe the nature of these persons' claims against the bankruptcy estate.

a) Bank's claims The debt to Bank is the total amount owed on the loans originally secured by trucks 001 and 002. Clearly, if Max had not sold the trucks, Bank would have a claim for each of the truck loans. Each of these claims would be a secured claim to the extent of the value of the collateral. Any deficiency would be an unsecured claim.

But the trucks were sold before bankruptcy. Max had no rights in them when he filed. Bank's security interest continued in the proceeds, but this collateral, too, was gone before bankruptcy. So, the bankruptcy estate acquired no interest in the trucks or the proceeds.

A secured claim requires that the creditor have a lien on property of the estate. 11 U.S.C. §506(a)(1). Because the estate had no interest in the trucks or the proceeds, Bank has two totally unsecured, contract claims for the total amount Max owes on the two truck loans.

(Probably, though, Bank's security interest continued in the trucks. Bank can therefore enforce its interest against the buyers. Bank probably lost its interest in the proceeds Max spent. The persons he paid would almost certainly take free of Bank's interest.)

Bank may have a tort claim, too. Max's unauthorized sale of the trucks (and spending the proceeds) likely amounts to conversion. It would seem that such a tort claim is unhelpful to Bank because this claim, too, is unsecured.

However, Bank can possibly argue that this claim is excepted from the discharge Max receives. 11 U.S.C. §523(a)(6) (excepting from discharge any debt for willful and malicious injury to another entity *or to the property of another entity*). If so, Bank can enforce the tort claim against bankruptcy despite the discharge.

b) Lender's claims   Lender has a claim with respect to each of the three trucks.

The claim for the debt owed on the loan originally secured by truck 003 is the amount of the deficiency (amount still owed after auction sale) and any finance charges accrued before bankruptcy. However, the low sale price suggests (but is not conclusive in itself) that the sale may not have been in compliance with applicable law. If so, state law would likely give Max an offsetting claim for damages for wrongful sale. This claim is property of the bankruptcy estate that the trustee can enforce to reduce Bank's claims, as by objecting to Bank's claim if and when Bank files the claim. See 11 U.S.C. §§541(a); 502(b); see also 11 U.S.C. §558 (giving trustee power to assert debtor's *defenses*).

The claim with respect to truck 004 is a secured claim to the extent of the value of the collateral and an unsecured claim with respect to the balance. 11 U.S.C. §506(a). In practice, either the trustee or Lender will sell the truck, and the estate gets any surplus (amount received that exceeds secured debt). The same is true with respect to truck 005.

c) Landlord's claim   In this case, explanation of the landlord's claim is simple. She has an unsecured claim for the accrued rent.

If the lease had been for a term that had not expired, section 365 would apply. 11 U.S.C. §365. Generally speaking, in such a case, the trustee can reject or assume the lease and, if the lease is assumed, can assign the lease. If the lease is rejected, the lease is deemed breached, *id.* §365(g)(1), and the landlord has a claim that includes both accrued, unpaid rent and also damages with respect to the landlord's loss of expected future rents subject to limitations the Bankruptcy Code imposes. 11 U.S.C. §502(b)(6).

d) GMAC's claim   GMAC has a secured claim to the extent of the value of the collateral and an unsecured claim for the balance. 11 U.S.C. §506(a)(1).

e) Mortgagees' claims   Each mortgagee has a secured claim to the extent of the value of Max's interest in the house collateral and an unsecured claim for the balance. 11 U.S.C. §506(a)(1). The second mortgagee's claim, however, is based on the value of the property in excess of the amount of the first mortgage. For example, suppose that the value of Max's interest in the property is $300,000. The first mortgage debt is $250,000. The second mortgage debt is $100,000. The first mortgagee has a fully secured claim for $250,000. The second mortgagee has a secured claim for $50,000 and an unsecured claim for $50,000.

f) Brother's claim   A surety that pays the debt is subrogated to the rights of the creditor. So, if Max had already paid the unsecured debt owed Third Bank, the brother would be the creditor with respect to this debt and have an unsecured claim against the estate in the same amount.

In this case, the brother has not yet paid the debt. However, and very likely, Third Bank will eventually enforce the debt against him, and Max will be required to pay. Until the brother pays, his liability is secondary or contingent and so is Max's liability to him. Nevertheless, the brother has a claim against the estate. "Claim" is defined as, 11 U.S.C. §101(5), "right to payment, *whether or not* such right is reduced to judgment, liquidated, unliquidated, fixed, *contingent*, matured, *unmatured*, disputed, undisputed, legal, equitable, secured, or unsecured. . . ."

g) Wife's claims   There are two types of claims to consider. First, prepetition, unsecured domestic support obligations based on state law that arise from the dissolution of the marriage. These claims are priority claims, 11 U.S.C. §507(a)(1), which mean they are paid before the claims of other unsecured creditors. Postpetition domestic support obligations are excepted from the discharge, which means they can be enforced against Max despite the discharge. 11 U.S.C. §523(a)(5).

Max's liability to Mary based on his unilateral promise to pay her $1000 (which he has probably stopped paying) is treated differently if it falls outside of the definition of "domestic support obligation." There is no claim whatsoever based on this promise if the promise is not enforceable. Debt means liability on a *claim*, 11 U.S.C. §101(12) (emphasis added), and there is no claim unless there is a "right to payment." Max's promise was a unilateral promise. It may be unenforceable for lack of consideration. If so, the trustee can object to Mary's claim based on this promise, assert the state-law defense of unenforceability, 11 U.S.C. §558, and the claim will not be allowed. If it is allowed and is not a domestic support obligation, the claim is likely an unsecured claim with no priority and no protection from the discharge.

h) Employees' claims   Before bankruptcy, as part of his effort to stay alive, Max had laid off some employees and still owes them wages they earned before bankruptcy. These employees have unsecured claims for the wages owed them. To some extent, these claims, though unsecured, are also entitled to priority payment from the estate. 11 U.S.C. §507(a)(4).

QUESTION #4

Scope and Effect of the Discharge

How does the bankruptcy discharge in Max's case affect these claims?

a) Secured claims (over and under)   In a Chapter 7 case, the Bankruptcy Code requires the court to grant an individual debtor a discharge, subject to some limited, specific reasons for not granting a discharge, 11 U.S.C. §727(a) (*objections* to discharge), and a few debts that are not affected by any discharge. 11 U.S.C. §523(a) (*exceptions* to discharge).

Part of the effect of the discharge is to operate "as an injunction against the commencement or continuation of an action, the employment of process, or an act, to collect, recover or offset any such debt as a personal liability of the debtor, whether or not discharge of such debt is waived. . . ." 11 U.S.C. §524(a)(2). For this reason, because the debtor is personally liable for an unsecured claim, the holder of such a claim cannot do anything to enforce or collect it.

On the other hand, if the claim is secured, the holder of the secured claim can enforce its lien despite the discharge. The reason: the creditor is enforcing a property interest, not personal liability. The discharge does not affect the enforcement of liens that survive bankruptcy.

But, to the extent the value of the collateral proves less than the debt, the deficiency is personal liability that is discharged. Assume the total debt owed the creditor is $100,000, which is secured by an interest in some property. The automatic stay stops the creditor from enforcing the lien during bankruptcy. Upon discharge, the stay ends but the discharge injunction begins. The creditor is free to enforce the lien in compliance with state-law rights. Assume the creditor enforces its lien by selling the property, and the sale produces $80,000. The creditor gets the $80,000 but cannot do anything to enforce or collect the $20,000 deficiency because this debt is personal liability and discharged.

What happens in the unlikely opposite case in which the collateral's value increases after bankruptcy? For example, assume that before and throughout the Chapter 7 case, the house that secures the two mortgages is worth $300,000. At the time, the second mortgagee's secured claim is $50,000. If these facts remain unchanged after bankruptcy and the mortgages are foreclosed at a sale producing $250,000, the first mortgagee gets $250,000 and is fully satisfied. The second mortgagee gets $50,000 of the proceeds. The $50,000 deficiency owed the second mortgagee is discharged.

Assume, however, that for a time after bankruptcy, the debtor continues voluntarily to make payments on the debt. (The discharge does not prevent the debtor from voluntarily paying any debt. 11 U.S.C. §524(f). Paying discharged debts after bankruptcy based on an agreement with the creditor is a different story. *Id.* §524(c).) Therefore, the mortgagees take no action to enforce their liens.

After several months, the debtor defaults. The house is sold at a forced sale that produces $350,000. The first mortgagee undoubtedly gets $250,000 of the proceeds. The second mortgagee undoubtedly gets $50,000 of the proceeds. Who gets the $50,000 surplus, the second mortgagee or the debtor? The second mortgagee gets it. The second mortgage lien is not frozen at the value of the collateral during bankruptcy. If the property appreciates, the lien swells to the extent of the amount of the debt. And this fattened lien is fully enforceable to the same extent. Dewsnup v. Timm, 502 U.S. 410 (1992).

b) Bank's claim for conversion (basis for "objecting" to discharge or "excepting" the debt)   Bank probably has a tort claim against the estate based on Max's unauthorized sale of Bank's collateral: the trucks and the proceeds thereof. This conduct likely amounts to conversion and gives Bank a tort claim against the estate. The claim is unsecured, however, and is not likely to be satisfied from the probably tiny estate. Also, Max's liability on a tort claim is personal liability that will be discharged.

However, Bank can possibly argue (probably in good faith but with unfavorable odds) that this tortious conduct is a reason for not discharging any of Max's debts (denying him a discharge altogether) or, more narrowly, is a reason for not discharging just the tort liability to Bank.

In a Chapter 7 case, the court must give an individual debtor a discharge unless the debtor has engaged in certain (usually objectionable) conduct before or during bankruptcy. The kinds of conduct that will result in denying the debtor a discharge are described by section 727(a). They are commonly known as "objections" to discharge. If any of them is proved, there is no discharge of any debt. All of the debtor's obligations, including personal liabilities, survive bankruptcy and are unaffected by the discharge.

The objections to discharge include:

- the debtor, with intent to hinder, delay, or defraud a creditor or an officer of the estate charged with custody of property under this title, has transferred, removed, destroyed, mutilated, or concealed, or has permitted to be transferred, removed, destroyed, mutilated, or concealed—
  — property of the debtor, within one year before the date of the filing of the petition; or
  — property of the estate, after the date of the filing of the petition;
- the debtor has concealed, destroyed, mutilated, falsified, or failed to keep or preserve any recorded information, including books, documents, records, and papers, from which the debtor's financial condition or business transactions might be ascertained, unless such act or failure to act was justified under all of the circumstances of the case;
- the debtor knowingly and fraudulently, in or in connection with the case—
  — made a false oath or account;
  — presented or used a false claim;
  — gave, offered, received, or attempted to obtain money, property, or advantage, or a promise of money, property, or advantage, for acting or forbearing to act; or
  — withheld from an officer of the estate entitled to possession under this title, any recorded information, including books, documents, records, and papers, relating to the debtor's property or financial affairs;
- the debtor has failed to explain satisfactorily, before determination of denial of discharge under this paragraph, any loss of assets or deficiency of assets to meet the debtor's liabilities;
- the debtor has refused, in the case—
  — to obey any lawful order of the court, other than an order to respond to a material question or to testify;
  — on the ground of privilege against self-incrimination, to respond to a material question approved by the court or to testify, after the debtor has been granted immunity with respect to the matter concerning which such privilege was invoked; or
  — on a ground other than the properly invoked privilege against self-incrimination, to respond to a material question approved by the court or to testify;
- the debtor has been granted a discharge under this section, under section 1141 of this title, or under section 14, 371, or 476 of the Bankruptcy Act, in a case commenced within 8 years before the date of the filing of the petition;

- the debtor has been granted a discharge under section 1228 or 1328 of this title, or under section 660 or 661 of the Bankruptcy Act, in a case commenced within six years before the date of the filing of the petition [with some exceptions]. . . .
- the court approves a written waiver of discharge executed by the debtor after the order for relief under this chapter; [or]
- after filing the petition, the debtor failed to complete an instructional course concerning personal financial management. . . .

11 U.S.C. §727(a)(2)-(6), (8)-(11). The objections to discharge are usually interpreted very narrowly, and denying the debtor a discharge for any of these reasons is uncommon. Bank can argue that the conversion of its collateral fits within the objection for fraudulent transfers, but the creditor is required to prove actual fraudulent intent, which is probably lacking in Max's case.

Even when a debtor receives a discharge, certain debts are excepted from the effects of the discharge. These debts are called "exceptions" to discharge and are described in section 523. 11 U.S.C. §523(a). Excepted debts include debts for:

- certain taxes;
- money, property, or services obtained by certain fraud;
- fraud or defalcation while acting in a fiduciary capacity, embezzlement, or larceny;
- a domestic support obligation;
- for willful and malicious injury by the debtor to another entity or to the property of another entity;
- STUDENT LOANS; and
- death or personal injury caused by the debtor's operation of a motor vehicle, vessel, or aircraft if such operation was unlawful because the debtor was intoxicated from using alcohol, a drug, or another substance.

11 U.S.C. §523(a)(1)-(2), (4)-(6), (8)-(9).

Bank could argue that the conversion claim is "excepted" under section 523 as a debt "for willful and malicious injury by the debtor to another entity or to the property of another entity." *Id.* §523(a)(6). This exception probably does not apply to the judgment against Joel Manfried for malicious negligence, as discussed in Essay Exam #1, even though punitive damages were awarded. The Supreme Court in Kawaauhau v. Geiger (In re Geiger), 523 U.S. 57 (1998), made clear that for section 523(a)(6) to apply, the actor must intend the consequences of the act, as with an intentional tort.

Bank's claim in this case is different. In this case, Max's conduct was intentional, but intentional does not mean willful. And, the Supreme Court in *Geiger* was clear that in order for the injury to be "willful and malicious," the debtor must intend the injury itself. The Restatement (Second) of Torts §8A, a comment to which the Supreme Court cites favorably in *Geiger*, defines "intent" as "denot[ing] that the actor desires to cause consequences of his act, or that he believes the consequences are substantially certain to result from it." Additionally, this requisite intent is not sufficient to block discharge under section 523(a)(6). Both willfulness *and maliciousness* must also be proven.

With respect to maliciousness, "[m]alice does not mean the same thing for nondischargeability purposes under §523(a)(6) as it does in contexts outside of bankruptcy. In bankruptcy, debtor may act with malice without bearing any subjective ill will toward plaintiff creditor or any specific intent to injure same. The Fourth Circuit defines malice as an act causing injury without just cause or excuse. Debtor's subjective mind set is central to the inquiry as to whether debtor acted deliberately in knowing disregard of a creditor's rights in property." In re Wooten, 423 B.R. 108, 130 (Bankr. E.D. Va. 2010).

So, the issue in this case is whether Max's technically intentional conduct of conversion was sufficiently willful and malicious within the peculiar meaning of section 523(a)(6).

To begin with, conversion requires acting knowingly or intentionally, but not necessarily with wrongful intent. Conversion can result from perfectly innocent, unknowing conduct by the actor. So, conversion is not always a willful and malicious injury to property of another. It requires, at least, that the conversion is done without the victim's knowledge or consent, for the purpose of inflicting the injury *or* knowing that the debtor's act was substantially certain to result in injury, which did occur, and without justification and excuse.

The problem for Bank fitting its conversion claim against Max within section 523(a)(6) is that conversion, including conversion of collateral, does not necessarily produce harm. And, the argument for willfulness and maliciousness is weakened if the debtor was acting with the hope and expectation of saving the business and also if the debtor had no real understanding of breach of legal rights that was occurring when she transferred property. Cutting the other way is the fact of the debtor using proceeds for personal reasons, not just business purposes.

So, was Max's conduct in selling the Bank's collateral, and not remitting the proceeds, willful and malicious within section 523(a)(6)? It's hard to say. The bankruptcy court deciding yes or no — either way — would almost certainly be upheld on appeal.

c) Third Bank's claim against Max's brother as a surety on the loan to Max (a/k/a effect of discharge on third-party nondebtors)   The discharge works as an injunction with respect to enforcing or collecting personal liability *of the debtor.* 11 U.S.C. §524(a). With narrowly confined exceptions typically in Chapter 11 cases, "discharge of a debt of the debtor does not affect the liability of any other entity on, or the property of any other entity for, such debt." *Id.* §524(e).

Therefore, as is true with respect to the automatic stay, the discharge in Max's bankruptcy case does not prevent Third Bank from going to Max's brother, the surety, to collect the loan debt. And, if the brother paid the debt and was thereby subrogated to Third Bank's claim against Max as the principal obligor on the debt, the discharge would prevent the brother from trying to recoup from Max. The principal purpose of suretyship is to shift, from the creditor to the surety, the risk of the principal obligor's bankruptcy and discharge.

QUESTION #5

Dismissal of the Case

a) Can Max freely dismiss the bankruptcy case?   Max filed Chapter 7 but never intended to go through with liquidation. His plan was to file the case, take advantage of the automatic stay to stop his creditors' collection efforts and buy himself some time, get better financially, work out matters with his creditors, and then dismiss the case. Many assumptions underlie this plan, including the assumption that a Chapter 7 debtor can freely dismiss the case. He can't.

The decision whether or not to grant a motion to dismiss a Chapter 7 case lies within the discretion of the bankruptcy court but, says section 707(a), "only for cause." 11 U.S.C. §707(a). Showing cause is required of any party in interest who wants to dismiss a case, even the debtor.

> While the section [707(a)] does not expressly refer to voluntary dismissals, the courts have held that it is applicable to such requests as well as to requests filed by creditors. The debtor thus has no absolute right to dismiss a Chapter 7 proceeding and must demonstrate cause for dismissal. Even if cause is shown, however, the court may deny the motion if creditors may be prejudiced by dismissal of the case.

In re Foster, 316 B.R. 718, 720 (Bankr. W.D. Mo. 2004); see also Blumeyer v. Sosne (In re Blumeyer), 383 B.R. 457, 2008 WL 657862, at *3 (B.A.P. 8th Cir. Mar. 13, 2008); In re Cohara, 324 B.R. 24 (BAP 6th Cir. 2005) (debtor does not have an absolute right to voluntarily dismiss his/her Chapter 7 case but, as party moving to dismiss, bears burden of showing "cause" for dismissal); In re Hopper, 404 B.R. 302 (Bankr. N.D. Ill. 2009) (debtor does not have an absolute right to dismiss a Chapter 7 case even if begun on a voluntary petition). Similarly, the debtor has no absolute right to dismiss a Chapter 13 case, In re Caola, 422 B.R. 13 (Bankr. D.N.J. 2010); In re Armstrong, 408 B.R. 559 (Bankr. E.D.N.Y. 2009); to convert a case from Chapter 7 to Chapter 13, Marrama v. Citizens Bank, 549 U.S. 365 (2007); or to convert a Chapter 11 case to Chapter 7, Monroe Bank & Trust v. Pinnock, 349 B.R. 493 (E.D. Mich. 2006).

Accordingly, the Federal Rules of Bankruptcy Procedure mandate that a motion for dismissal by a debtor must be predicated on cause and may only be granted after notice and a hearing. Fed. R. Bankr. P. 1017(a). In determining whether to grant such a motion, the courts have generally looked at the following factors:

- whether all of the creditors have consented;
- whether the debtor is acting in good faith;
- whether dismissal would result in a prejudicial delay in payments;
- whether dismissal would result in a reordering of priorities;
- whether there is another proceeding through which the payment of claims can be handled; and
- whether an objection to discharge, an objection to exemptions, or a preference claim is pending.

In re Foster, 316 B.R. 718, 720-21 (Bankr. W.D. Mo. 2004). The key is whether or not dismissal will prejudice creditors, and the debtor bears the burden of proving lack of such prejudice.

Generally, however, "creditors are . . . not prejudiced by dismissal since they will no longer be stayed from resorting to the state courts to enforce and realize upon their claims." In re Bruckman, 413 B.R. 46, 50 (Bankr. N.D. 2009). But, they "may be prejudiced 'if the motion to dismiss is brought after the passage of a considerable amount of time and they have been forestalled from collecting the amounts owed to them.' " *Id.*

Especially if his creditors don't agree, Max is likely unable freely to dismiss his case for two principal reasons.

- First, "it is well established and supported by legislative history that the fact that a debtor is willing and able to pay his debts outside of bankruptcy does not constitute adequate cause for dismissal under Section 707(a)." Kirby v. Spatz (In re Spatz), 221 B.R. 992, 994 (Bankr. M.D. Fla. 1998); see also In re Perrine, 369 B.R. 571 (Bankr. C.D. Cal. 2007) (In this case, the debtor anticipated that there would be funds available to pay unsecured creditors, at least in part; but dismissal would have resulted in prejudice to creditors because there was no guarantee that Perrine would have paid their claims outside of bankruptcy.); In re Foster, 316 B.R. 718 (Bankr. W.D. Mo. 2004) (the ability of a debtor to pay his debts is not cause for dismissal).

- Second, the delay that Max caused his creditors in filing bankruptcy may have prejudiced them; and, the courts often say, as though an independent rule, that "[d]ismissal of a bankruptcy petition that was filed principally to forestall creditors should not be permitted after the delay sought has been achieved." In re Bruckman, 413 B.R. 46, 50 (Bankr. N.D. 2009).

b) Could the court dismiss the case for bad faith sua sponte *or on motion by a party in interest?*   Suppose Max decided not to ask for dismissal of his case or had his motion to dismiss denied. He filed the case with no intention of liquidating but now will not or cannot stop the case on his own. Maybe he even discovers that there is unexpected advantage to him in completing the Chapter 7 case. Can the court on its own, or upon motion by the trustee or a creditor, dismiss the case for bad faith because of Max's arguably disingenuous filing?

Undoubtedly, the bankruptcy court is empowered to dismiss a case for bad faith. Section 707(a) allows dismissal for cause, and the courts long ago decided that bad faith is "cause." 11 U.S.C. §707(a). Also, in 2005, the Bankruptcy Code was amended to provide explicitly that in a case filed by an individual with primarily consumer debts, a court can dismiss a Chapter 7 case if granting relief to the debtor would be an abuse of Chapter 7; and for this purpose abuse includes the debtor filing "the petition in bad faith" or if "the totality of the circumstances . . . of the debtor's financial situation demonstrates abuse." 11 U.S.C. §707(b)(3). Finally, dismissal for bad faith is within the inherent judicial authority of the bankruptcy court.

The issue is whether or not Max's motive for filing bankruptcy translates into filing in bad faith or lacking good faith.

The courts always wrestle with defining a bad faith filing, as in In re Hornung, 425 B.R. 242 (Bankr. M.D.N.C. 2010):

> In the context of bankruptcy, a "bad faith filing" is defined as "[t]he act of submitting a bankruptcy petition that is inconsistent with the purposes of the Bankruptcy Code or is an abuse of the bankruptcy system (that is, by not being filed in good faith)." Black's Law Dictionary 149 (8th ed. 2004). Good faith is defined as a "state of mind consisting in (1) honesty in belief or purpose, . . . or (4) absence of intent to defraud or to seek unconscionable advantage." . . . "Bad faith may involve a dishonest debtor or nefarious acts, but such motivation or intent is not necessary. Bad faith exists if the filing of the bankruptcy was for a purpose not consistent with the Bankruptcy Code or policy even though the purpose may otherwise be lawful." In determining whether a debtor filed her petition in bad faith, courts should look to the debtor's intent and purpose at the time of commencing the bankruptcy, focusing upon the debtor's conduct. An analysis of bad faith under Section 707(b)(3)(A) may look outside a debtor's financial situation.

Id. at 248-49. And the courts regularly recite lists of factors to consider based on the "totality of circumstances," even though "totality" is supposedly a separate independent basis for dismissal in some cases.

> "[A] debtor's bad faith acts or omissions may, in the totality of the circumstances, constitute cause for dismissal in the sound discretion of the bankruptcy court." . . . [M]ost courts "sensibly employ a totality of the circumstances test focusing on a variety of factors," [including:]
> (1) The debtor's concealment or misrepresentation of assets and/or sources of income, such as the improper or unexplained transfers of assets prior to filing;
> (2) The debtor's lack of candor and completeness in his statements and schedules, such as the inflation of his expenses to disguise his financial well-being;
> (3) The debtor has sufficient resources to repay his debts, and leads a lavish lifestyle, continuing to have excessive and continued expenditures;
> (4) The debtor's motivation in filing is to avoid a large single debt incurred through conduct akin to fraud, misconduct, or gross negligence, such as a judgment in pending litigation, or a collection action;
> (5) The debtor's petition is part of a "deliberate and persistent pattern" of evading a single creditor;
> (6) The debtor is "overutilizing the protection of the Code" to the detriment to his creditors;
> (7) The debtor reduced his creditors to a single creditor prior to filing the petition;
> (8) The debtor's lack of attempt to repay creditors;
> (9) The debtor's payment of debts to insider creditors;
> (10) The debtor's "procedural gymnastics" that have the effect of frustrating creditors;
> (11) The unfairness of the debtor's use of the bankruptcy process.

In re Remember Enterprises, Inc., 425 B.R. 757, 762-63 (Bankr. M.D.N.C. 2010).

But, at core, "good faith is an 'amorphous notion, largely defined by factual inquiry' and 'no list is exhaustive of all the conceivable factors that could be relevant in analyzing a particular debtor's good faith.' " Haney v. Clippard, 2007 WL 781321, *3 (W.D. Ky. 2007). Generally, however, "dismissal based on lack of good faith should be 'confined carefully and . . . utilized only in . . . egregious cases that entail concealed or misrepresented assets and/or sources of income, and excessive and continued expenditures, lavish lifestyle, and intention to avoid a large single debt based on conduct akin to fraud, misconduct, or gross negligence." *Id.*

Not surprisingly, therefore, filing bankruptcy to thwart creditors' collection efforts is not, by itself, bad faith.

> [C]reditors complaining about a debtor's bad faith are able to argue that the debtor filed bankruptcy in response to just about any action they might take, whether it is filing suit, a motion for summary judgment, setting a matter for trial, following trial or judgment or following proceedings to enforce a judgment. Thus, whenever a debtor files it can stand condemned in creditors' eyes. The only way to avoid such criticism would be to file bankruptcy when creditors are not taking any action to collect their debts, and that hardly seems particularly useful.

In re Kane & Kane, 406 B.R. 163, 170 (Bankr. S.D. Fla. 2009). And specifically, "the fact that Debtor may have effectively put creditors on hold and delayed their pursuit of state law claims is a mere by-product of having filed bankruptcy and thereby invoked the automatic stay of Section 362. This delay in collecting debts, without more, cannot alone constitute cause for dismissal." In re Aiello, 2010 WL 1718203, *3 (Bankr. E.D.N.Y. 2010); see also In re 15375 Memorial Corp. v. Bepco, L.P., 589 F.3d 605 (3d Cir. 2009) (The protection of the automatic stay is not *per se* a valid justification for filing bankruptcy; rather, it is a consequential benefit of an otherwise good faith filing.); In re Burton, 2009 WL 2912901 (Bankr. W.D.N.C. 2009) (The ability to stay collection actions by filing bankruptcy is a central tool of the bankruptcy system. If the bankruptcy case itself is meritorious, there is nothing improper about filing to avert foreclosure.).

On the other hand, "it is well-established that filing a bankruptcy petition on the eve of foreclosure (or eviction) solely to obtain an automatic stay constitutes 'bad faith' and 'cause' to dismiss a Chapter 13 case." In re Watkins, 2008 WL 708413 (E.D.N.Y. 2008).

In the end, Max's filing was probably not in bad faith, but not certainly. And, if the case is dismissed, the dismissal is not the only consequence. Sanctions against the debtor are possible on the basis of section 105(a) and the rules of bankruptcy procedure. 11 U.S.C. §105(a) ("The court may issue any order, process, or judgment that is necessary or appropriate to carry out the provisions of this title."); Fed. R. Bankr. P. 9011(b)(1) (A petition, pleading, a written motion or other paper filed with the Court contains an implicit specification that it is not being presented for any purpose, such as to harass or to cause unnecessary delay or needless increase in the cost of litigation.). These sanctions can include paying the fees of the law firm that represented the creditor who successfully moved to dismiss the case. It's not cheap. See In re Hydretech Utilities, Inc., 391 B.R. 473 (Bankr. M.D. Fla. 2008) ($36,363).

BANKRUPTCY ESSAY EXAM #3 [CHAPTER 13]

QUESTION #1

Choosing Between Chapter 7 and Chapter 13

a) Why does Ms. Burnett believe Chapter 13 is better for Steve than Chapter 7? In Chapter 7, when the petition is filed, all of the debtor's interests in property pass by law to the bankruptcy estate, 11 U.S.C. §541(a), except for a usually small subset of property excluded from the estate. *Id.* §541(b). The debtor is left with nothing except any such excluded property and any property she exempts. The trustee liquidates the balance of the estate and distributes the proceeds to unsecured creditors. In exchange, the debtor is granted a discharge. Unsecured creditors are paid from prepetition property, and the debtor reciprocally gets postpetition income and other postpetition wealth.

So, for the debtor, the "game" in Chapter 7 is to exclude and exempt as much property as possible from the estate and receive the widest possible discharge that thereby frees the most future income from creditors' claims. In short, walk away with as much property and as few liabilities as the law permits and thereby reduce the cost of the discharge as much as possible.

In purely rational, economic terms, Chapter 7 is often better for a debtor who would have a small bankruptcy estate with potential postpetition income.

In Chapter 13, the same property as in Chapter 7 fills a bankruptcy estate, but the debtor gets to keep and use the property. Prepetition debts are paid as far as possible from future, disposal income earned during the next three to five years. At the end of this period, the debtor is discharged from the unpaid balance of the unsecured debts, the bankruptcy ends, and the debtor's income is thereafter unburdened by prepetition debts.

Chapter 13 is often better for a debtor with substantial property and, considering legitimate expenses, little disposable income.

On these facts, none of Steve's property would be excluded from the bankruptcy estate; and, nothing would be exempted. There is no exemption for the MMW stock. And, the lighthouse is no longer his homestead. All of Steve's "substantial equity" would pass to the estate, and he couldn't exempt a dime.

Even if the trailer and lot are or will become his homestead or are otherwise exempt, Steve lacks any equity in the property. Again, there is nothing for the estate and nothing for Steve to exempt. The same is true with respect to the new car.

If Steve filed Chapter 7, he would escape the "crushing" unsecured debt but at the cost of his equity in the lighthouse and the MMW stock. Perhaps Steve could keep the lighthouse by refinancing and buying his equity from the estate, but refinancing is uncertain considering the down economy and Steve's low credit score. If he could refinance, even with the salary from his new job, Steve would have trouble paying the increased mortgage payment and covering the expenses of the lighthouse as vacation rental property.

If Steve filed Chapter 13, he would keep all of the property. He would not lose the lighthouse equity or anything else. His payments to secured creditors would not increase and, at worst, stay the same. And, because payments on secured debts are considered legitimate expenses that reduce disposable income that is paid under the plan to unsecured creditors, all of Steve's secured debt (lighthouse, new car and trailer, and inland lot) will substantially shrink the amount of his future "disposable" income he must pay his unsecured creditors.

You can see from this short analysis why Ms. Burnett thinks Chapter 13 may be better for Steve than Chapter 7. In Chapter 13, Steve keeps everything, and the bite out of future income is very small compared to huge amount of debt that will be discharged.

b) Why does Ms. Burnett believe Chapter 13 may be Steve's only choice? She's worried that if Steve files Chapter 7, the court will dismiss his case because his income is too high (under the statutory "means test") or for some other reason. Here's why she worries.

Steve qualifies for filing a Chapter 7 case, 11 U.S.C. §109(a) & (b). The possibility is high, however, that his case would be dismissed or, with his agreement, converted to Chapter 13, i.e., that the court would kick him out of Chapter 7.

If Steve's "current monthly income" exceeds the median family income for one earner in North Carolina, he cannot maintain a Chapter 7 case, even though he can file the case, unless he passes a "means test." The test is whether or not his income less allowed expenses multiplied by 60 is equal to or greater than the lesser of:

(I)   25 percent of the debtor's nonpriority unsecured claims in the case, or $6,000, whichever is greater; or
(II) $10,000.

To pass the test and stay in Chapter 7 (unless there is some other reason for dismissal), Steve's net income must be below the calculated amount. If his net income is equal to or greater than the calculated amount, Steve fails the means test, abuse of Chapter 7 warranting dismissal is presumed, and his case is dismissed or converted to Chapter 13 (unless one of a few, tiny exceptions applies).

Before doing the math, determine if the means test even applies in his case. It applies only if Steve's income exceeds the median income for one person in North Carolina, which is $38,656. The income from his new job is $55,000. It seems clear that Steve is subject to the means test, *but* there is more involved in comparing his income to the state median.

The comparison is based on Steve's "current monthly income" which is a backward-looking, historical amount, not Steve's current or future salary. The term means:

(A) . . . the average monthly income from all sources that the debtor receives (or in a joint case the debtor and the debtor's spouse receive) without regard to whether such income is taxable income, derived during the 6-month period ending on—

(i) the last day of the calendar month immediately preceding the date of the commencement of the case if the debtor files the schedule of current income required by section 521(a)(1)(B)(ii); . . .

(B) includes any amount paid by any entity other than the debtor (or in a joint case the debtor and the debtor's spouse), on a regular basis for the household expenses of the debtor or the debtor's dependents (and in a joint case the debtor's spouse if not otherwise a dependent), but excludes benefits received under the Social Security Act. . . .

11 U.S.C. §101(10A).

Steve's only income during the relevant six-month period before the bankruptcy case is Joel's charity payments and any MMW dividends Steve received during the period. This calculation of Steve's income would likely yield an amount less than the state median.

Even if the means test were applied in Steve's case, calculating Steve's net or disposable income to see if he earns too much money is based on essentially the same historical test of "current monthly income" less expenses the statute allows. These expenses include standardized allowances for housing, transportation, and other expenses; and also "the debtor's average monthly payments on account of secured debt," which is high in Steve's case.

Because Steve's "current monthly income" is low and his expenses are high, Steve would likely pass the means test as literally calculated according to the Bankruptcy Code formula. If so, Steve could file and stay in Chapter 7.

However, even if a debtor avoids presumed abuse of Chapter 7 by passing the means test, the court can dismiss the case for abuse based on the debtor having filed the case in "bad faith" or because abuse is demonstrated by "the totality of circumstances . . . of the debtor's financial situation." Ms. Burnett worries that somebody in Steve's case will make a motion, or the court will act on its own, to dismiss Steve's case (or convert it to Chapter 13) for abuse based on the totality of Steve's financial situation considering (among other things):

- Steve's present and future income from his new job;
- the prospect of eventual, substantial rental income from the lighthouse;
- the value of the real and personal property Steve owns, including the dormant tort cause of action against Joel; and
- Steve's now healthy condition and his status as a professional with a good job.

The reason Ms. Burnett worries is that passing the means test is no guarantee of staying in Chapter 7. The courts have dismissed or converted Chapter 7 cases based on the totality of circumstances after deciding that despite not having too much income under the means test, the debtor is otherwise too wealthy for Chapter 7.

Ms. Burnett does not want to take this risk, and Chapter 13 is probably the better choice for Steve anyway. She'll file under Chapter 13.

QUESTION #2

Aspects of the Chapter 13 Plan

a) Outline the overall structure and likely main components of Steve's Chapter 13 plan. Broadly speaking, the plan must submit some part of the debtor's future income (known as "disposable income") over the "applicable commitment period" (three to five years) to fund the obligations the plan covers in the amounts the plan specifies. The Chapter 13 trustee (one is appointed in every Chapter case) has a say in shaping the debtor's plan and is responsible for insuring that creditors are paid every month according to the terms of the plan.

The "applicable commitment period" is

> (i) 3 years; or
> (ii) not less than 5 years, if the current monthly income of the debtor and the debtor's spouse combined, when multiplied by 12, is not less than —
>> (I) in the case of a debtor in a household of 1 person, the median family income of the applicable State for 1 earner. . . .

11 U.S.C. §1325(b)(4).

Generally speaking, secured claims must be paid in full with interest. However, if the term of a secured debt is longer than the term of the plan, the plan can provide for maintaining payments on the debt during the term of the plan. 11 U.S.C. §1322(b)(5). Typically, in providing for mortgage or other long-term debt, the debtor does not accelerate the debt but continues to make scheduled payments in due course.

The plan must provide for paying in full, in deferred cash payments, unsecured claims entitled to priority under section 507. 11 U.S.C. §§1322(a)(2) & (4); 507(a). Steve's only priority claims are the administrative expense of the bankruptcy.

Ms. Burnett's fee will be paid in installments during the first several months of the plan as money becomes available for this purpose.

Minimally, the plan must provide for paying non-priority, unsecured claims, including the medical debts, an amount that, "as of the effective date of the plan, . . . is not less than the amount that would be paid on such claim if the estate of the debtor were liquidated under chapter 7 of this title on such date." 11 U.S.C. §1325(a)(4). So, the plan must provide for paying the holder of each unsecured claim, over the term of the plan, the same amount the holder would have been paid from the bankruptcy estate had Steve filed Chapter 7 bankruptcy and liquidated, plus interest.

Typically, this total amount is far less than the full amount of an unsecured claim. Unsecured creditors are therefore unhappy. If they object to this treatment under the plan, and they always do, the plan must provide "that all of the debtor's *projected disposable income* to be received in the *applicable commitment period* beginning on the date that the first payment is due under the plan will be applied to make payments, on a generally pro rata basis, to unsecured creditors under the plan." 11 U.S.C. §1325(b)(1)(B) (emphasis added).

Disposable income is defined to mean:

current monthly income received by the debtor (other than child support payments, foster care payments, or disability payments for a dependent child made in accordance with applicable nonbankruptcy law to the extent reasonably necessary to be expended for such child) **less amounts reasonably necessary** to be expended—
- for the maintenance or support of the debtor or a dependent of the debtor, or for a domestic support obligation, that first becomes payable after the date the petition is filed; and
- for [a certain percentage of certain] charitable contributions . . . ; and
- if the debtor is engaged in business, for the payment of expenditures necessary for the continuation, preservation, and operation of such business.

11 U.S.C. §1325(b)(2) (emphasis added). As already discussed, Steve's current monthly income is low because the amount is based on the months before bankruptcy when Steve wasn't working. His monthly expenses will be higher if he is considered "engaged in business" because he operates the lighthouse as rental income. Engaged in business means the debtor "incurs trade debt in the production of income from such employment." 11 U.S.C. §1304(a).

The net monthly amount is Steve's disposable income that the plan will provide for paying unsecured creditors every month during the term of the plan. When the required payments are completed, the debtor is discharged even though the full amount of unsecured claims has not been paid. The discharge depends on Steve paying unsecured claims in whatever amounts the Chapter 13 plan provides, not the full amount of the unsecured claims. So, the unsecured creditors get more than had Steve liquidated but less than the full amounts of the amounts owed them.

b) Can the plan "strip down" Ford Credit's security interest to the value of the collateral (the new car and trailer)? A Chapter 13 plan cannot freely discount secured claims. They must be paid in full during the term of the plan or in accordance with any longer, contract term. 11 U.S.C. §§1325(a)(5); 1322(b)(5).

The amount of a secured claim, however, is not necessarily the amount of the secured debt. If the value of the collateral is less than the secured debt, the secured claim is reduced or "stripped down" to the value of the collateral. So says section 506(b). 11 U.S.C. §506(b). The balance of the debt is an unsecured claim, *id.*, which can be reduced to the amount the creditor would have received in Chapter 7 and discharged. The coupling of sections 506(b) and 1325(a)(5) allows Steve's plan to strip down Ford Credit's secured claim to the value of the new car and trailer.

However, Chapter 13 decouples these two sections (11 U.S.C. §§506(b) & 1325(a)(5)) with respect to certain secured claims because of this paragraph dangling at the very end of section 1325(a):

For purposes of paragraph (5) [and determining how a plan must treat a secured claim], section 506 shall not apply to a claim described in that paragraph if the creditor has a purchase money security interest securing the debt that is the subject of the claim, the debt was incurred within the 910-day period preceding the date of the filing of the petition, and the collateral for that debt consists of a motor vehicle (as defined in section 30102 of title 49) acquired for the personal use of the debtor, or if collateral for that debt consists of any other thing of value, if the debt was incurred during the 1-year period preceding that filing.

11 U.S.C. §1325(a). When this dangling paragraph applies, section 506(b) does not apply, and the size of the secured claim is the amount of the secured debt even though the value of the collateral is less. The plan cannot strip down the secured claim. The claim is the amount of the debt and must be provided for in full.

The dangling paragraph has a reach-back period of about two and one-half years (exactly 910 days) with respect to a purchase money security interest in a *motor vehicle* acquired for the debtor's personal use. The reach-back period is only one year for a purchase money security interest in "*any other thing of value.*"

The reach-back period for motor vehicles for personal use is longer, and the meaning of the term "motor vehicle" is peculiarly wide. For this purpose, it means "a vehicle driven or drawn by mechanical power and manufactured primarily for use on public streets, roads, and highways, but does not include a vehicle operated only on a rail line." 49 U.S.C. §30102(a)(6). The regulatory history of this definition has included passenger cars, multipurpose passenger vehicles, trucks, buses, motorcycles, *and trailers.*

Deciding if Steve's Airstream or the combination of truck and Airstream is a "motor vehicle" for purposes of section 1325(a) is unnecessary. The trailer and the truck were acquired within one year before bankruptcy. The dangling paragraph applies to a purchase money security interest in *anything* acquired within one year before bankruptcy.

The only issue is whether or not Ford Credit's security interest is a purchase money interest. State law labels a security interest in goods as purchase money "to the extent that the goods are purchase-money collateral with respect to that security interest." Uniform Commercial Code (UCC) §9-103(b)(1). " '[P]urchase-money collateral' means goods or software that secures a purchase-money obligation incurred with respect to that collateral." *Id.* §9-103(a)(1). And " 'purchase-money obligation' means an obligation of an obligor incurred as all or part of the price of the collateral or for value given to enable the debtor to acquire rights in or the use of the collateral if the value is in fact so used." *Id.* §9-103(a)(2).

The only reason "purchase money" status is questionable for Ford Credit's security interest is that the secured debt includes the negative equity associated with Steve's trade-in. The argument is that the negative equity was not itself a purchase money obligation and, therefore, that this non-purchase money piece transformed the whole debt into non-purchase money. The courts generally have disagreed and found, for one reason or another, that including negative equity in new vehicle financing does not deny purchase money status to the secured debt. For example, the Eighth Circuit reasoned:

> Since the parties here agreed to include the negative equity as part of the total sale price of the new vehicle, the negative equity was "an integral part of" and "inextricably intertwined" with the sales transaction. The negative-equity financing of the trade-in and the new-car purchase were a "package deal." Therefore,

> there was "a close nexus" between the acquisition of the new vehicle and the negative-equity financing.
>
> The amount financed to pay off the negative equity in the trade-in is "part of the price" of the new car, so it is a purchase-money obligation. The new car is purchase-money collateral securing the purchase-money obligation. Thus, Ford Credit has a PMSI securing the negative-equity financing.

In re Mierkowski, 580 F.3d 740, 742-43 (8th Cir. 2009); see also In re Howard, 597 F.3d 852 (7th Cir. 2010) (purchase money security interest in vehicle includes negative equity).

Therefore, Ford Credit's security interest in the truck and trailer is a purchase money security interest, the section 1325(a) dangling paragraph applies, and the secured claim equals the amount of the secured debt. The claim cannot be stripped down to the lower value of the collateral.

   c) How much, if any, interest is paid on Ford Credit's secured claim?   Separate from the issue of the size of a secured claim, which must be paid fully under the plan, is the closely related issue of the rate of interest that must be paid on the secured claim. The size of the secured claim determines the principal amount of the debt to be paid. The plan will provide, however, for paying this debt over the period of the plan, which is usually 36 to 60 months. Whatever the size or amount of the secured claim, the plan must provide for paying interest on the amount.

   In effect, section 1325(b)(5) requires that the plan compensates the secured creditor (through interest) due to the delay in getting its claim fully paid because the creditor receives payments over the life of the plan. So, what's the rate of interest the plan must pay? There are several possibilities: the contract rate of interest; the market rate of interest; the prime rate of interest; the cost-of-funds rate of interest; the coerced-loan rate of interest; some other rate of interest; and some combination of these rates. The secured creditor wants the rate that yields the highest amount of interest; the debtor wants the opposite.

   The Supreme Court "decided" this issue in 2004 in Till v. SCS Credit Corp., 541 U.S. 465 (2004). The Supreme Court adopted the "formula" or "risk plus" analysis in determining the appropriate rate of interest, which means that the prime rate serves as a base rate and is adjusted for the risk of default associated with payments over the term of a Chapter 13 plan. The size or amount of "adjust-ment" is decided by the bankruptcy court on a case-by-case basis.

   Under *Till,* "prime rate" means the "national prime rate, reported daily in the press, which reflects the financial market's estimate of the amount a commercial bank should charge a creditworthy commercial borrower to compensate for the oppor-tunity costs of the loan, the risk of inflation, and the relatively slight risk of default." *Id.* at 479. The "adjustment" is added "[b]ecause bankrupt debtors typically pose a greater risk of nonpayment than solvent commercial borrowers. . . ." *Id.*

   How much is the adjustment? "The appropriate size of that risk adjustment depends, of course, on such factors as the circumstances of the estate, the nature of the security, and the duration and feasibility of the reorganization plan." *Id.*

   How is the adjustment decided? "The [bankruptcy] court must . . . hold a hearing at which the debtor and any creditors may present evidence about the appropriate risk adjustment. Some of this evidence will be included in the debtor's bankruptcy filings, however, so the debtor and creditors may not incur significant additional expense." *Id.*

Who has the burden of proof? Well, "starting from a concededly *low* estimate [e.g., the prime rate] and adjusting *upward* places the evidentiary burden squarely on the creditors, who are likely to have readier access to any information absent from the debtor's filing . . ." *Id.*(emphasis in original).

Some lawyers have argued that *Till* doesn't apply after the 2005 amendments to the Bankruptcy Code, at least not with respect to secured claims on vehicles that cannot be stripped down because of the 910-day rule. See 11 U.S.C. §1325(a) (dangling paragraph). This argument has been especially popular with lawyers for secured creditors when the contract rate of interest is more than the "prime rate plus" rate of interest under *Till*. So far, most courts have rejected the argument that *Till* no longer applies. They reason that the 2005 amendments did not change the key language of section 1325 that requires paying interest on secured claims. So, *Till* continues to apply; and the applicable interest rate on secured claims in Chapter 13 plans is "prime rate plus" without regard to the contract rate (whether higher or lower) or any other rate of interest.

In a typical case involving this issue, In re Soards, 344 B.R. 829 (Bankr. W.D. Ky. 2006), Bankruptcy Judge Joan Cooper summed it up: "Simply stated, where the plan proposes to pay the secured claim in installments over time, the *Till* rate of interest must be added to the payment [of the secured claim] to arrive at the present value of the claim and the contract rate of interest is irrelevant to the analysis." *Id.* at 832.

Judge Cooper also concluded in *Soards* that "[i]n the absence of evidence of the risks associated with a default, . . . [adding] an additional two percentage points to the prime rate is the appropriate rate to be applied on . . . [secured] claims in these cases." *Id.* Other courts applying the prime rate plus approach "have generally approved adjustments of 1% to 3%." Till v. SCS Credit Corp., 541 U.S. 465, 480 (2004).

Therefore, Steve's Chapter 13 plan will likely commit to pay Ford Credit the amount of Ford Credit's secured claim in 60 monthly installments. The interest rate is the prime rate at the time they filed their plan plus about 2 percent or so.

d) Explain (i) how the circumstances in Steve's case could possibly result in Ms. Burnett proposing a "zero percent" plan for her client and (ii) whether or not the court will likely confirm such a plan over the creditors' objections. A "zero percent" Chapter 13 plan is a plan that provides for fully paying priority claims and secured claims but paying nothing — zero — to general, unsecured creditors. It's possible when the debtor's disposable income, which the plan must pay to unsecured creditors, is zero: the debtor's allowed expenses equal or exceed the debtor's current monthly income. It's possible in Steve's case because current monthly income is based on a six-month period before bankruptcy when Steve wasn't working; and also because his expenses, which include the monthly average of payments on secured debts, are high.

The Bankruptcy Code does not prohibit zero percent plans. The principal question about zero percent plans, as might be proposed in Steve's case, is how to determine "income" in calculating "disposable income" in order to decide if the amount available for unsecured creditors is really zero.

In Steve's case, the possibility of a zero percent plan depends largely on sticking close to the literal definition of "current monthly income," which means:

> the average monthly income from all sources that the debtor receives . . . during the 6-month period ending on — the last day of the calendar month immediately preceding the date of the commencement of the case if the debtor files the schedule of current income required by section 521(a)(1)(B)(ii). . . .

11 U.S.C. §101(10A). During this six-month period, Steve earned nothing beyond the stock dividends and what Joel gave him. So, his current monthly income is low, and, after subtracting his allowed expenses, his disposable income could very much be zero or less. Some courts, using what is called a "mechanical approach," would approve a zero percent plan that calculates disposable income in this way.

The rub is that his actual income at the time of bankruptcy and start of the plan is pretty good. And, if this income were used in calculating his disposable income, the difference when expenses are subtracted would likely be a noticeable, positive sum. Other courts, therefore, have decided that in calculating disposable income, the historical "current monthly income" is not the beginning and end but only the beginning. The court determines this amount as the statute describes it but also considers the debtor's actual circumstances in calculating disposable income.

How do these courts get around the plain language of section 101 that defines current monthly income only in terms of the approximate 60-day period before commencement of the case? They focus on the plain language of section 1325. This section literally provides that when objecting unsecured creditors are not fully paid under the plan (which they never are), the plan must commit to unsecured creditors "*as of the effective date of the plan* . . . all of the debtor's *projected* disposable income" that is "*received in the applicable commitment period.*" 11 U.S.C. §1325(b)(1)(B) (emphasis added). The emphasized language and statutory context, these courts say, allow them to consider and use the debtor's actual income at the time of bankruptcy to calculate the disposable income the plan must commit to unsecured creditors.

These courts, using a so-called forward-looking approach, would not approve a zero percent plan in Steve's case that was based solely on the historical current monthly income and failed to account for Steve's actual, present income. This approach was adopted by the court in In re Lanning, 545 F.3d 1269 (10th Cir. 2008), cert. granted in part, 130 S. Ct. 487 (2009), where the court explained:

> The main problem with the analysis in decisions adopting the mechanical approach is that little heed is given to three statutory phrases: "as of the effective date of the plan," 11 U.S.C. §1325(b); "to be received in the applicable commitment period," *id.* §1325(b)(1)(B); and "will be applied to make payments," *id.* "[A] cardinal principle of statutory construction [is] that a statute ought, upon the whole, to be so construed that, if it can be prevented, no clause, sentence, or word shall be superfluous, void, or insignificant." We think that these textual problems, discussed below, outweigh the concern about implying a presumption.
>
> Under §1325(b)(1)(B), a bankruptcy court may not approve a Chapter 13 plan over objection unless "**as of the effective date of the plan**" the plan

"provides that all of the debtor's projected disposable income **to be received in the applicable commitment period** beginning on the date that the first payment is due under the plan **will be applied to make payments** to unsecured creditors under the plan." (Emphasis added.) The first emphasized phrase, "as of the effective date of the plan," indicates that the court should determine, at that time, whether the plan meets the remaining requirements of subparagraph (b)(1)(B). The term "effective date" is not defined in the Bankruptcy Code, but for purposes of §1325(b)(1), "the most logical interpretation . . . is the date of plan confirmation, as a chapter 13 plan is not binding on the debtor and other interested parties until it is confirmed." In re Pak, 378 B.R. at 265 (relying on 11 U.S.C. §1327(a)), abrogated on other grounds, In re Kagenveama, 541 F.3d 868. The date of plan confirmation is practically certain to be later than the date on which the petition is filed, and it is the filing date that starts the backward-looking assessment of "current monthly income." Thus, determining whether or not a debtor has committed all projected disposable income to repayment of the unsecured creditors "as of the effective date of the plan" suggests consideration of the debtor's actual financial circumstances as of the effective date of the plan.

In turn, the remaining statutory requirements are subject to conflicting interpretations. As viewed by mechanical-approach courts, "projected" could mean that a plan simply must project the Form B22C disposable income over the applicable commitment period to determine the amount that "will be applied to make payments" to the unsecured creditors. Alternately, under the forward-looking approach, "projected" links "disposable income" and "to be received in the applicable commitment period," requiring the debtor to commit all "disposable income" (as defined by §1325(b)(2) and its reliance on the definition of "current monthly income") that is "projected . . . to be received in the applicable commitment period." Under this reading, the debtor's actual circumstances at the time of plan confirmation are taken into account in order to "project" (in other words, to "forecast") how much income the debtor will actually receive during the commitment period, which, after deducting permitted expenses, then "will be applied to make payments" to the unsecured creditors, as the statute requires.

The second reading, i.e., the forward-looking approach, strikes us as the better one. . . . Congress defined "disposable income," not "projected disposable income," meaning that "Congress must have intended 'projected disposable income' to be different than 'disposable income'" when it chose to define only the latter term for purposes of §1325(b). . . . [W]e do not think the forward-looking approach leaves the definition of "disposable income" floating with no apparent purpose. Through its reliance on the statutory definition of "current monthly income," the definition of "disposable income" serves to "describe[ ] the sources of revenue that constitute income, as well as those that do not."

Also, the forward-looking approach gives effect to the phrase "to be received in the applicable commitment period," which otherwise would be rendered superfluous. Under the mechanical approach, the amount "to be received in the applicable commitment period" would be a fiction if, as of the effective date of the plan, the debtor had no realistic expectation of earning enough to produce the amount of "disposable income" calculated on Form B22C. Furthermore, such a debtor could not get the plan confirmed due to infeasibility. *See id.*

§1325(a)(6). This undermines the importance given to historical income as a "better" predictor of "projected disposable income. . . ." . . .

Finally, we note that the mechanical approach advocated by the Trustee would effectively foreclose bankruptcy protection to debtors like Ms. Lanning, who lack adequate income going into the commitment period to pay the amount of disposable income on Form B22C, while at the same time permitting above-median debtors who have greater income at the time of plan confirmation to pay less to unsecured creditors than they are able to. While the latter situation could be rectified by post-confirmation modification of the plan under 11 U.S.C. §1329, the former situation cannot be addressed in this manner because the plan would be infeasible and therefore unconfirmable in the first place. A Chapter 13 debtor may modify the plan prior to confirmation under 11 U.S.C. §1323(a), but any effort by the debtor to deviate from Form B22C "disposable income" through pre-confirmation modification begs the question of whether the forward-looking approach is proper or not.

Id. at 1279-82 (emphasis added). The Supreme Court granted certiorari in this case to decide: "Whether, in calculating the debtor's 'projected disposable income' during the plan period, the bankruptcy court may consider evidence suggesting that the debtor's income or expenses during that period are likely to be different from her income or expenses during the pre-filing period." Hamilton v. Lanning, 130 S. Ct. 487 (2009).

QUESTION #3

Post-Confirmation Issues

a) Before payments under the plan are completed, can Steve obtain credit to finance the acquisition or improvement of property or services? Between the times of getting the plan confirmed and completing it, Steve must live on the balance of his income that remains after making the required, monthly payments under the plan. Living on this balance is often difficult and challenging. Help in the form of increases in actual income is very unlikely and even rare and, in any event, is discounted because the court would most likely modify the plan to increase the dividend paid to unsecured creditors.

Help in the form of new credit is also not likely. The reason is not that new credit is unavailable. The main reason is the order of confirmation, which usually commands: "[a]ll credit cards shall be canceled and surrendered immediately" and "[t]he Debtor shall not incur any indebtedness without the approval of the Trustee or this Court."

In the event a debtor disobeys and incurs new debt without the necessary approval, the creditor faces major problems in collecting the debt. First, the creditor can't expect to receive anything from the trustee because the plan does not provide for paying this creditor. Second, the creditor is stopped from collecting directly from the debtor because the automatic stay remains in effect.

Section 1305 provides some relief for creditors in the event of postpetition *consumer* debts "for property or services necessary for the debtor's performance under the plan." 11 U.S.C. §1305(a). Such a creditor can file a proof of claim for the postpetition debt. If the claim is allowed, provision can be made for paying the debt within and under the plan and the debt is excepted from the Chapter 13 discharge.

The claim will be disallowed, however, "if the holder of such a claim knew or should have known that prior approval by the trustee of the debtor's incurring the obligation was practicable and was not obtained." *Id.* §1305(c). In this event, the creditor gets nothing under the plan, the stay stops collection efforts, and the debt is excepted from the discharge. So, creditors who know that the trustee's approval is required for new credit are strongly encouraged to get this approval. Otherwise, they risk getting nothing of the new credit repaid.

On the other hand, if the creditor lacked this knowledge and the claim for new consumer debt is allowed, the debt is excepted from the discharge if the debtor failed to obtain trustee's approval when doing so was practicable. The intended effect, of course, is to encourage debtors to get the trustee's approval. Otherwise, the debtor's Chapter 13 discharge will have a large hole that leaves the debt for new credit unaffected.

b) Is there any effect on the Chapter 13 case if after a year or so, the lighthouse becomes a successful investment and creates a source of substantial income for Steve? In this event, the trustee or an unsecured creditor will request the court to modify the plan for the purpose of increasing the payments made to unsecured creditors. Section 1329 clearly creates a right for the trustee or an unsecured creditor to make such a request for this reason. 11 U.S.C. §1329(a)(1). The statute does not clearly, expressly say that in such a case the court must modify the plan to increase the dividend to unsecured creditors. Section 1322 requires the plan to provide for the submission of all future income necessary to carry out the plan, *id.* §1322(a)(1), and section 1325 requires the plan to commit all of the debtor's projected disposable income. *Id.* §1325(b). On the other hand, whether and how these requirements exactly apply to modifications under section 1329 is uncertain. Nevertheless, in practice, creditors — not the debtors — get the benefit of increases in actual, future income that were not anticipated at the time of confirmation but occur during the performance of a plan.

c) Is there any effect on the Chapter 13 case if after a year or so, a hurricane washes away the lighthouse and all vacation rentals, the MMW dividends drop to zero, or Steve loses his job? When the debtor's financial situations worsens after confirmation and during performance of the plan, the debtor has three basic options.

i) Steve's first choice is to ask the court for a "hardship" discharge.

Ordinarily, the Chapter 13 debtor earns a discharge only at the end of the plan when the debtor has completed all the payments required by the plan. 11 U.S.C. §1328(a). The discharge covers all debts provided for by the plan and also a discharge of all debts for claims the court has disallowed.

The section 1328(a) discharge is triggered by the debtor completing all payments *required by the plan.* So, the discharge is not conditioned on paying creditors everything the creditors are owed under state or other nonbankruptcy law. The discharge is earned by paying creditors whatever the confirmed Chapter 13 plan requires paying them. Therefore, if Steve were to complete his plan, he would receive a discharge even though his unsecured creditors were paid only a percentage of the debts owed them.

Like a discharge under Chapter 7, the section 1328(a) discharge is subject to section 523(a) exceptions, i.e., debts that are unaffected by the discharge. The section 1328(a) discharge, however, is wider: it is subject to fewer 523(a) exceptions. For example, because of section 523(a)(6), a Chapter 7 discharge excepts, i.e., does not affect, a debt "for willful and malicious injury by the debtor to another entity or to the property of another entity." Chapter 13 discharges this kind of debt.

For the most part, however, the exceptions that apply in Chapter 7 but not in Chapter 13 are typically insignificant. As a result, the wider discharge in Chapter 13 is not usually sufficient to lure into Chapter 13 a debtor who could liquidate under Chapter 7.

In theory, Steve or any other Chapter 13 debtor can earn a discharge even without completing all the payments required by the plan. It's called a "hardship" discharge under section 1328(b) but is available only if three tough requirements are satisfied:

- Modifying the plan so that the debtor can complete all the required payments is not practicable; AND
- Each unsecured creditor has been paid the present value of what she would have been paid if the debtor had liquidated under Chapter 7; AND
- The debtor's failure to complete all of the payments required by the plan is due to circumstances for which the debtor should not justly be held accountable.

In practice, a hardship discharge is rare. And, when such a discharge is granted under section 1328(b), it is subject to all of the section 523(a) exceptions to discharge that apply in a Chapter 7 case. A hardship discharge for a Chapter 13 debtor under 1328(b) is therefore narrower than the 1328(a) discharge that occurs when the debtor completes all payments required by the plan.

Also, although objections to discharge that apply in Chapter 7 don't generally apply in Chapter 13, some reasons exist for denying a discharge of any debts under either 1328(a) or (b). These reasons are, in effect, conditions to discharge. Two of them are most important.

- First, the debtor cannot be discharged under Chapter 13 unless and until she has completed "an instructional course concerning personal financial management." This "course" is different from, and in addition to, the credit counseling "briefing" that is a condition on an individual filing a bankruptcy case.
- Second, the debtor cannot be discharged in Chapter 13 if she has previously received a discharge (1) in another Chapter 13 case filed within two years before the present case was filed or (2) in any other kind of bankruptcy case filed within the preceding four years. These time limitations

don't prevent the debtor from filing a later Chapter 13 case; they only prevent a discharge in the later-filed case.

The option of getting a hardship discharge isn't likely to work for Steve or any other debtor because of the tough conditions on such a discharge and, practically speaking, won't ever work in the absence of a fortuitous loss of income that the debtor can't reasonably replace.

ii) Steve's second-best choice is to request the court to modify the plan to reduce the amount of payments to unsecured creditors.

Section 1329 provides that "[a]t any time after confirmation of the plan but before the completion of payments under such plan, the plan may be modified, upon request of the debtor, the trustee, or the holder of an allowed unsecured claim, to — increase or reduce the amount of payments on claims of a particular class provided for by the plan. . . ." 11 U.S.C. §1329(a)(1).

Not all of the requirements that apply to plan confirmation also apply to plan modification. In re Stonier, 417 B.R. 702, 704 (Bankr. M.D. Pa. 2009) (requirements of 1325(a) apply, but not 1325(b)). So, in this sense, modification is less difficult. However, some courts have held that in order to modify their plan, debtors must prove that they have experienced a substantial or material and unanticipated change in their post-confirmation financial condition. Other courts require only that debtors demonstrate some post-confirmation change in circumstances that justifies the proposed plan modification. Basically, though, the debtor must show either that the original plan was not realistically, accurately predictive or that some change of circumstances has occurred which, though not justifying a hardship discharge, nevertheless justifies a reduction in payments. Either showing is difficult to make.

And even though section 1329 includes the option of extending the time for payments on claims, debtors like Steve, whose plan is probably five years, cannot avoid an adverse change in circumstances simply by extending the length of the plan. The court can extend a three-year plan but not a five-year plan. 11 U.S.C. §1329(c).

iii) Steve's final option is procedural: either dismiss the Chapter 13 case or convert it to Chapter 7.

A Chapter 13 debtor enjoys a largely unfettered right to have the court dismiss the case, but the consequences are not good. 11 U.S.C. §1307(b). The debtor loses the benefit of bankruptcy protections, including the stay and discharge; and her creditors enjoy an almost unfettered right to collect their debts.

According to Chapter 13, the debtor's right to have the court convert the case to Chapter 7 is largely unfettered, too, id. §1307(b), as long as the debtor acts in good faith; and, upon conversion, she gets the benefits of Chapter 7 bankruptcy. However, she must pay the "costs" of Chapter 7. The principal cost is loss of title and possession to the debtor's property that becomes property of the estate, which upon conversion includes property of the estate on and after the filing of the Chapter 13 petition that remains in the possession of or is under the control of the debtor on the date of the conversion. Also, upon conversion, any valuation of collateral and lien stripping done in Chapter 13 is undone for purposes of the Chapter 7 case, which reinvigorates the strength of any affected secured creditor.

Beyond such costs is a possible problem for a Chapter 13 debtor wanting to convert her case to Chapter 7. The problem is section 707(b) "means testing," which limits the availability of Chapter 7 relief. 11 U.S.C. §707(b). When a case is converted from 13 to 7, "means testing" may still apply according to the circumstances existing at the time the case was filed or the time of conversion. If so, and to this extent, "means testing" effectively limits converting a case from Chapter 13 to Chapter 7. The reason is that under the right circumstances, a debtor who cannot complete the payments required by a Chapter 13 plan may also fail the Chapter 7 "means test," which means she cannot sustain a case under Chapter 7. Practically speaking, therefore, the debtor's only options are to dismiss the case and get out of bankruptcy altogether or "gut it out" under Chapter 13. This Hobson's choice may prove to be an important, unintended consequence of Chapter 7 means testing: the test can force a debtor into Chapter 13, and it can also keep her there.

> ## BANKRUPTCY ESSAY EXAM #4 [CHAPTER 13]

> ### QUESTION #1

Providing for the Three Mortgage Debts in the Chapter 13 Plan

a) How does the plan deal with the default on the first mortgage?   Generally, a Chapter 13 plan can "modify the rights of holders of secured claims" but not a claim "secured only by a security interest in real property that is the debtor's personal residence . . ." 11 U.S.C. §1322(b)(2). The first mortgage on Ms. Jack's home is fully secured, and the amount of the secured claim is the same as the full mortgage debt. And the collateral is a mortgage (which is a kind of security interest) on Ms. Jack's personal residence. Therefore, the plan cannot modify in any way the state law, contract rights of the first mortgagee's secured claim. However, section 1322(b)(3) provides "for the curing or waiving of any default" in a Chapter 13 plan. 11 U.S.C. §1322(b)(3). Likewise, section 1322(b)(5) states that notwithstanding section 1322(b)(2), a plan may "provide for the curing of any default within a reasonable time . . ." 11 U.S.C. §1322(b)(5).

For this reason, Ms. Jack's plan can cure her default in the Chapter 13 plan and, in effect, ignore the likelihood that the entire mortgage debt, by terms of the mortgage itself, was accelerated and is due in full. The amount necessary to cure the default is determined in accordance with the underlying agreement and applicable nonbankruptcy law. How the plan cures the default is not prescribed by statute. A common way is rolling the missed payments into the secured claim or otherwise providing for paying them during the term of the plan. The effect is to thereby de-accelerate and reinstate the original terms of the mortgage.

b) How does the plan deal with the term of the first mortgage that is much longer than the term of the Chapter 13 plan?   The mortgage will be de-accelerated by curing the prepetition default, but 20 years remain on the term of the mortgage. Ms. Jack is not required to shorten the term and pay off the mortgage during the term of her Chapter 13 plan. Section 1322(b) allows a Chapter 13 plan "to provide for . . . maintenance of payments while the case is pending on any unsecured or secured claim on which the last payment is due after the date on which the final payment under the plan is due."

Therefore, with respect to the first mortgagee's secured claim, Ms. Jack will propose paying the claim according to the exact terms of the mortgage. In other words, Ms. Jack will make her usual, monthly payments of principal and interest.

However, she is not required to include these payments within the plan itself. Instead, Ms. Jack can propose paying the mortgage "outside" the plan, which will reduce administrative costs. Paying outside the plan means the debtor pays the mortgagee directly. The trustee would not disburse the payments to the mortgagee and, as a result, the Chapter 13 trustee's fee in the case could be reduced. The trustee usually only gets a percentage of funds paid by her under and through the plan.

Several provisions of Chapter 13 seem to imply that all payments in Chapter 13 should be made through the plan. Section 1326(a) provides that "[e]xcept as otherwise provided in the plan or in the order confirming the plan, the trustee shall make payments to creditors under the plan." 11 U.S.C. §1326(c). Section 1322(a)(1) provides: "The plan shall (1) provide for the submission of all or such portion of future income of the debtor to the supervision and control of the trustee as is necessary for the execution of the plan." 11 U.S.C. §1322(a)(1). Section 1326(a)(2) provides that upon confirmation of a Chapter 13 plan, "the trustee shall distribute any such payment in accordance with the plan as soon as is practicable." 11 U.S.C. §1326(a)(2).

On the other hand, section 1326(c) provides that the plan or the order confirming a plan can "otherwise provide" for payments to creditors under the plan. So, the Bankruptcy Code doesn't prohibit payments outside the plan. The judge in her discretion can allow it. And, in practice, courts have generally allowed debtors to pay secured claims outside the plan and directly to the secured creditors if the claims have not been modified in any way.

You might think Ms. Jack wouldn't care about this issue and would just as soon pay the mortgage through the plan. She does care. The commission the trustee is paid for administering a Chapter 13 plan is paid by the debtor. So, by paying the mortgages outside the plan, the debtor pays lower administrative expenses.

c) Can the plan strip down the second mortgage and entirely strip off the third mortgage?   Generally, a Chapter 13 plan can "modify the rights of holders of secured claims" but not a claim "secured only by a security interest in real property that is the debtor's personal residence . . ." 11 U.S.C. §1322(b)(2). This provision is not limited, by its terms, to first mortgagees but *is* limited to *claims secured by the real property*. Ordinarily, a claim is secured only to the extent of the value of the collateral, as section 506 provides:

> An allowed claim of a creditor secured by a lien on property in which the estate has an interest . . . is a secured claim to the extent of the value of such creditor's interest in the estate's interest in such property . . . and is an unsecured claim to the extent that the value of such creditor's interest is less than the amount of such claim. Such value shall be determined in light of the purpose of the valuation and of the proposed disposition or use of such property, and in conjunction with any hearing on such disposition or use or on a plan affecting such creditor's interest.

11 U.S.C. §506(a)(1). Thus, under section 506(a), an allowed claim secured by a lien on the debtor's property is a secured claim to the extent of the value of the property; to the extent the claim exceeds the value of the property, it is an unsecured claim.

However, section 1322(b)(2), which applies only to Chapter 13 bankruptcy, provides that even though the plan can generally modify the rights of holders of any and all secured claims, the plan cannot modify the rights of a claim secured only by a security interest in real property that is the debtor's principal residence. 11 U.S.C. §1322(b)(2).

Therefore, Ms. Jack's lawyer, Kate Epstein, may well reason that because the second mortgage is undersecured, the secured claim that is protected by section 1322(b)(2) is limited to the amount of the value of the property in excess of the first mortgage, which is also consistent with section 506(a). Therefore, consistent with the very language of section 1322(b)(2), Ms. Jack's plan can strip down the second mortgage to the value of the property exceeding the first mortgage and treat the balance as an unsecured claim. And, with the same reasoning, the plan can entirely strip down and off the third mortgage so that the entire, third mortgage debt is unsecured.

In Nobelman v. Am. Sav. Bank, 508 U.S. 324 (1993), the Supreme Court analyzed the interplay between claim bifurcation under section 506(a) and the anti-modification clause of section 1322(b)(2) to determine whether a debtor could bifurcate a single, undersecured residential mortgage claim into secured and unsecured components pursuant to section 506(a). The debtor in *Nobelman* had a primary residence valued at $23,500 and a first mortgage claim for $71,335. The debtors' Chapter 13 plan proposed to bifurcate the mortgagee's claim under section 506(a) into a secured claim of $23,500 and an unsecured claim of $47,835. The debtor asserted that section 1322(b)(2)'s anti-modification provision applied only to the secured component, as that term was defined in section 506(a), of her mortgage claim.

The Court concluded in *Nobelman* that where a creditor's lien is at least partially secured, section 506(a) does not operate to eliminate the creditor's rights with respect to the unsecured component. *Id.* at 332.

The *Nobelman* decision left open the question of whether or not the holding extends to junior lienholders who are completely underwater, that is, who hold a wholly unsecured mortgage lien on the debtor's principal residence. The courts are divided on this issue. A few of them prohibit the avoidance of a wholly unsecured homestead lien. The large majority of courts (including six Courts of Appeals) have held that the anti-modification provision in section 1322(b)(2) protects only those homestead liens that are at least partially secured — as that term is defined by section 506(a) — by some existing equity after accounting for encumbrances that have senior priority.

So, Ms. Jack's plan cannot strip down the second mortgage, which must be treated as a fully secured claim. However, the plan can completely strip off the third mortgage and treat the entire mortgage debt as an unsecured claim.

QUESTION #2

Providing for Any Unsecured, Priority Claims

Are there any unsecured, priority claims that must be paid in full? With respect to unsecured claims, the debtor's plan will pay them, as far as possible, with disposable income. Balances remaining after payments under the plan are completed will be discharged.

Some unsecured claims, however, are given priority payment under section 507. 11 U.S.C. §507(a) (1)–(10). They are given priority over and paid from the estate before other unsecured claims. The Chapter 13 plan must provide for paying these priority claims in full, albeit in deferred cash payments. 11 U.S.C. §1322(a)(2).

Two kinds of priority claims are most common in typical Chapter 13 cases: administrative expenses (including the debtor's lawyer's fees paid through the plan), 11 U.S.C. §507(a)(2), and certain taxes. *Id.* §507(a)(8).

The most common kinds of tax claims in typical Chapter 13 cases are claims for property and income taxes. A property tax debt entitled to priority payment is "a property tax incurred before the commencement of the case and last payable without penalty after one year before the date of the filing of the petition." 11 U.S.C. §507(a)(8)(B). Priority claims for income taxes are mainly limited to:

- Income taxes for tax years ending on or before the date of filing the bankruptcy petition for which a return is due within three years of the filing of the petition;
- Income taxes assessed within 240 days before the date of filing the petition; and
- Income taxes that were not actually assessed before the petition date but were assessable as of the petition date.

Id. §507(a)(8)(A). The priority amount includes the taxes themselves and the interest due on the taxes to the date of filing on the tax. Penalties associated with a priority tax are not priority claims and are treated just as any other unsecured debt, which means they may get little or nothing through the plan.

Priority tax claims are also excepted from discharge. Non–priority taxes, unpaid interest, and tax penalties, are discharged at the completion of the plan.

However, taxes secured by liens are not entitled to section 507 priority, which covers only unsecured claims. The reason is that secured claims are fully protected by their collateral, even if the underlying debt is discharged. Therefore, liens securing non–priority, unsecured tax claims that would be discharged by the bankruptcy are enforceable, to the extent of the value of the collateral, after bankruptcy and despite the discharge. Personal liability for the taxes is discharged but not the liens enforcing them.

Of course, to the extent that a tax lien is undersecured, the Chapter 13 plan can strip down the lien to the value of the collateral as of the commencement of the case. The portion of the tax claim exceeding the value of the collateral is an unsecured claim that is entitled to priority to the extent covered by section 507(a)(8) and otherwise is treated as an unsecured claim that shares in the disposable income during the commitment period of the plan.

Ms. Jack owes "some back taxes." What the taxes are, how far "back" they go, and whether or not they are secured by liens will determine if the tax debts are entitled to priority.

QUESTION #3

The Effect of Bankruptcy on the Student Loan

a) Is the student loan discharged along with other general, unsecured claims? In a Chapter 13 case, the discharge does not accompany confirmation of the plan. Rather, the discharge is generally delayed until the debtor fully completes all payments under the plan, 11 U.S.C. §1328(a), except in the rare case of a "hardship discharge" when "the debtor's failure to complete such payments is due to circumstances for which the debtor should not justly be held accountable." *Id.* §1328(b).

The good news is that not all of the exceptions to a Chapter 7 discharge apply in Chapter 13, which means that the Chapter 13 discharge is somewhat wider than in Chapter 7. 11 U.S.C. §§523(a) & 1328(a). For example, a debt "for willful and malicious injury by the debtor to another entity or to the property of another entity" is excepted from discharge in a Chapter 7 case but not in Chapter 13. A Chapter 13 debtor who completes payments on such a debt under her plan will be discharged from the balance of the tort debt.

However, most of the common, important section 523 exceptions to discharge fully apply in Chapter 13 cases. For example, priority claims for taxes are excepted from discharge in Chapter 13 and also student loans, which are excepted by this language:

> unless excepting such debt from discharge under this paragraph would impose an undue hardship on the debtor and the debtor's dependents, [bankruptcy does not discharge an individual debtor from any debt] for—
>
>> (A)(i) an educational benefit overpayment or loan made, insured, or guaranteed by a governmental unit, or made under any program funded in whole or in part by a governmental unit or nonprofit institution; or
>>
>>> (ii) an obligation to repay funds received as an educational benefit, scholarship, or stipend. . . .

11 U.S.C. §523(a)(8).

Triggering the exception to the exception, i.e., getting a discharge of student loans because not discharging them "would impose an undue hardship," requires (1) commencing an adversary proceeding to determine the issue of dischargeability by serving summons and complaint on the affected creditors and (2) the debtor satisfying the so-called *Brunner* test, which means the debtor must make a three-part showing:

(1) that the debtor cannot maintain, based on current income and expenses, a "minimal" standard of living for herself and her dependents if forced to repay the loans;

(2) that additional circumstances exist indicating that this state of affairs is likely to persist for a significant portion of the repayment period of the student loans; and

(3) that the debtor has made good faith efforts to repay the loans.

Brunner v. New York State Higher Educ. Services Corp., 831 F.2d 395, 396 (1987), which most courts have adopted.

The *Brunner* test is difficult to satisfy. And, if the debtor does satisfy the test, the court can limit the discharge: instead of discharging all of the student loan or loans, discharge only as much as creates the hardship. It's called a partial discharge. The balance is not discharged. The statute does not provide for the partial discharge. The courts do it on the basis of inherent and supplemental powers. Finally, in any event, the time for deciding if Ms. Jack qualifies for a student loan discharge is far away. Almost certainly, though, she will not qualify if she completes her plan and still has a $50,000-a-year income.

b) Can the plan reduce the student loan?   A claim for student loans is not a priority claim that must be paid in full. And, the plan is not required to pay a debt in full simply because the debt is non-dischargeable. Rather a student loan claim seems to fall within the general authority to modify the rights of holders of unsecured claims so long as the requirements for confirmation are satisfied.

Suppose, therefore, that Ms. Jack's plan provides for treating her student loan as any other general, unsecured claim. Her hope is that nobody notices, nobody objects, the plan is confirmed; and the balance of the loan not paid under the plan will be discharged when the plan is completed.

It looks like a good idea, but it won't work if proper procedure is followed.

In *United Student Aid Funds, Inc. v. Espinosa*, 130 S. Ct. 1367 (2010), the debtor Espinosa's Chapter 13 plan provided for repaying the principal of his student loan debt and discharging the interest on the debt when the debtor completed the payments the plan required. The clerk of the bankruptcy court mailed notice and a copy of Espinosa's plan to the student loan creditor, United Student Aid Funds, Inc. (United). In boldface type immediately below the caption, the plan stated: "WARNING IF YOU ARE A CREDITOR YOUR RIGHTS MAY BE IMPAIRED BY THIS PLAN." The plan also noted the deadlines for filing a proof of claim or an objection to the plan.

The debtor did not commence an adversary proceeding at which the court would decide the issue of undue hardship, which is usually necessary to determine the dischargeability of student loans.

Nevertheless, when United received notice of the plan, United responded only by filing a proof of claim for $17,832.15, an amount representing both the principal and the accrued interest on Espinosa's student loans. United did not object to the plan's proposed discharge of Espinosa's student loan interest. The bankruptcy court confirmed Espinosa's plan in due, ordinary course.

Espinosa completed payments under the plan and was discharged. Thereafter, the United States Department of Education, which was the assignee of Espinosa's loans, commenced efforts to collect the unpaid interest on the loans. In response, Espinosa filed a motion asking the bankruptcy court to enforce its discharge order by directing the Department and United to cease all efforts to collect the unpaid interest on his student loan debt.

On ultimate appeal, the Supreme Court determined that "the Bankruptcy Court's failure to find undue hardship before confirming Espinosa's plan was a legal error." *Id.* at 1380. However, the creditors lost on procedural grounds: the discharge order was a final judgment that "remains enforceable and binding on United because United had notice of the error and failed to object or timely appeal." *Id.*

So, if a debtor's Chapter 13 plan provides for discharging any part of student loans, the plan will fail if the creditor timely objects or appeals. The only way to discharge a student loan is by adversary proceeding in which the court determines that not discharging the debt would create an "undue hardship."

QUESTION #4

Classifying and Treating Some Debts Differently (Paying Them More)

a) Can the plan provide for paying the student loan fully or more completely than other general, unsecured claims? The student loan debt is nondischargeable except on determination of undue hardship. And, the plan cannot provide for discharging any part of the debt without determining undue hardship. The bottom line is: in the vast majority of cases, the debtor cannot get out of a student loan. Any amount of the loan not paid under the plan will not be affected by the discharge when the debtor completes payments under the plan.

Therefore, why not provide in the plan for paying the student loan in full or in larger percentage than other general, unsecured claims? These other creditors would receive much less of the debtor's disposable income that will fund the plan. But, the balance of their claims will be discharged. So, why not pay down the nondischargeable debt as much as possible? The total disposable income the debtor must pay does not change.

There's a problem. Chapter 13 does allow the plan to provide for different classes of creditors and to treat the classes differently. 11 U.S.C. §1322(b)(1). However, the plan cannot "discriminate unfairly" between classes. A number of tests have emerged to assess whether a classification discriminates unfairly under section 1322(b)(1), and, thus, whether separate classification should be disallowed. Some commonly accepted factors to consider are:

- Whether there is a rational basis for the classification;
- Whether the classification is necessary to the debtor's rehabilitation under Chapter 13;
- Whether the discriminatory classification is proposed in good faith;
- Whether there is a meaningful payment to the class discriminated against; [and]
- The difference between what the creditors discriminated against will receive as the plan is proposed, and the amount they would receive if there was no separate classification.

In re Husted, 142 B.R. 72 (Bankr. W.D.N.Y. 1992). "'The debtor bears the burden of showing that the proposed classification does not discriminate unfairly. While the *Husted* factors are helpful, they do not constitute bright-line standards. Accordingly, the court must conduct a flexible case-by-case analysis in determining whether a plan discriminates unfairly and must consider all pertinent factors.'" In re Caccamise, 2009 WL 5205980, *1-3 (Bankr. E.D. Va. 2009), quoting In re Delauder, 189 B.R. 639, 643-44 (Bankr. E.D. Va.1995).

With respect to paying student loans disproportionately more than other claims, the courts have said that in general and in principle, "if discrimination furthers the goals of the debtor, satisfies the purposes behind Chapter 13, and does not require any creditor or group of creditors to bear an unreasonable burden, the debtor may be able to make greater payments to the student loan creditors under the plan." In re Coleman, 560 F.3d 1000, 1011 n.26 (9th Cir. 2009); see also In re Orawsky, 387 B.R. 128 (Bankr. E.D. Pa. 2008) (approved plan paying more on student loans because debtor had no disposable income and all the money funding the plan was voluntarily contributed). However, "non–dischargeability alone is not a sufficient reason for permitting debtors to classify student loans differently from other debt. . . ." In re Coleman, 560 F.3d 1000, 1011 n.26 (9th Cir. 2009). Indeed, a common refrain is that courts "do not permit payment of a student loan at a higher rate than other unsecured debts. This discriminates unfairly against other similarly sited creditors. . . ." In re Siler, 426 B.R. 167 (Bankr. W.D.N.D. 2010).

b) Can the plan treat the debt owed Ms. Jack's parents more favorably? The answer is maybe, but maybe not with additional, favorable facts. Generally speaking, although the plan can create and treat differently classes of unsecured creditors, the plan cannot discriminate unfairly between the classes. There is an explicit proviso, however, with respect to sureties on consumer debts: a "plan may treat claims for a consumer debt of the debtor if an individual is liable on such consumer debt with the debtor differently than other unsecured claims. . . ." 11 U.S.C. §1322(b)(1). Here's the explanation for the proviso:

> The legislative history of section 1322(b)(1) indicates that Congress was concerned that a debtor would feel the moral obligation to protect family or friends who had obligated themselves for the debtor's benefit. The repayment of such a debt might be outside the plan, and therefore jeopardize the reorganiza-tion effort. The same moral obligation does not exist when the debtor is not the beneficiary of the obligation. Also, Congress was concerned that the failure of a debtor to completely pay off a cosigned obligation would lead to a "ripple effect" driving codebtors into bankruptcy as the creditor looked to the cosigner for satisfaction of any debt unpaid under the plan. This presumes that the debtor would be primarily liable, and that the creditor would turn to the codebtor only in the event that the debtor fails to pay. Most courts already require that the debtor be the beneficiary of the obligation in order to separately classify the debt for disparate treatment. This, therefore, is nothing more than a restatement of existing law.

In re Beauchamp, 283 B.R. 287, 289 (Bankr. D. Minn. 2002). Nevertheless, "[f]avorable treatment of cosigned debt still depends on its not being unfairly discriminatory. That is, the treatment must have a legitimate purpose." *Id.*

Therefore, even when the surety is a family member, treating the surety more favorably than other unsecured creditors is not necessarily always, carte blanche allowed. There is authority that the debtor must show that the disparate treatment is "essential to the success of the plan and necessary to protect the cosigner from financial ruin." In In re Thompson, 191 B.R. 967 (Bankr. S.D. Ga. 1996), the debtor's plan proposed a 100 percent distribution on a consumer note cosigned by the debtor's mother while paying nothing on other general unsecured claims. The court would not confirm the plan with this distribution on the basis of the lack of good faith.

> This plan takes the wisdom of Congress in allowing the separate classification of codebtor claims and turns it upside down to suggest that the right to separately classify the codebtor claim creates the right to eliminate the claims of other creditors. Until the congressional mandate is rendered more specific to that effect

by some amendment, the provisions of the present Code will not be interpreted by this Court to accomplish that result. The effect of Debtors' proposal in this case is to preserve the wealth of the codebtor at the expense of the other unsecured creditors. This objective is particularly unattractive when it is apparent that the wealth of the codebtor might reasonably be considered to be a financial resource of Debtors themselves.

Id. at 975. On the facts of Ms. Jack's case, as stated, there is no evidence of a legitimate purpose in favoring the claim of her parents. Without more and favorable facts, Ms. Jack's plan cannot discriminate by paying a disproportionately larger amount on her parents' claim.

QUESTION #5

Maximizing Expenses Associated with the Two Vehicles in Calculating Disposable Income

a) Is the debtor allowed vehicle expenses for the Jeep that she owns? To compute the amount of "disposable income" the debtor must commit to fund the Chapter 13 plan, the debtor's gross, current monthly income is reduced by "amounts reasonably necessary to be expended — for the maintenance or support of the debtor or a dependent of the debtor, or for a domestic support obligation, that first becomes payable after the date the petition is filed. . . ." 11 U.S.C. §1325(b)(2). If the debtor's annualized, current monthly income is more than the comparable "median family income," these "amounts reasonably necessary" are based on allowable expenses relevant to the "means test" under Chapter 7. *Id.* §1325(b)(3). These expenses include certain standardized amounts for housing, transportation, and other expenses, i.e., "the *debtor's applicable* monthly expense amounts specified under the National Standards and Local Standards, and the debtor's actual monthly expenses for the categories specified as Other Necessary Expenses issued by the Internal Revenue Service for the area in which the debtor resides. . . ." *Id.* §707(b)(2)(A)(ii) (emphasis added).

The Local Standards provide for transportation expenses in varying amounts depending on where the debtor lives and how many vehicles she owns:

The transportation standards consist of nationwide figures for monthly loan or lease payments referred to as **ownership costs**, and additional amounts for monthly **operating costs**. The operating costs include maintenance, repairs, insurance, fuel, registrations, licenses, inspections, parking and tolls (These standard amounts do not include personal property taxes).

The ownership costs provide maximum allowances for the lease or purchase of up to two automobiles, if allowed as a necessary expense. A single taxpayer is normally allowed one automobile.

If a taxpayer has a car payment, the allowable ownership cost added to the allowable operating cost equals the allowable transportation expense. The taxpayer is allowed the amount actually spent, or the standard, whichever is less.

> If a taxpayer has a car, but no car payment, only the operating costs portion of
> the transportation standard is used to figure the allowable transportation expense.
> The taxpayer is allowed the amount actually spent, or the standard, whichever is
> less.

IRS.gov (http://www.irs.gov/businesses/small/article/0,,id=104623,00.html).

In this case, the standardized, allowed expenses for two cars are $992 for ownership costs and $468 for operating costs. For one car, it's half of each amount.

However, if the debtor's actual car payment to the secured creditor is more than the standardized ownership expense, the debtor is allowed to deduct the amount of the actual payment in calculating disposable income. Actually, the statute allows the debtor to deduct the "debtor's average monthly payments on account of secured debts . . . contractually due to secured creditors in each month of the 60 months following the date of the petition" and some additional payments to secured creditors. 11 U.S.C. §707(b)(2)(A)(iii).

Ms. Jack's Jeep is unencumbered. She is not making payments on it. So, throughout the Chapter 13 plan, Ms. Jack will not be making secured car payments. There is no doubt that she is entitled to deduct operating expenses for the Jeep. The issue is: can Ms. Jack also deduct the standardized ownership expense in calculating disposable income? If so, the disposable income paid under the plan will be artificially low, which naturally benefits the debtor.

The courts are split on the issue. The probable majority of courts, including some circuit courts, have taken a "plain meaning" approach to interpreting the statute and allowed the deduction of an "ownership cost" for a vehicle that is subject to neither secured debt nor a lease. Other courts have not, including the Ninth Circuit in In re Ransom, 577 F.3d 1026 (9th Cir. 2009), cert. granted sub nom. Ransom v. MBNA, 2010 WL 333672 (2010). In *Ransom*, the court reasoned:

> Congress has deemed the expense of owning a car to be a basic expense that
> debtors can deduct in calculating what they can afford to pay to their creditors.
> However, in making that calculation, what is important is the payments that
> debtors actually make, not how many cars they own, because the payments that
> debtors make are what actually affect their ability to make payments to their
> creditors.
>
> The statute is only concerned about protecting the debtor's ability to con-
> tinue owning a car, and if the debtor *already* owns the car, the debtor is ade-
> quately protected. . . . When the debtor has no monthly ownership expenses, it
> makes no sense to deduct an ownership expense to shield it from creditors.
>
> Section 707(b)(2)(A)(ii)(I) provides, in relevant part, that "[t]he debtor's
> monthly expenses shall be the debtor's applicable monthly expense amounts
> specified under . . . the Local Standards." As set forth in the statute, the adjective
> "applicable" modifies the meaning of the noun "monthly expense amounts;" it
> indicates that the deduction of the monthly expense amount specified under the
> Local Standard for the expense becomes relevant to the debtor (i.e., appropriate
> or applicable to the debtor) when he or she in fact has such an expense.
>
> The ordinary, common meaning of "applicable" further impels us to this
> conclusion. "Applicable," in its ordinary sense, means "capable of or suitable
> for being applied." Merriam-Webster's Collegiate Dictionary 60 (11th ed.

2005). Given the ordinary sense of the term "applicable," how is the vehicle ownership expense allowance *capable of being applied* to the debtor if he does not make any lease or loan payments on the vehicle? In other words, how can the debtor assert a deduction for an expense he does not have? If we granted the debtor such an allowance, we would be reading "applicable" right out of the Bankruptcy Code.

577 F.3d at 1030-31. In other words, the ownership expense is only "applicable" and therefore allowable if the debtor actually owes loan or lease payments on a vehicle. The courts going the other way on this issue and allowing the deduction read the word "applicable" to mean the Local Standard vehicle ownership deduction "applies" to the debtor by virtue of his geographic region and number of cars, regardless of whether that deduction is an "actual expense." The Supreme Court will decide the debate in Ransom v. MBNA, 2010 WL 333672 (2010), granting cert. sub nom. in In re Ransom, 577 F.3d 1026 (9th Cir. 2009). Ms. Jack's lawyer, Ms. Epstein, will certainly argue for Ms. Jack taking the ownership expense, but how a bankruptcy court decides the issue is uncertain until the Supreme Court decides *Ransom*.

b) Is the debtor allowed vehicle expenses for the Lexus if she surrenders it? Ms. Jack's plan provides for surrendering the Lexus. Surrender means that the debtor gives up possession and responsibly for the collateral to the secured party. Thereafter, the debtor will no longer make the secured car payments. The issue here is different from the issue about the Jeep. With respect to the Jeep, the debtor wants ownership expenses for a car she already owns. Here, with respect to the Lexus, the debtor wants expenses for a car she will not have. The issue in this problem is: can the debtor deduct the ownership and operating expenses for the Lexus she is surrendering in calculating disposable income? If so, as the debtor hopes, the disposable income paid under the plan will be artificially low and her real income actually higher.

With respect to the ownership expense, the argument is that the above-median income debtor can deduct from current monthly income, as provided by section 1325(b)(2), "the higher of the Local Standards amount or the debtor's average monthly payments on account of secured debts . . . *contractually due* to secured creditors . . . *following the date of the petition* . . ." 11 U.S.C. §707(b)(2)(A)(iii)(I). When Ms. Jack filed the petition and up until she actually surrenders the Lexus, the secured vehicle payments for the Lexus are "contractually due." It doesn't matter that when the plan is confirmed and the Lexus surrendered, such payments will no longer be due. She is free of them.

The same issue arises and a debtor makes the same kind of argument for deducting ownership expenses if she plans to abandon real estate for which, at filing, she is contractually bound to pay the secured creditor, even though she will not be required to make the payments after abandonment.

In In re Smith, 418 B.R. 359 (9th Cir. BAP 2009), in calculating their disposable income, the debtor's deductible expenses included about $7,000 in monthly payments on two houses and a vehicle that their Chapter 13 plan proposed to surrender. Together with other variables, the debtors' monthly disposable income was −$1,749.00. There is nothing to pay unsecured creditors. On the other hand, if the secured payments on the houses and vehicle to be surrendered were excluded as expenses, the debtors would have a positive monthly disposable income of about $4,000.

The bankruptcy court allowed the deductions. The Bankruptcy Appellate Panel reversed. The key to the Panel's decision was the connection between subsections 1325(b)(2) and (b)(3). Subsection (b)(2) defines disposable income as the debtor's current monthly income "less amounts reasonably necessary . . . for the maintenance or support of the debtor or a dependent. . . ." Subsection (b)(3) then explains how to determine "amounts reasonably necessary" under (b)(2). It is (b)(3) that references and incorporates the allowable expenses described in section 707(b), including "contractually due" payments on secured debts.

The Panel reasoned that (b)(2) imposed a predicate requirement that any expense claimed under (b)(3) is "reasonably necessary . . . for . . . maintenance or support." The Panel then concluded:

> [T]he debtors found their two houses and one vehicle so *unnecessary* to their maintenance and support they surrendered them to the lenders. They made that decision, not the court. Thus they had no payments to make. . . .
>
> Items that a debtor has surrendered or intends to surrender are not necessary for his or her support or maintenance. The concepts — surrender and necessity — are mutually exclusive of one another. Phantom payments for the surrendered item are not reasonably necessary for a debtor's support and maintenance. Therefore, secured debt payments on property to be abandoned or surrendered could not be deducted in calculating disposable income.

Id. at 368-69.

Although the Lexus and the Jeep raise different issues, the Panel's reasoning could apply equally with the same result on both issues and deny allowing Ms. Jack to claim the questionable expenses when calculating disposable income. But wait and see how and why the Supreme Court decides the Jeep-like issue in Ransom v. MBNA, 2010 WL 333672 (2010), granting cert. sub nom. In re Ransom, 577 F.3d 1026 (9th Cir. 2009) (whether or not debtor can claim ownership expense for vehicle that is not encumbered).

QUESTION #6

Post-Discharge

a) What is the effect of Ms. Jack winning a discrimination action against MMW after she completes all the payments under the plan and is discharged? A bankruptcy case is closed when the "estate is fully administered and the court has discharged the trustee." 11 U.S.C. §350(a). "A case may be reopened in the court in which such case was closed to administer assets, to accord relief to the debtor, or for other cause." *Id*. §350(b). These reasons include administering assets for the benefit of creditors. In fact, there is authority that the court is obligated to do so.

The principal issue here is whether or not the estate or creditors have any rights with respect to the proceeds of the discrimination action. When Ms. Jack filed bankruptcy, the cause of action against MMW became part of the bankruptcy estate,

11 U.S.C. §§541 & 1306(a), and she would have been required to disclose the property in the schedule of assets filed with her bankruptcy petition. Section 541 defines property of the estate to includes proceeds of such property; and section 1306 includes all property listed as property of the estate under 541 "that the debtor acquires after the commencement of the case but before the case is closed, dismissed, or converted . . . whichever occurs first. . . ." 11 U.S.C. §1306(a)(1). However, Chapter 13 also provides that "[e]xcept as otherwise provided in the plan or the order confirming the plan, the confirmation of a plan vests all of the property of the estate in the debtor."

Nevertheless, if Ms. Jack had won the lawsuit and recovered the damages during the term of the Chapter 13 case, the plan could have been modified to account for the money to increase payments to creditors, 11 U.S.C. §1329, whether or not the money was property of the estate and whether or not the money is properly labeled "income" or "earnings."

In this problem, however, the recovery was received after the case was closed. In In re Thompson, 344 B.R. 461 (Bankr. W.D. Va. 2004), the court refused to reopen a closed Chapter 13 case to allow the trustee to administer a claim that had existed prepetition but had not been recovered then, even though the debtor had never disclosed the claim. The court reasoned:

> [N]either the Chapter 13 Plan nor the order confirming it provided "otherwise" with respect to property of the bankruptcy estate. Accordingly, the confirmation of the Chapter 13 Plan vested in the Debtor the property of the bankruptcy estate, including the "qui tam" claim. . . . If the Debtor had filed a Chapter 7 petition, control of the "qui tam" claim would have passed to the Chapter 7 Trustee and, because the claim was undisclosed, would not have been "abandoned" to [the debtor] at the conclusion of the case.
>
> Furthermore, the time period of a Chapter 13 case is limited while that of a Chapter 7 is not. The normal length of a Chapter 13 case, as contemplated in the Bankruptcy Code, is a period of three years, although the Court "for cause" may approve a period up to "five years". 11 U.S.C. §1322(d). A Chapter 13 Plan can be modified even after its confirmation, but the Code expressly prohibits any modification which would provide "for payments over a period . . . that expires after five years after [the time that the first payment under the original confirmed plan was due]." 11 U.S.C. §1329(c). As pertinent to this case, the Chapter 13 Plan was originally confirmed on September 17, 1998. . . . [T]he first payment was due no later than June 26, 1998. As of the date of this Decision, we are just shy of *six* years after the date the first payment was due. The Court is without authority to modify the Debtor's Chapter 13 Plan to provide additional payments to creditors more than five years after June 26, 1998. Moreover, if a Chapter 13 Plan is to be modified, it must be done "before the completion of payments under such plan." 11 U.S.C. §1329(a).

Id. at 464-65.

To the contrary is Matter of Tarrer, 273 B.R. 724 (Bankr. N.D. Ga. 2001). The court allowed a Chapter 13 case to be reopened after the debtor had successfully completed his confirmed plan and received a discharge for the purpose of administering recovery on a prepetition arbitration claim for the benefit of his creditors.

> In considering the question of whether to reopen a closed bankruptcy case, courts have generally considered the following three interests: 1) the benefit to the debtor; 2) the prejudice or detriment to the defendant in the pending litigation; and 3) the benefit to the debtor's creditors. . . .
>
> [In this case,] . . . the potential benefit to the creditors would appear to be the most important factor in this analysis. Assuming the Debtor recovers on his claims, the creditors, who are owed approximately $105,000 worth of debt, would receive payment. In *In re Daniel*, 205 B.R. 346 (Bankr. N.D. Ga. 1997), while the court did not explicitly consider the three factors, it essentially weighed the potential benefit to the creditors against the detriment to the defendant in the litigation. The court noted that "[a] denial in the instant case of Debtor's motion to reopen would deprive Debtor's creditors of an opportunity to share in the fruits of any recovery Debtor may obtain." *Id.* at 348. This Court agrees with Judge Murphy's statement in *In re Daniel*, that "[r]eopening may be detrimental to [the defendant] . . . [,] but this court cannot countenance depriving Debtor's creditors of the opportunity to share in damages to which Debtor is entitled. . . ."

Id. at 732-33. The court noted that a bankruptcy court may in fact have a duty to reopen a case in which new assets have been discovered in order to ensure that the assets are administered for the benefit of the debtor's creditors. *Id.* at 732. It should be said, however, that any such duty is less strongly implied in Chapter 13 cases than in Chapter 7 cases in which property of the Chapter 7 estate is generally never returned to the debtor.

b) What happens if a creditor sues Ms. Jack, after she is discharged, for personal liability on a prepetition debt that the plan provided for and that was paid according to the plan, though not paid fully according to the terms of the contract between the parties? With some exceptions, the Chapter 13 discharge affects "all debts provided for by the plan or disallowed under section 502. . . ." 11 U.S.C. §1328(a). The discharge "operates as an injunction against the commencement or continuation of an action, the employment of process, or an act, to collect, recover or offset any such debt as a personal liability of the debtor, whether or not discharge of such debt is waived. . . ." 11 U.S.C. §524(a)(1).

There are two principal answers when a creditor violates the discharge injunction by filing an action on a discharged debt. First, the discharge of the debt is a defense to the creditor's action, which the debtor can assert directly and immediately without regard to the court in which the suit has been filed. There is generally no need to return to the bankruptcy court for the benefit of this defense.

Second, the violation is a contempt of court that the debtor will bring to the bankruptcy court's attention. Typically, the court will issue a show cause order requiring the creditor to explain why the actions are not in violation of the stay and why the court should not hold the creditor in contempt if the stay has been violated.

This proceeding is not pursued as a private cause of action that belongs to the debtor for the creditor's violation of the stay. The Bankruptcy Code does not provide for such an action, and the courts have refused to infer a cause of action for the debtor.

Rather, the contempt proceeding is in aid of and supplemental to section 524 and is based on section 105(a), which empowers the court to "issue any order, process, or judgment that is necessary or appropriate to carry out the provisions of this title." 11 U.S.C. §105(a).

> "[Section] 105 does not itself create a private right of action, but a court may invoke §105(a) if the equitable remedy *utilized* is demonstrably necessary to preserve a right elsewhere provided in the Code. . . ." These powers are "in addition to whatever inherent contempt powers the court may have" and "must include the award of monetary and other forms of relief to the extent such awards are necessary and appropriate to carry out the provisions of the Bankruptcy Code and provide full remedial relief." (internal quotation marks and citations omitted). We therefore must reject Kalikow's argument that §105 serves as an independent basis for awarding sanctions without violation of §524(a)(2) or another provision of the Bankruptcy Code.

In re Kalikow, 602 F.3d 82, 97 (2010). These sanctions, however, are typically compensatory only. "The power of a bankruptcy court to find a party in criminal contempt of court [and impose punitive sanctions] remains unsettled, and the different circuits have resolved this question differently. It is undisputed that '[c]ourts . . . have embraced an inherent contempt authority that encompasses the ability to impose civil and criminal contempt.' The Supreme Court explained that courts' inherent powers 'necessarily result . . . from the nature of their institution . . . [and] cannot be dispensed with in a Court, because they are necessary to the exercise of all other[ ] [powers].' However, the extent of this inherent power [and whether it supports criminal contempt] is a source of debate as it relates to non-Article III courts such as the Bankruptcy Courts." Walton v. Countrywide Home Loans, Inc., 2009 WL 1905035, ★7 (S.D. Fla. 2009) (concluding that pursuant to 11 U.S.C. §105, the Bankruptcy Court has the authority to impose criminal contempt sanctions).

c) What happens if she defaults on the mortgages after discharge, the mortgages are foreclosed, and the property is more valuable now than at the time Ms. Jack filed her Chapter 13 case? The answer with respect to each of the three mortgages depends on the size or amount of the secured claim. In particular, it turns on whether or not the secured claim could be and was stripped down. Generally, in a Chapter 13 plan, secured claims can be stripped down to the value of the collateral if this value is less than the contract amount of the secured debt. In other words, an undersecured debt is bifurcated: there is a secured claim equaling the amount of the value of the collateral and an unsecured claim for the balance. When bifurcated and stripped down, the lien can never be enforced beyond the stripped down amount.

However, a very big exception to strip down lurks in Chapter 13: the plan cannot strip down or otherwise "modify the rights of [a] holder[] of . . . a claim secured only by a security interest in real property that is the debtor's principal residence. . . ." 11 U.S.C. §1322(b)(2). The secured claim is never lower than the amount of the contract secured debt, even though the value of the collateral is lower.

The first mortgagee was fully secured even during the bankruptcy. So, the appreciation is irrelevant to the first mortgagee. Despite the discharge, the mortgagee can enforce its mortgage to the full amount of the mortgage debt that is fully secured. There is no violation of the discharge because in foreclosing, the mortgagee is not suing the debtor for personal liability. The mortgagee is enforcing a property interest, which the discharge does not disturb.

The second mortgage was partly secured. But, section 1322(b)(2) nevertheless fully applies. The plan could not strip down the second mortgage. So, the amount of the second mortgagee's secured claim, during and after bankruptcy, equals the amount of the contract debt because the debtor could not strip down the mortgage in the Chapter 13 plan. So, the second mortgage can enforce the mortgage, to the extent of the secured debt, in any and all of the foreclosure surplus that remains after paying the first mortgage. Any deficiency that remains is unsecured and discharged.

In the unlikely event that a surplus remains after satisfying the secured claims of the first and second mortgagees, whether or not the third mortgagee can get to this remaining surplus depends on whether or not the third mortgage was stripped down in the Chapter 13 plan, which depends on whether or not section 1322(b)(2) applies to a mortgage that, during the bankruptcy, was fully under water, i.e., fully unsecured. If section 1322(b)(2) applies, the Chapter 13 plan could not strip down the third mortgage. So, the third mortgagee can enforce the mortgage, to the extent of the secured debt, in any and all of the foreclosure surplus that remains after paying the first and second mortgages. Any deficiency that remains is unsecured and discharged. If section 1322(b)(2) does not apply and the Chapter 13 plan stripped down and completely away the third mortgage, there is no third mortgage to foreclose after bankruptcy ends. The third mortgagee's claim was fully unsecured and completely discharged.

The courts are split on whether or not section 1322(b)(2) applies to a home mortgage that is fully underwater and unsecured, i.e., there is no value in the property to support the mortgage above the value supporting senior encumbrances. The large majority of courts have held that the anti-modification provision in section 1322(b)(2) protects only those homestead liens that are at least partially secured — as that term is defined by section 506(a) — by some existing equity after accounting for encumbrances that have senior priority.

> ## BANKRUPTCY ESSAY EXAM #5 [CHAPTER 11 (PART 1)]

> ### QUESTION #1

Managing the Process

a) Explain the role and importance of the debtor-in-possession (DIP) in the Chapter 11 process.   Based on the bare language of Chapter 11, the dominate player in a Chapter 11 case is a trustee because it is a trustee who, by the terms of the statute, is given rights and powers to drive the process. However, no trustee is appointed in the typical Chapter 11. Instead, "a debtor in possession . . . [has] all the rights . . . and powers, and shall perform all the functions and duties . . . of a trustee serving in a case under this chapter." 11 U.S.C. §1107(a). Functionally, the debtor — with the same officers, directors, and managers at the time the company files bankruptcy — is the debtor in possession (DIP). Most courts seem to agree that "the debtor in possession [] is the same person for bankruptcy purposes as . . . the pre-bankruptcy corporation." Bilmore Associates, LLC v. Twin City Fire Ins. Co., 572 F.3d 663, 671–72 (9th Cir. 2009), citing NLRB v. Bildisco & Bildisco, 465 U.S. 513, 528 (1984) ("it is sensible to view the debtor-in-possession as the same 'entity' which existed before the filing of the bankruptcy petition").

The most important roles of DIP include:

- overseeing the operation of the business, including deciding if and how to obtain financing, sell assets, and continue operations;
- selecting and hiring the professionals that assist with the bankruptcy and appointing other persons to perform functions for the business and the estate;
- having the exclusive right during the first 120 days of the bankruptcy case to propose the Chapter 11 reorganization plan, *id.* §1121(b);
- having the opportunity to sue or be sued in the same manner as a trustee, *id.* §323(b);
- exercising the powers to reject or assume leases and executor contracts and the powers to avoid prepetition transfers;
- disclosing the financial condition of the debtor entity by periodic reporting to interested parties;
- protecting and preserving the assets; and
- prosecuting the bankruptcy case in an expeditious manner.

In sum, the DIP takes the company into bankruptcy; runs the business during the bankruptcy; has a lead run in directing the bankruptcy process; and makes decisions that greatly influence, as much or more than any other player, the form, structure, and direction of the debtor and its business after bankruptcy.

b) Identify critical counterweights to the DIP's control of the process.   The authority of the DIP to run the debtor's business during bankruptcy and to control the bankruptcy process is not absolute. Principal limitations on this authority include:

- the pervasive power of the court to review and approve or disapprove discretionary actions of the debtor in possession;
- the DIP's role as a fiduciary for creditors of the estate, which means the DIP cannot act totally in its own interests and must take into account the often adverse interests of creditors;
- the creation of committees of unsecured creditors to monitor the bankruptcy process, which collectively leverages their importance in influencing the DIP's conduct and the court's review of this conduct;
- the risk that the court will revoke the DIP's right to operate the business, will convert the case from Chapter 11 to Chapter 7, or dismiss the case;
- the court's recently enlarged power to appoint an examiner or replace the DIP with a trustee; and
- the need for other parties in interest to agree to some matters, especially including the requirement that a certain level of creditors accept even a Chapter 11 plan proposed by the debtor.

The most important limitations, however, are the increasing power of the debtor's lenders and their changing roles. Lenders are more involved and more in control of the process because their liens fully encumber the debtor's property and leave little or no room for the debtor to operate without their consent. And, the increasing role of hedge funds and other non-traditional lenders, as opposed to the single, dominate bank or syndicate, has generated more reason for lenders to exercise their control of the reorganization process chiefly by insisting on the court enforcing the limits on the DIP.

> Banks make their profit by lending money and having it paid back. They do not seek to own and operate the business. Not so with hedge funds. A hedge fund may buy the loan with the view that in the event of default it would be left with the business, and given the amount at which it purchased the notes, it would not be a bad price at which to acquire it even if it were in financial distress. Banks want their money back; hedge funds loan to own. The same dynamic that plays out with respect to publicly traded unsecured debt now plays out with respect to traditional bank debt as well.
>
> . . . Far from having a liquidation bias, a hedge fund may affirmatively want to advance a reorganization plan in which it ends up with the equity of the business. Rather than push for a market sale, it prefers a judicial process it can control. Not only can it push for a low valuation, but the managers of the business (individuals whose options will be reset upon emergence from Chapter 11) will push for a low valuation as well.
>
> In short, the senior lender in the identical place within the capital structure is doing exactly the opposite of its traditional counterpart. Instead of fleeing from the Chapter 11 process, it embraces it. Rather than terminating its relationship with the business, the hedge fund wants to run it. Rather than fighting the managers, it takes control both through conditions imposed on debtor-in-possession financing and by installing new officers, most typically a chief restructuring officer (CRO).

Douglas G. Baird & Robert K. Rasmussen, *Antibankruptcy*, 119 Yale L.J. 648, 670-71 (2010).

QUESTION #2

Continuing Operations

a) What property of the estate can the DIP use to continue MMW's business? Generally speaking, the debtor in possession "may enter into transactions" and "may use property of the estate in the ordinary course of business without notice or a hearing." 11 U.S.C. §363(c)(1). So, the DIP can pretty much freely use property of the estate in whatever ways are common and ordinary in operating the debtor's business. Property can also be used, sold, or leased out of the ordinary course but only with the court's approval after notice and hearing. *Id.* §363(b)(1).

Sometimes, the property is subject to the rights and interests of third parties and, almost always, is largely or wholly encumbered, that is, subject to the liens of creditors with secured claims. At any time, on request of a creditor or other entity that has an interest in property the DIP is using or proposing to use, the court must prohibit or condition such use, sale, or lease as is necessary to provide "adequate protection" of the lien or other interest.

And, a tighter rule applies when the property the DIP wants to use is cash collateral, which means "cash, negotiable instruments, documents of title, securities, deposit accounts, or other cash equivalents whenever acquired in which the estate and an entity other than the estate have an interest. . . ." *Id.* §363(a). The debtor in possession cannot touch cash collateral for its own use without getting the creditor's consent beforehand or getting the court's prior approval, which depends on ensuring that the creditor's interest is adequately protected. *Id.* §363(c)(2). Pending this consent or approval, the DIP must segregate and account for all cash collateral in its possession, custody, or control. *Id.* §363(c)(4).

Adequate protection implies giving the secured creditor substitute property or some other form of compensation or insurance that replaces the amount of any decrease in the lien or other third-party interest in the property the DIP wants to use. To the extent that the DIP's use of estate property will result in a decrease in the value of a third person's interest in the property, the DIP may provide adequate protection by:

- Making a cash payment or periodic cash payments to the creditor;
- Giving the creditor an additional or replacement lien; or
- Providing such other relief as will result in the realization by such entity of the indubitable equivalent of such entity's interest in such property.

Id. §361.

The debtor's operating funds and other deposit accounts are cash collateral. The business will close if the debtor cannot use the cash collateral. Understandably, bankruptcy judges are sympathetic to the debtor's argument that unless it is permitted to use cash collateral, the debtor will close and all of its employees will lose their jobs, their health insurance, their retirement benefits, etc. Understanding the court's sympathy and knowing the odds of defeating this sympathy, creditors generally agree to the debtor's use of cash collateral in exchange for some sort of replacement lien on postpetition inventory and receivables and some sort of administrative expense priority. Thus, most court orders approving the use of cash collateral are consent orders. Use of cash collateral is typically the debtor's initial source of credit for continuing the business in bankruptcy, as by paying suppliers and employees.

b) Explain why paying the prepetition debts of critical vendors and suppliers is more likely objectionable than paying employees' wages, including accrued prepetition wages. Smoothly continuing the debtor's business often requires keeping many of the same suppliers of goods and services, including employees. The costs of goods and services provided *postpetition* are administrative expenses and, traditionally, are paid when or soon after the costs are incurred, not later as part of the Chapter 11 plan.

Not surprisingly, some of these suppliers will nevertheless be reluctant to provide anything postpetition until they are paid for whatever they provided prepetition. For this reason, as soon as bankruptcy is filed, a debtor in possession may ask the court for permission to pay the prepetition, unsecured debts of suppliers whom the DIP says are critical to the success of the reorganization. The Bankruptcy Code does not condone such payments. Indeed, unsecured debts are to be provided for and paid according to the Chapter 11 plan, which the court must have confirmed. Paying these suppliers earlier and in amounts larger than other unsecured creditors is forbidden discrimination.

Nevertheless, many courts for many years routinely approved these immediate payments of prepetition suppliers' debts on the basis of section 105(a) and an implied or conjured "doctrine of necessity."

> The Doctrine of Necessity is a principle used in bankruptcy law . . . ostensibly in contradiction to other law in order to accomplish a vital objective in a bankruptcy case. The Doctrine exists simply because it works. The proper use of the Doctrine helps to stabilize a debtor's business relationships without significantly hurting any party.

Russell A. Eisenberg & Frances F. Gecker, *The Doctrine of Necessity and Its Parameters*, 73 Marq. L. Rev. 1, 2 (1989). "[T]he Necessity Doctrine may be used to permit a debtor to pay the pre-petition claims of suppliers or employees whose continued cooperation is essential to the debtor's successful reorganization . . . [and] may also be used, however, to justify post-petition payment of a wide variety of other types of pre-petition claims, as long as payment of those claims will help to 'stabilize [the] debtor's business relationships without significantly hurting any party.'" In re UNR Industries, Inc., 143 B.R. 506, 520 (Bankr. N.D. Ill. 1992), rev'd on other grounds sub nom. UNR Industries, Inc. v. Bloomington Factory Workers, 173 B.R. 149 (N.D. Ill. Sept. 22, 1994). The underlying rationale is that "[s]ometimes immediate payment to a prepetition creditor will make the creditors as a group better off." Russell A. Eisenberg & Frances F. Gecker, *The Doctrine of Necessity and Its Parameters*, 73 Marq. L. Rev. 1, 3 (1989).

In In re Kmart Corp., 359 F.3d 866 (7th Cir. 2004), the court rejected the necessity doctrine and the practice of paying the prepetition debts of critical suppliers.

> A "doctrine of necessity" is just a fancy name for a power to depart from the Code. Although courts in the days before bankruptcy law was codified wielded power to reorder priorities and pay particular creditors in the name of "necessity."

Id. at 871. And the court concluded that the only provision of the Code that possibly supports preferring critical suppliers is section 363(b)(1):

> "The trustee [or debtor in possession], after notice and a hearing, may use, sell, or lease, other than in the ordinary course of business, property of the estate." This is more promising, for satisfaction of a pre-petition debt in order to keep "critical" supplies flowing is a use of property other than in the ordinary course of administering an estate in bankruptcy.

Id. at 872. However, to pay critical suppliers on this basis, the debtor in possession must make a certain showing:

> The foundation of a critical-vendors order is the belief that vendors not paid for prior deliveries will refuse to make new ones. Without merchandise to sell, a retailer such as Kmart will fold. If paying the critical vendors would enable a successful reorganization and make even the disfavored creditors better off, then all creditors favor payment whether or not they are designated as "critical." This suggests a use of §363(b)(1) similar to the theory underlying a plan crammed down the throats of an impaired class of creditors: if the impaired class does at least as well as it would have under a Chapter 7 liquidation, then it has no legitimate objection and cannot block the reorganization. For the premise to hold true, however, it is necessary to show not only that the disfavored creditors *will* be as well off with reorganization as with liquidation . . . but also that the supposedly critical vendors would have ceased deliveries if old debts were left unpaid while the litigation continued. If vendors will deliver against a promise of current payment, then a reorganization can be achieved, and all unsecured creditors will obtain its benefit, without preferring any of the unsecured creditors.

Id. at 872-73. In the *Kmart* case, this showing was not made. It was therefore wrong to pay the critical suppliers' prepetition debts because there is no other lawful basis for doing so. The same is true in any other case.

Paying the prepetition wages of employees is often treated differently and allowed. To some extent, a claim for prepetition wages is a given priority over the payment of other unsecured debts. 11 U.S.C. §507(a)(4) (fourth priority to the extent of $10,000 earned within 180 days before bankruptcy for wages, salaries and the like). For this reason and to this extent, prepetition wages are rightly preferred to other creditors and can be paid early in the bankruptcy without any special showing or proof.

QUESTION #3

Staying Unsecured Creditors

a) Can critical suppliers simply refuse to do further business with the debtor?   The automatic stay prevents a creditor from doing just about anything to collect a prepetition debt. Specifically, the stay forbids "any act to collect, assess, or recover a claim against the debtor that arose before the commencement of the case under this title." 11 U.S.C. §362(a)(6). Does "*act to collect*" include refusing to sell property and services or otherwise deal with the debtor? Suppose, for example, that the creditor is a long-time supplier of goods on open account that are critically important to MMW's business. MMW can most efficiently deal with this creditor because of their experience together and well-established course of conduct. Continuing this relationship is thus financially important to the debtor. However, after MMW filed bankruptcy, the creditor refuses to sell to the debtor even for cash. Finding another supplier will cost time and money that MMW's bankruptcy probably cannot afford.

If the creditor were contractually obligated to continue supplying the debtor, the debtor could assume the contract. 11 U.S.C. §365. By complying with section 365 the debtor could force the creditor to continue to perform. Even apart from section 365, the contract would become property of the estate; and it is arguable that the creditor would be barred from cancelling or breaching the contract by section 362(a)(3), which prohibits interference with property of the estate. 11 U.S.C. §362(a)(3) ("any act to obtain possession of property of the estate or of property from the estate or to exercise control over property of the estate"). By this argument, section 362(a)(3) alone would shield the contract from cancellation or breach.

In this problem, however, section 362(a)(3) is not implicated. By refusing to deal with MMW, the supplier has not breached a contractual commitment as to future performance; is not otherwise exercising control over any estate property or property of the debtor; and is not otherwise keeping, withholding, or interfering with something to which the debtor or the estate is legally entitled.

Whether or not section 362(a)(6) covers this precise situation was almost decided in In re Sportfame of Ohio, Inc., 40 B.R. 47 (Bankr. N.D. Ohio 1984). The critical facts of *Sportfame* are these:

> Plaintiff, Sportfame of Ohio, Inc. (Sportfame), runs four retail sporting goods stores in Ohio, three of which are located in Toledo, one in Findlay. Plaintiff carries a wide variety of goods and, in addition to supplying customers at its stores, employs salespeople to call on schools and institutions with sports programs directly.
>
> Defendant, Wilson Sporting Goods Company (Wilson), has sold its line of sporting goods to plaintiff at wholesale for almost 10 years until recently when it refused to ship any further goods to plaintiff. Defendant had supplied plaintiff with a wide variety of its name brand products which are widely advertised and promoted.
>
> On February 14, 1983 plaintiff filed a voluntary petition under Chapter 11 of the Bankruptcy Code. In the twelve month period prior to the filing of the petition, plaintiff had purchased some $45,000 worth of goods from defendant at wholesale and sold them at retail to its customers for approximately $70,000. Sometime prior to the filing of the petition, plaintiff became in arrears with defendant for shipments of goods in the amount of approximately $18,000. Due to the arrearage, defendant ceased shipping goods to plaintiff prior to the filing of the petition.
>
> In March and April of 1983 Sam R. Shible, president of Sportfame, contacted defendant's credit manager by telephone in an attempt to have shipments of

inventory resumed. On these occasions, Mr. Shible attempted to buy goods from defendant for cash. Defendant, while aware of the Chapter 11 proceeding, refused to resume shipments of goods unless plaintiff brought its account current or made arrangements to pay 100% of the arrearage.

As a result of defendant's refusal to fill plaintiff's orders, plaintiff can no longer supply its customers with the Wilson line of sporting goods. According to the evidence adduced at trial, many of plaintiff's individual and institutional customers have asked for certain Wilson goods by name. These same customers many times either refuse or are reluctant to accept as replacements other lines of goods carried by plaintiff. Plaintiff's president testified that its inability to fill orders for Wilson goods will result in customer dissatisfaction and loss of profits.

Id. at 48-49. The court decided that Wilson violated section 362(a)(6) but circumscribed its holding: the violation occurred "by refusing to enter into *cash* transactions with debtor *absent payment of its prepetition debt* where its *sole* motivation was to collect its prepetition debt." *Id.* at 48-49. The key to this decision is not Wilson's refusal to deal but Wilson's repeated coercive demands for payment. It was irrelevant to the court that the coercion was by carrot rather than stick. The effect was the same because of the debtor's extraordinary dependency on Wilson.

A similar case is In re Mathson Industries, Inc., 423 B.R. 643 (E.D. Mich. 2010). The defendant, NegriBossi USA, Inc., had an unsecured claim against the estate for machines sold to the debtor. In the Chapter 7 bankruptcy, the trustee proposed to sell the machines for the benefit of the estate. "Defendant attempted to control bidding on the machines by telling potential purchasers that it would not provide necessary services and parts — referred to in this case as 'servicing capabilities' — for machines purchased from [the trustee]. By its actions, Defendant intended to suppress bidding on the machines so that it could purchase the machines at a low price from the estate and then resell them to the potential purchasers at or near full-price. In this way, Defendant would basically be able to recover all of its unsecured claim against Mathson." *Id.* at 645-46. The bankruptcy court decided that the defendant had violated section 362(a)(6) and therefore enjoined the defendant from (a) communicating to potential purchasers of the machines that NegriBossi will not provide servicing capabilities to them if they purchase one or more of the machines from the trustee; and (b) refusing to provide servicing capabilities to the purchaser of one or more of the machines at the same cost that it charges its other customers in the ordinary course of its business for such servicing capabilities.

The district court affirmed, agreeing that the defendant suppliers violated section 362(a)(6) because:

> the conduct allows Defendant to recover its pre-petition debt at the expense of other creditors, not because Defendant expressed an intention to obtain such a result. Had Defendant expressed an intention to recover a pre-petition claim without engaging in any conduct to effectuate that intent, there would be no violation of the stay. Conversely, by engaging in an act to recover a pre-petition claim, Defendant violated the stay regardless of its expressed intentions. Admittedly, a defendant's express intentions will normally be relevant to determining whether an act is taken "to collect, assess, or recover" a pre-petition debt. Ultimately, though, . . . it is not the mere expression of intent that makes a creditor's conduct unlawful; the proper analysis focuses on whether the conduct in question actually violates a provision of the bankruptcy code.

In this case, Defendant did more than simply express an intent to collect a pre-petition debt; Defendant engaged in conduct in furtherance of that intent. Specifically, Defendant (1) informed a prospective purchaser that it would not provide support or maintenance for machines purchased from the bankruptcy estate, and (2) offered to purchase the machines from Plaintiff for far less than their value, knowing other purchasers would require the assistance Defendant refused to provide. In this way, Defendant sought to pursue its own remedy against the debtor's property to the detriment of other creditors. The conduct more specifically violates §362(a)(6) in that it (1) could reasonably be expected to have a significant impact on the creditor's ability to collect, assess, or recover a pre-petition debt, and (2) is contrary to what a reasonable person would consider fair under the circumstances. Having identified a violation of the bankruptcy code, the Court now turns to consider the appropriateness of injunctive relief.

Id. at 652-53.

Neither the *Sportfame* nor *Mathson Industries* case decides our problem in which the supplier has simply refused to deal with MMW. Probably, though, the supplier has not violated section 362(a)(6), not even if the supplier's reason for refusing to deal is MMW's default and bankruptcy. This conduct may well constitute an act, but not an act to collect or recover a claim that (a)(6) requires and that was at the bottom of *Sportfame*. The court in *Sportfame* itself recognized:

> Wilson could have simply refused, for any reason, to sell goods to debtor or offered no explanation for its refusal. Instead, its sole reason for refusing to sell goods to debtor was its desire to collect its prepetition claim.

If any violation of section 362(a)(6) occurred in *Sportfame*, which is unlikely, it was Wilson's act of attempting to collect by insisting on payment. Refusing to deal, for any reason or no reason, is not itself prohibited by subsection (a)(6) or even by section 362(a) in whole absent a contractual or other legal commitment of future performance. As the Third Circuit has so clearly said,

> Nothing in the bankruptcy code requires [a] creditor to do business with [a] debtor. . . . [A] mere refusal to do business does not amount to improper coercion. The refusal can be "designed to protect the . . . coffers against repeated defaults, a permissible purpose."

Brown v. Pennsylvania State Employees Credit Union, 851 F.2d 81, 85-86 (3d Cir. 1988). Reading section 362(a)(6) otherwise would seriously undermine freedom of and from contract without the very clear and very strong justification that should be required to do so. Cf. In re Coachlight Dinner Theatre of Nanuet, Inc., 8 B.R. 657 (Bankr. S.D.N.Y. 1981) (radio station could not be compelled to accept advertisements even on a cash in advance basis).

b) In terms of statutory language and underlying policy, explain whether or not critical suppliers can likely convince the court to lift the automatic stay so they can prosecute their claims in state court. Sometimes, the purpose for generally staying a certain act is overcome by a circumstantially more compelling reason for permitting the act to be done. The Code recognizes this possibility by empowering the bankruptcy court, in section 362(d)(1), to lift the stay "for cause." Specifically, section 362(d)(1) provides:

> On request of a party in interest and after notice and a hearing, the court shall grant relief from the stay provided under subsection (a) of this section, such as by terminating, annulling, modifying, or conditioning such stay—
>
> (1) for cause, including the lack of adequate protection of an interest in property of such party in interest. . . .

11 U.S.C. §362(d)(1).

Basically, section 362(d)(1) works very simply. A person affected by the stay asks the court, by motion, for permission to do whatever the stay prevents her from doing. If her reason is sufficient, i.e., she establishes "cause," the court will grant her request by formally ordering that she can proceed to the extent and in the manner provided in this order. This order is the grant of relief that section 362(d)(1) mentions. Everybody refers to this process as *lifting the stay*, and the motion requesting the relief is called a *lift-stay motion*.

In truth, very few reasons are sufficient cause to lift stay. Relief is usually reserved for people who have property interests that the stay threatens to erode by delaying resort to the property. *Unsecured creditors seldom get relief from the stay.*

The general explanation is that bankruptcy honors the interests of third parties in the debtor's property. The bankruptcy itself does not affect their interests. Even the property that comprises the estate is limited to the debtor's interests. Third-party interests generally survive the bankruptcy whether they are legal or equitable, recorded or secret, large or small. These interests are sometimes avoided by the trustee but only exceptionally. Avoidance is based on relatively narrow concerns that do not significantly undermine the respect of the Bankruptcy Code for the huge, general policy of derivative title.

The stay itself does not offend this policy. It does not cut off or reduce any third-party interest in property that is affected by the bankruptcy.

Yet, the stay can stop third parties, temporarily, from taking action with respect to their interests in the property that could affect the debtor's interest, the debtor herself, or her bankruptcy case. This delay by itself can reduce a third party's interest, most commonly when it is a security interest or lien. The costs of time and the depreciation of the collateral consume the security, and, when the declining value falls below increasing debt, the size of the secured creditor's interest begins to shrink.

In theory, bankruptcy law protects against this erosion by providing the secured creditor with two shots at relief from the stay. "Cause" under (d)(1) is actually the creditor's second shot or fall-back position. Her first shot is usually section 362(d)(2), which is essentially a standardized cause or reason for giving relief with respect to an act against property. Under (d)(2) the stay is lifted if:

> (A) the debtor does not have an equity in such property; and
> (B) such property is not necessary to an effective reorganization.

11 U.S.C. §362(d)(2). Property that lacks equity is useless in bankruptcy unless the debtor is reorganizing and needs the property itself in order to make it. There is no reason to continue the stay with respect to property that the bankruptcy cannot use.

Even if equity exists or the property is needed for reorganization or both, the secured creditor's interest will shrink if the bankruptcy's use of her collateral or other circumstances will consume any equity and further devalue the collateral so as to cut into her interest. Proving that this risk to her interest is likely to occur is "cause" for relief under section 362(d)(1). The court must lift the stay to permit the secured creditor to realize on her collateral unless the debtor provides the creditor with "adequate protection" against the loss of value that would result from the erosion of the creditor's interest.

Unsecured creditors have no property interests to protect so that relief from the stay under section 362(d)(2) is never possible. Their other concerns are usually unimportant against the stay because the bankruptcy will discharge the debts owed them. Essentially, these creditors' reasons for wanting relief from the stay contradict the fundamental purposes of the bankruptcy. Typically, therefore, they lack "cause" for relief under section 362(d)(1). About the only halfway common reason to lift the stay for an unsecured creditor is to permit liquidation of the claim in a forum that is substantially more appropriate than the bankruptcy court, or because the debtor filed bankruptcy in bad faith. *Even these reasons are seldom established, and the bottom line is that relief from the stay for any reason is rare for the unsecured creditor.*

Unsecured creditors have nevertheless argued for section 362(d)(1) relief because of another right, though not a property interest, with respect to the collateral that is not adequately protected: it is the right to immediate foreclosure that the stay suspended. Adequately protecting this right would require paying the secured creditor interest for the term of the stay on the proceeds that the immediate foreclosure, at the beginning of the case, would have produced.

The Supreme Court faced this issue in United Savings Association of Texas v. Timbers of Inwood Forest Associates, Ltd., 484 U.S. 365 (1988). At bottom, the base issue in *Timbers* was whether or not an undersecured creditor is entitled to postpetition interest on its secured claim. The Court answered no. The short reason is that the Code clearly provides for paying interest that accrues postpetition to oversecured creditors and is silent, at best, on paying the same to undersecured creditors. See 11 U.S.C. §506(b).

QUESTION #4

Lifting the Stay for Secured Creditor FNB

Discuss whether or not the court will likely grant or deny an early motion by FNB to lift the stay in order to enforce its security interest against the collateral. Whether or not RFB carries through on buying most of MMW's debt to FNB, FNB has a secured claim to some extent. MMW's bankruptcy should not continue to keep FNB from its collateral when the property cannot serve the reorganization aims of the bankruptcy. The property lacks any liquidation value if the debtor owns no equity in it; and the property lacks any other value for bankruptcy purposes if the property is not needed for a reorganization. Therefore, section 362(d)(2) provides for lifting the stay:

> with respect to an act against property under subsection (a) of this section, if—
>> (A) the debtor does not have an equity in such property; and
>> (B) such property is not necessary to an effective reorganization.

11 U.S.C. §362(d)(2). Both elements must be established to lift the stay under (d)(2), but the secured creditor or other person seeking the relief is burdened to prove only the debtor's lack of equity. The burden of proof is on the party opposing relief from stay, who wants to keep the property in the bankruptcy, to prove that the property is needed for a reorganization.

Significantly, subsections (d)(2) and (1) are disjunctive: they provide entirely alternate grounds for relief. Thus, the stay should be lifted if (d)(2) is met even if the secured creditor's interest is adequately protected within the meaning of (d)(1). Remember that (d)(2) is really a specific expression of (d)(1). The circumstances of (d)(2) are themselves, by operation of law, sufficient cause for relief from the stay. The absence of any other cause, such as lack of adequate protection, can (practically) influence the decision whether or not (d)(2) is met, but cannot trump relief under (d)(2) when its requirements are proved.

Deciding if the debtor lacks equity in the collateral under section 362(d)(2)(A) is mechanical and easy once certain values are determined. Equity basically "is the value, above all secured claims against the property [including both security interests and liens], that can be realized from the sale of the property for the benefit of the unsecured creditors." In re Mellor, 734 F.2d 1396, 1400 n.2 (9th Cir. 1984). Thus, section 362(d)(2)(A) is decided by determining the market value of the property and subtracting the amount of debts that it secures. The debtor has no equity in the property if the difference is zero or less.

In deciding if MMW lacks any equity in the collateral, the secured debt that is subtracted from the market value of the property is the sum of all valid liens and security interests against the property, not just the encumbrance of the person who wants the stay lifted. Even junior claims are included. At bottom, accounting for all secured claims is the only way to determine if the property holds value that the bankruptcy can use.

It is likely, even almost certain, that MMW lacks any equity in the collateral, meaning that the value of the property is fully encumbered by the combined liens of FNB and RFB. However, in a Chapter 11 case, the debtor's lack of an equity in the property is not sufficient for relief under section 362(d)(2). A second, equal requirement, imposed by (d)(2)(B), is that "such property is not necessary to an effective reorganization." 11 U.S.C.A. 362(d)(2)(B). In other words, (d)(2) allows the bankruptcy to keep property that is needed to reorganize even though the debtor lacks any equity in it.

The trustee or debtor bears the burden of proving two points. First, the property must be important to the reorganization. Merely helpful or convenient is not enough. The debtor or trustee must also prove a second point, that the planned reorganization is feasible. In truth, (d)(2) relief in Chapter 11 business cases usually turns solely on this issue, which the Supreme Court more fully described in United Savings Association of Texas v. Timbers of Inwood Forest Associates, Ltd., 484 U.S. 365 (1988):

> Once the movant under §362(d)(2) establishes that he is an undersecured cred-itor, it is the burden of the debtor to establish that the collateral at issue is "necessary to an effective reorganization." What this requires is not merely a showing that if there is conceivably to be an effective reorganization, this prop-erty will be needed for it; but that the property is essential for an effective reorganization that is in prospect. This means, as many lower courts, including the en banc court in this case, have properly said, that there must be a "reasonable possibility of a successful reorganization within a reasonable time."

Id. at 375-76. This rule or test of feasibility — whether or not a successful reorgani-zation is reasonably possible within a reasonable time — was merely dicta in *Timbers*, but was the law that most courts followed before *Timbers* and that everybody follows now.

In deciding feasibility, timing is very important. The detail and soundness that are required to show feasibility are affected by when in the bankruptcy, early or late, relief is sought and the debtor's showing is responsively made. The principle is:

> The debtor's burden of demonstrating a reasonable possibility of a successful reorganization increases with time. "During the early stages of a proceeding, a less detailed showing may succeed. The same showing at a later time, however, may be insufficient."

In re Ritz-Carlton of D.C., Inc., 98 B.R. 170, 172 (S.D.N.Y. 1989), quoting In re Grand Sports, Inc., 86 B.R. 971, 974 (Bankr. N.D. Ind. 1988). The showing of feasibility "necessarily must be stronger as the case ages or if the financial information shows a marginal operation." In re Northgate Terrace Apartments, Ltd., 126 B.R. 520, 523 (Bankr. S.D. Ohio 1991), related proceeding, 126 B.R. 762 (Bankr. S.D. Ohio 1991).

Very often, therefore, part of the reason for granting relief under section 362(d)(2) is that the debtor's plan falls short compared to the length of the case, or simply that the case has continued so long that the absence of success so far argues against any possibility of success in the future. By contrast, a court may well deny relief at a "relatively early stage" in the case based on the debtor showing feasibility "not by a very comfortable margin." In re Swansea Consolidated Resources, Inc., 127 B.R. 1, 3 (Bankr. D.R.I. 1991).

In most cases, when a secured party moves to lift stay early in the case, the odds strongly favor the court finding that the collateral, whatever it is, is property that is important for the reorganization and also that, at the current point, the planned organization is feasible. So, FNB's early motion to lift stay in the MMW bankruptcy case will likely fail *unless FNB's interest is not adequately protected*.

Even if property is necessary for an effective reorganization, the court must lift the stay if using the property in the bankruptcy or merely keeping it from the secured creditor can imperil the lien or other interest of a third party in the collateral. Harming the interest would violate bankruptcy's usual policy of honoring third parties' claims to property that is affected by the case.

Section 362(d)(1) therefore trumps (d)(2) and orders relief for the secured creditor or other third-party claimant who can show a threat to its interest that is not adequately protected. This exposure, called "lack of adequate protection," is actually only a specific example of reason for relief under section 362(d)(1). Its few words are much wider and appear very generous in ordering relief

> *for cause*, including the lack of adequate protection of an interest in property of such party in interest [who requests the relief].

11 U.S.C. §362(d)(1) (emphasis added). For purposes of (d)(1), " '[c]ause' has no clear definition and is determined on a case-by-case basis," In re Universal Life Church, Inc., 127 B.R. 453, 455 (E.D. Cal. 1991), in light of "all the facts and circumstances of the case, taking into account the purposes of the automatic stay, the behavior of the parties, considerations of judicial efficiency, and the balance of hardships involved." In re Sonnax Industries, Inc., 99 B.R. 591, 595 (D. Vt. 1989), aff'd, 907 F.2d 1280 (2d Cir. 1990).

In theory, cause is endless: "*any* reason cognizable to the equity power and conscience of the court as constituting an abuse of bankruptcy process." Little Creek Dev. Co. v. Commonwealth Mortgage Corp., 779 F.2d 1068, 1072 (5th Cir.1986) (emphasis added). Even in practice section 362(d)(1) has justified relief in a wide range of circumstances and for many reasons. In truth, however, for creditors in typical cases, few causes regularly trigger relief under section 362(d)(1) other than lack of adequate protection, which only secured creditors can claim.

In very general terms, adequate protection means that the value of an interest is reasonably well insured. If the circumstances do not naturally provide this insurance and the debtor cannot realistically propose buying or otherwise supplying adequate protection, the interest is not adequately protected and this lack of protection itself justifies relief "for cause" under section 362(d)(1). The secured creditor can then grab her collateral and apply its value to the secured debt.

Determining if an interest is adequately protected involves these three basic steps, reported by the Eighth Circuit in In re Martin, 761 F.2d 472 (8th Cir.1985):

(1) establish the value of the secured creditor's interest,
(2) identify the risks to the secured creditor's value . . . , and
(3) determine whether the debtor's adequate protection proposal protects value as nearly as possible against risks to that value. . . .

Id. at 477. The burden of non-persuasion is on the trustee or debtor: to defeat relief under (d)(1) she is burdened to prove that the creditor's interest is adequately protected. 11 U.S.C. 362(g).

The Supreme Court explained in United Savings Association of Texas v. Timbers of Inwood Forest Associates, Ltd., 484 U.S. 365 (1988), that "the 'interest in property' referred to by 362(d)(1) includes the right of a secured creditor to have the security applied in payment of the debt. . . ." *Id.* at 370. The value of this interest is measured by the secured debt but is naturally limited by the value of the collateral. The value of the interest is also reduced by the amount of senior encumbrances. If they exceed the collateral's value, the creditor's junior interest lacks any value that (d)(1) is designed to protect. She is essentially unsecured. Therefore, relief is impossible under (d)(1) for lack of adequate protection, as is true for any unsecured creditor.

In the case of MMW's bankruptcy, even if the debtor lacks equity in the property, FNB is adequately protected if its security interest retains priority over RFB's security interest. If FNB's interest is subordinate and there is no value in the collateral beyond the amount of RFB's secured claim, FNB's claim is completely unsecured, it has no interest to adequately protect, and the stay will not be lifted.

However, if FNB has a secured claim to any extent and circumstances threaten to shrink this interest, FNB is entitled to adequate protection and MMW must provide it.

How can MMW provide protection adequate to protect FNB's interest? The debtor and creditor very often negotiate and settle the issue through an adequate protection agreement that is filed as an agreed order of adequate protection and approved by the court upon proper notice. The debtor's breach of the agreement and order is itself reason to lift the stay.

Often enough, the creditor rejects the debtor's offer of adequate protection and takes the issue to court. On the creditor's lift-stay motion, the court will decide if the debtor's proposal is sufficient, can order additional protection, and will grant relief from the stay if adequate protection is not forthcoming. If the creditor's interest is adequately protected, her motion is denied unless she establishes other "cause" for relief under section 362(d)(1) or that the grounds for relief under (d)(2) are satisfied.

An important key to understanding and deciding adequate protection is that the actual purpose is not to protect the creditor's interest itself, but to insure the value of the interest. Therefore, many different kinds of protection are possible. The Code gives examples in section 361:

> When adequate protection is required . . . of an interest of an entity in property, such adequate protection may be provided by —
> (1) requiring the trustee to make a cash payment or periodic cash payments to such entity, to the extent that the stay under section 362 of this title, use, sale, or lease under section 363 of this title, or any grant of a lien under section 364 of this title results in a decrease in the value of such entity's interest in such property;
> (2) providing to such entity an additional or replacement lien to the extent that such stay, use, sale, lease, or grant results in a decrease in the value of such entity's interest in such property; or
> (3) granting such other relief, other than entitling such entity to compensation allowable under section 503(b)(1) of this title as an administrative expense, as will result in the realization by such entity of the indubitable equivalent of such entity's interest in such property.

11 U.S.C. §361. Behind this veneer of a list in section 361 are the thick, heavy reason and purpose of adequate protection. They confirm that providing equivalent value to insure an interest is sufficient rather than preserving the interest in specie. This substitution is even necessary to allow the flexibility that is often essential to the bankruptcy process. Moreover, adequate protection can and should differ among cases and between proceedings. It "must . . . be determined on a case-by-case basis,

permitting the debtors 'maximum flexibility in structuring a proposal for adequate protection' . . . [i]n order to encourage reorganization. . . ." In re Martin, 761 F.2d 472, 474, 476 (8th Cir. 1985).

Still, the protection that is provided, though it can be different from the creditor's interest, must be equivalent — the "indubitable equivalent" — in terms of the power to guarantee and realize the value of the interest. This requirement of equivalency can affect the nature of the protection that is appropriate. Its larger role is to test the protection for safety and reliability in preserving an amount of value that equals the creditor's interest.

In the typical case, the threat to the creditor's encumbrance is a decline in the value of the collateral. Adequate protection to counter this threat is most commonly provided in any one of these forms or by a combination of them:

- identifying an equity cushion, which is the value of the collateral in excess of the secured debt;
- making cash payments (commonly called a "stream of payments") to satisfy interest and, more certainly, to reduce the principal in sufficient amount to keep it below declining value;
- transferring the encumbrance to other collateral or creating a security interest in additional collateral; or
- proposing to use the original collateral, or otherwise affect it, in such a way that its value is enhanced.

Acting to enhance the collateral's value is the most *un*common form of adequate protection, especially in a common bankruptcy case. The opportunities and possibilities for it are small, and the risk is large. It usually involves repairing, improving, or developing the collateral and sometimes uses money that the creditor also claims as proceeds. The expected return should be sufficient to recover the proceeds as well as to protect the value of the interest in the collateral.

An equity cushion is undoubtedly the single most common form of adequate protection. An existing cushion works even more fundamentally in determining when the creditor's interest is threatened. Measuring a cushion for any purpose under section 362(d)(1) is very different from determining if the debtor has equity for purposes of (d)(2). The debtor's equity is calculated by totaling all of the encumbrances on the property and subtracting the sum from the property's value. A creditor's equity cushion in the collateral is found by subtracting from the property's value only the creditor's lien or interest and any senior encumbrances.

Whenever an equity cushion is proposed as adequate protection, the question is seldom asked if a cushion is an appropriate means of protection. Always asked, and often hotly debated, is the question of how much cushion is enough. Obviously, the necessary size of the cushion depends on several factors, including mainly the certainty of a drop in the collateral's value, how quickly it will drop and how far. Equally important are the effect and strength of other protections that are proposed in combination with an equity cushion. Every situation is different, posing an entirely fresh guessing game every time the necessary size of an equity cushion is calculated. Nevertheless, there are general rules of thumb, as reported in In re Kost, 102 B.R. 829 (D. Wyo. 1989): "Case law has almost uniformly held that an equity cushion of

20% or more constitutes adequate protection. Case law has almost as uniformly held that an equity cushion under 11% is insufficient to constitute adequate protection. Case law is divided on whether a cushion of 12% to 20% constitutes adequate protection." *Id.* at 832-33. In sum, it is a "general law of bankruptcy" that "the likelihood of lift of stay is inversely proportional to the amount of equity that the debtor possesses in the collateral." In re Novak, 121 B.R. 18, 19 (Bankr. W.D. Mo. 1990).

On the other hand, it is not a general rule of bankruptcy law that a cushy equity cushion is always adequate protection in itself that bars relief under section 362(d)(1). Uncertainty can falsely inflate the cushion. Time will usually deflate it. Moreover, an equity cushion does not always respond to or answer fully the whole range of risks to the value of the creditor's encumbrance, such as the threat of calamitous loss because of the lack of casualty insurance. Finally, an equity cushion solves only the problem of the lack of adequate protection, which is "'but one "cause" for which relief can be granted under 362(d)(1).'" In re Wieseler, 934 F.2d 965, 968 (8th Cir. 1991). In sum, "[t]he mere fact that the debtor enjoys a so-called equity cushion above the secured claim of [the creditor] Citibank does not mean that the debtor may float on this cushion out of the troubled waters stirred up by Citibank's request for relief from the stay." In re Westchester Ave. Marina Realty, Inc., 124 B.R. 161, 166 (Bankr. S.D.N.Y. 1991).

In MMW's bankruptcy case, FNB clearly enjoys a huge equity cushion if its security interest enjoys priority over RFB's interest. The cushion is the value of the property above the amount of FNB's secured claim. If RFB's interest has priority, the equity cushion for FNB's interest is the value of the property above the amount of the combined interests of RFB and FNB, which is likely very small or non-existent. In this event, MMW will likely make cash payments to FNB to offset erosion in the value of FNB's interest. But these payments could not be proceeds of collateral to which FNB was already entitled, or subject to a lien as proceeds or otherwise in favor of someone else with priority. In its role as refinancing lender, RFB could make the offsetting payments to FNB from proceeds of RFB's collateral or other property of RFB.

Another alternative for adequate protection is giving FNB a compensating lien on other property in which there is sufficient equity to support such a lien. This alternative is not realistic if, as is often the case, there is no free equity because all of the estate property is fully encumbered. If so, RFB, again in the role of refinancing lender, might be willing to help by subordinating its interest to FNB to the extent necessary to provide adequate assurance for FNB's interest.

QUESTION #5

DIP Financing

a) What collateral is available to secure the DIP financing? In MMW's bankruptcy, the DIP financer, RFB, will have acquired most of the debt owed FNB and, along with the debt, FNB's security interest in the property that secures the debt.

Nevertheless, MMW needs new advances from RFB, and RFB needs as much insurance against non-payment as possible.

Section 364 allows the debtor in possession to obtain credit and provides incentives for suppliers and lenders to extend credit.

- The DIP can obtain unsecured credit that is treated as an administrative expense and therefore entitled to priority payment. But, having a priority right to payment is not backed by specific property and is no absolute guarantee of payment.
- The DIP can also obtain secured credit using property of the estate as collateral, but estate property is often already encumbered. The lien would be subordinate to existing claims to the property, which has insufficient value to fully support the new, subordinate lien.
- Therefore, the court is authorized to secure new credit with a superior or priming lien on collateral that trumps existing liens, but only if the existing subordinated liens are provided adequate protection. Again, there is the problem of satisfactorily compensating these subordinated liens.

For these reasons, unsecured credit treated as an administrative expense and credit secured by liens on existing property of the estate are often not sufficient to lure DIP financing. Finding fresh, unencumbered collateral or other ways to reduce credit risks are also needed.

There are three principal conventional sources of fresh collateral to secure DIP financing:

i) The most conventional source of fresh, unencumbered collateral is wealth the debtor creates postpetition by operating its business. The floating liens of prepetition creditors are not effective postpetition, 11 U.S.C. §552(a), except with respect to proceeds, products, offspring, or profits resulting from prepetition collateral. *Id.* §552(b)(1); and, even the exceptional reach of a prepetition lien to proceeds and the like can be limited by the court if the equities of the case so require. *Id.*

ii) Another conventional source of fresh property for paying or securing DIP financing are the proceeds of sales of assets, which are often required by the terms of the DIP financing agreement.

> Also known as an asset sale milestone, this covenant requires the debtor to sell assets within a specified time period through a Bankruptcy Code Section 363 sale. See 11 U.S.C. §363. A Section 363 sale allows the debtor, after notice and a hearing and with bankruptcy court approval, to sell assets outside the ordinary course of business. Through the prepayment provisions of the DIP credit agreement, the proceeds of these asset sales are applied to prepay the DIP loans, or reduce the commitments available under the facility. These asset sale milestones have gained increasing popularity during the recent credit crunch as a method to speed the process of repayment of the DIP lenders' loans and, if the proceeds are sufficient, the pre-petition lenders' (who are often the same or substantially the same entities as the DIP lenders) secured loans. The requirement to quickly sell assets

may prevent debtors from reorganizing pursuant to a stand-alone reorganization plan because the debtor must either sell the assets in accordance with the covenant or refinance its DIP facility with a new facility that does not require such a sale.

Opponents of tight asset sale covenants, notably debtors and their counsel, as well as unsecured creditors (and equity holders), who hope a turnaround of the company may lead to greater recovery on their claims or interests, argue that asset sale milestones give the DIP lenders too much control over the bankruptcy process. They further argue that DIP facilities with tight asset sale provisions do not provide debtors with enough time for a true operational restructuring; rather, they provide the company with enough funds to operate while it seeks a buyer. Their contention centers on the fact that such milestones often require the sale of assets in such a short period of time that the debtor and its advisers do not have the time to realistically attempt a turnaround of the company. This control by the DIP lenders (who are often also the pre-petition senior lenders) can be viewed as ensuring a quick return of the DIP lenders' money and some recovery for certain pre-petition senior lenders, but providing no value for unsecured creditors or equity holders.

Paul H. Zumbro, An Overview of Debtor-In-Possession Financing, 2010 WL 556188, at *12 (Aspatore, February 2010).

An advantage to selling assets in bankruptcy is suggested by MMW's plan to sell its FAO subsidiary. Sometimes, under state or federal nonbankruptcy law, causes of action against a company follow the sale of the company or its assets. However, under certain circumstances, a section 363 sale in bankruptcy of a company or its assets may be "*free and clear of any interest in such property* of an entity other than the estate. . . ." 11 U.S.C. §363(f) (emphasis added). Selling free and clear may also be independently allowed on the basis of the bankruptcy court's equitable or supplemental authority. See U.S.C. §105(a). The reason for clear and free sales is: "the potential chilling effect of allowing [claims] . . . subsequent to the sale would run counter to a core aim of the Bankruptcy Code, which is to maximize the value of the assets and thereby maximize potential recovery to the creditors." Douglas v. Stamco, 2010 WL 337043, 2 (2d Cir. 2010).

This language — "free and clear of any interest" — has been interpreted not only to cut off liens, but also to preclude successor tort liability against purchasers of assets under section 363. For instance, in In re Trans World Airlines, Inc., 322 F.3d 283 (3d Cir. 2003), the Third Circuit held that American Airlines, which had purchased assets of TWA "free and clear of any interest in such property" under section 363(f), could not be held liable for the undischarged employment discrimination claims of former TWA employees. The Third Circuit based its holding on the fact that section 363(f) authorized the sale of assets free and clear of "any interest" in the property, rather than of merely *in rem* interests. See *id. at* 289 (observing that "while the plain meaning of the phrase 'interest in such property' suggests that not all general rights to payment are encompassed by the statute, Congress did not expressly indicate that, by employing such language, it intended to limit the scope of section 363(f) to *in rem* interests, strictly defined"). The court reasoned that Congress intended the term "any interest" to be construed broadly so as to encompass "obligations that are connected to, or arise from, the property being sold." *Id.* at 289. Accordingly, the Third Circuit concluded that

> [w]hile the interests of the [plaintiffs] in the assets of TWA's bankruptcy estate are not interests in property in the sense that they are not *in rem* interests . . . they are interests in property within the meaning of section 363(f) in the sense that they arise from the property being sold.

Id. at 290.

Suppose, therefore, that Ms. Jack, from Essay Exam #4, had worked not for MMW itself but for its subsidiary, Fresh Air Oxygen (FAO). Her discrimination claim is actually against FAO. In this event, it's possible that FAO could be sold by the debtor in the MMW bankruptcy and that the sale would be free and clear of Ms. Jack's discrimination claim. Presumably, though, if her claim and like claims are conceptualized as "interests in property," they may be transferred and channeled to the proceeds of the sale but subordinated to any interests entitled to priority.

iii) Also, DIP financing is often secured by a superpriority claim superior to, or a lien on, "Chapter 5 claims," which are causes of action that arise under sections 544, 545, 547, 548, or 549. The Chapter 5 claims include preference, fraudulent transfers, and similar claims that may be pursued under the "strong arm" provisions of the Bankruptcy Code. See 11 U.S.C. §§544-49.

For example, the facts of Essay Exam #5 report that before MMW filed bankruptcy, the company "disproportionately paid accounts of certain critical suppliers who would be most important to the success of any reorganization plan should the company file Chapter 11 bankruptcy. The loan from RFB was also repaid (which was very good for the bank and also the surety, AVI, because MMW would end up filing bankruptcy a little more than three months later) before MMW filed bankruptcy." These prepetition payments are likely preferences that are avoidable in bankruptcy. See 11 U.S.C. §547(b).

Necessarily, to increase the value of the avoidance actions as collateral for a DIP financer, provision must be made for insuring that such actions can be brought after confirmation. According to section 1123, the plan may provide for "the retention and enforcement by the debtor, by the trustee, *or by a representative of the estate* appointed for such purpose, of any . . . claim or interest [belonging to the debtor or to the estate]." 11 U.S.C. §1123(b)(3)(B) (emphasis added). This statutory allowance covers avoiding powers, and whomever the plan appoints needs no further, separate authorization by the court to enforce whatever powers the plan gives her. However, a lender intending to rely on avoidance powers as collateral is not a representative of the estate. With respect to avoidance, the lender would act for itself. So, section 1123(b)(3)(B) does not seem to explicitly authorize using avoidance actions as collateral.

In fact, authority for a debtor in possession or trustee to assign avoidance claims outside section 1123 and Chapter 11 is uncertain and divided. The traditional, doctrinal rule is that avoidance claims are unassignable. However, substantial authority allows trustees or debtors in possession to sell or otherwise assign avoidance claims or interests in them under circumstances that are fair and benefit the estate. And, in actual practice, debtors in possession commonly secure postpetition financing with liens on avoidance claims or their proceeds.

b) To what extent can the DIP financing provide for securing any of the prepetition debt that RFB is buying from FNB? Sometimes, postpetition credit is provided by prepetition lenders. A prepetition lender who is unsecured or undersecured may attempt to improve its position on its prepetition claim by agreeing to lend postpetition funds to the debtor with "cross-collateralization." The same is true of a postpetition lender who has purchased prepetition undersecured debt, as in the case of RFB purchasing prepetition, unsecured debt from FNB.

The term "cross-collateralization" does not appear in the Bankruptcy Code. It is a creation and creature of the case law and commentary. In theory, cross-collateralization can take two different forms. First, cross-collateralization results when a postpetition extension of credit is secured by both prepetition collateral and postpetition collateral. A second form of cross-collateralization involves securing prepetition claims with postpetition collateral as a condition for new credit. It is this second form of cross-collateralization that is controversial.

Effectively, this second form of cross-collateralization by which a creditor gets new postpetition collateral to secure an old prepetition debt is inconsistent with the priority scheme of the Bankruptcy Code. The debtor is dealing with the prepetition debt owed to its postpetition lender more favorably than the debtor's other prepetition debts. The Bankruptcy Code nowhere deals with cross-collateralization. Relatively few reported cases deal with cross-collateralization.

There are two "leading" reported cases on this second form of cross-collateralization. The first is the Second Circuit's decision in In re Texlon Corp., 596 F.2d 1092 (2d Cir. 1979), which was decided under the Bankruptcy Act of 1898 and is generally read as (i) holding that a court cannot approve this second form of cross-collateralization without notice and hearing and (ii) reserving the question of whether a court can approve cross-collateralization with proper notice and hearing. The other leading cross-collateralization case is the Eleventh Circuit's decision in Shapiro v. Saybrook Mfg. Co. (In re Saybrook Mfg. Co.), 963 F.2d 1490 (11th Cir. 1992), which was decided under the Bankruptcy Code and held that this second form of cross-collateralization is not permitted. *Saybrook* is a case in which the appellate court took a strong stand against the second form of cross-collateralization.

In the *Saybrook* case, the debtor in possession (Saybrook) entered into post-petition financing under section 364 with Manufacturer's Hanover Bank (MHB). MHB was already a creditor to the tune of some $34 million, only $10 million of which was secured. So at filing, it had a secured claim of $10 million and an unsecured claim of $24 million. Under the terms of the DIP financing, MHB was to lend Saybrook an additional $3 million. For that additional loan, MHB demanded and received "cross-collateralization" of its debt; that is, not only was the $3 million of new money secured by postpetition assets, but MHB's entire $34 million prepetition debt was to be secured by estate assets. This would have resulted in an increase in collateral to MHB of some $24 million (and would certainly have increased their ultimate recovery). Two unsecured creditors complained and appealed.

The Eleventh Circuit Court of Appeals ultimately disapproved of cross-collateralization (at least of collateralizing old debt with new estate assets) on two grounds. First, the court noted that the Code does not specifically allow the practice. This creates a presumption against the practice. This presumption is not overcome by resort to section 105, in part because of the second ground: the effect of cross-collateralization is to force distributions that are in direct conflict with the Code's distribution scheme. As such, under *Saybrook*, cross-collateralization is not permitted, and orders incorporating it are not protected by section 364(e). Other courts have been less absolute in condemning *Saybrook*-like cross-collateralization, but it is everywhere viewed with suspicion and doubt absent exceptional, countervailing circumstances.

Partly because of judicial opposition to cross-collateralization, DIP lenders have attempted to improve their prepetition position by "rolling" their prepetition debt into the postpetition facility. A roll-up can be structured to occur all at once or over time as money is actually borrowed. However, depending on the language employed in the provision, the DIP lender does not necessarily need to advance new money in order to effectuate a roll-up, if cash collateral is "deemed" to be advanced.

The most recent variation of roll-up allows prepetition lenders to roll up $1 of prepetition debt for each $1 of new money loaned to the company as part of the DIP facility.

> The conversion of pre-petition debt to post-petition debt provides the lender with the benefit of administrative expense priority in the bankruptcy. The claim on such debt must therefore be paid in full in cash upon the company's emergence from bankruptcy unless the holder of such loan otherwise consents. In short, the claim cannot be compromised in the bankruptcy process. The recent downturn has given us the innovation of "modified" roll-up loans that do not have to be paid in cash in full at the conclusion of the bankruptcy case. Rather, these modified roll-up loans may be "termed out" and become post-emergence debt obligations of the reorganized company instead of being repaid in full in cash with the consent of two-thirds in amount and one-half in number of the roll-up class — that is, the requisite Bankruptcy Code class approval instead of individual lender consent to not receiving payment in full in cash.

Paul H. Zumbro, An Overview of Debtor-In-Possession Financing, 2010 WL 556188, at *7 (Aspatore, February 2010).

Despite judicial reservations, courts in several recent Chapter 11 cases have approved "roll-ups" of prepetition loan obligations into postpetition financing obligations under a postpetition financing facility. This approach is safer for RFB than proposing traditional cross-collateralization as condemned in *Saybrook*.

QUESTION #6

Rejecting or Assuming the Commercial Real Estate Leases

a) Explain (i) why and how MMW would reject the commercial real estate lease between MMW, as lessee, and the lessor, LDI and (ii) how LDI's damages would be limited (which is why the ability to reject a lease is a powerful reason in itself for many companies to file Chapter 11). A lease is a type of executory contract, which is a contract that is so far unperformed on both sides that the failure of either party to complete her performance would be a material breach excusing further performance from the other party. See Countryman, *ExecutoryContracts in Bankruptcy*, 57 Minn. L. Rev. 439 (1973); 58 Minn. L. Rev. 479 (1974). Under the lease between MMW and LDI, both parties owe reciprocal, unperformed obligations for the three years remaining under the terms of the lease.

MMW's bankruptcy does not terminate the lease. The debtor's remaining leasehold interest survives and is a property that passes to the bankruptcy estate. The lessor's right to payment under the lease is a claim against the bankruptcy estate.

The debtor in possession must decide how to handle the lease. If the lease has direct or indirect value to the debtor, the DIP can assume the lease and continue occupying and using the premises, as before, according to the terms of the lease. Or, after assuming the lease, the DIP can assign it to a person for an amount greater than the value to the debtor of continuing to occupy the premises.

On the other hand, the DIP can reject the lease if there is more value to the debtor in getting out of it and saving the costs of the lease, as when market rate is lower than the lease rate for the debtor's use or the use of any possible assignee.

The general rule is that a lease of nonresidential real property is *deemed* rejected unless it has been assumed within 120 days after bankruptcy is filed, 11 U.S.C. §365(d)(4), but the court can extend the 120 period by 90 days. The lessor must agree to any additional extension. The debtor can sooner reject a lease upon motion to and approval by the court, which will almost always go along with rejection. The courts routinely defer to the debtor's business judgment if there is any rational basis supporting it.

During the gap period between filing of bankruptcy and rejection or assumption, the statute requires a debtor/lessee to "timely perform" all obligations under a commercial real estate lease, specifically requiring the debtor to make all postpetition rent payments on commercial real estate and to start making such payments within 60 days. 11 U.S.C. §365(d)(3). Section 365 does not generally prescribe the performance obligations of the nondebtor party to a lease or executory during the gap period. The few cases that have expressly dealt with the question have held that the nondebtor party is obligated to perform its obligations under the lease. Section 365 does say, however, that if there has been a default under an unexpired lease, the lessor is not required to provide services or supplies incidental to the lease before assumption of the lease unless the lessor is compensated under the terms of such lease for the services and supplies. 11 U.S.C. §365(b)(4).

Upon rejection, however, the debtor's obligations under the lease are ended. The debtor therefore avoids and captures for other use the future rent payments and other costs.

However, if MMW rejects the lease with LDI, the result is NOT that MMW saves $540,000 ($15,000/month × 36 months). Rejection amounts to a breach of the lease, 11 U.S.C. §365(g), for which LDI has an unsecured claim against the estate determined as if the claim has arisen before the date bankruptcy was filed, *id.* §502(g); but, proper calculation of LDI's claim seriously reduces it. Here's how to calculate the claim:

- LDI's claim includes the amount of accrued unpaid (i.e., back) rent and the amount of expected (i.e., future) rent that state law allows as damages for breach, which usually accounts for actual or imagined mitigation.
- The state law recovery for future rent is then capped by federal law to "the rent reserved by [the] . . . lease, without acceleration, for the greater of one year, or 15 percent, not to exceed three years, of the remaining term of such lease. . . ." *Id.* §502(b)(6).

Therefore, if MMW rejects the lease, LDI's unsecured claim for future rent is limited to the lower of the recovery state law allows and the limit of section 502, which is $81,000. And, the amount of this claim that LDI will likely be paid depends on the terms of the Chapter 11 plan the court confirms. Ordinarily, a Chapter 11 plan need not pay unsecured claims in full but only "the amount that such holder would . . . receive . . . if the debtor were liquidated under chapter 7. . . ." *Id.* §1129(a)(7). The balance of the claim will be discharged.

So, in the end, the cost of rejecting an unfavorable lease in bankruptcy is much, much less than the cost of completing the lease or the cost of breaching the lease under state law; and therein is the reason for MMW to reject the LDI lease if the lease is unfavorable to MMW.

b) Explain (i) why and how MMW would assume and keep the lease or assume and assign it, and (ii) the principal limitations on assumption and assignment that protect the lessor, LDI. If the market rate of MMW's lease is higher than the contract lease rate, the debtor can usually assume the lease and lock in the favorable rate for the term of the lease. Assumption means the estate takes on the obligations of the lease, which continues according to its terms. On the other hand, the DIP cannot assume the lease without curing damages of default and providing adequate assurance of future performance. 11 U.S.C. §365(b). Also, if a lease is assumed, lease payments become an administrative expense of the bankruptcy case.

The favorable rate may also be exploited by assigning the lease and thereby capturing the excess value of the lease of premises not necessary for the debtor's business. Assignment requires and follows assumption. 11 U.S.C. §365(f)(2)(A). The debtor can assume a lease but not assign it, but the debtor cannot assign a lease without first assuming it. Neither assumption nor assignment is prevented by an "ipso facto" or "anti-assignment" clause in the lease. 11 U.S.C. §365(e)(1) & (f).

On the other hand, when originally pricing the lease, the lessor made a risk assessment based on the character and creditworthiness of the lessee. But, after assuming and assigning a lease, neither the debtor nor the estate has any further responsibilities under the lease. 11 U.S.C. §365(k). They are relieved of liability for future breaches of a lease after assignment, notwithstanding lease provisions to the contrary.

Therefore, to protect the lessor's expectations to some extent, section 365 includes safeguards designed to insure (but not guarantee) the original pricing:

- An unexpired lease can be assigned only if adequate assurance of future performance by the assignee of such contract or lease is provided, §365(f)(2); and
- The lessor of the property may require a deposit or other security for the performance of the debtor's obligations under the lease substantially the same as would have been required by the landlord upon the initial leasing to a similar tenant. §365(l).

In theory, however, the character, qualities, or other characteristics of the lessee can be so peculiar or unique that such monetary or financial guarantees are not sufficient to protect the lessor's interests. For this reason, adequate assurance of future performance must be provided not only with respect to the assignee's financial wherewithal, but also with respect to the assignee's ability and willingness to perform all of the terms of the lease that are materially and economically important, not just the price.

Also, as a further protection of the lessor, an executory lease cannot be assigned "if applicable law excuses a party, other than the debtor, to such contract or lease from accepting performance from or rendering performance to the trustee or to an assignee of such contract or lease, whether or not such contract or lease prohibits or restricts assignment of rights or delegation of duties; and such party does not consent to such assumption or assignment." 11 U.S.C. §365(c). Arguably, in such a case, even assumption of the lease is prohibited.

Section 365(c), however, mainly applies to contracts that are nondelegable because they involve unique personalization (In re Pioneer Ford Sales, 729 F.2d 27 (1st Cir. 1984) (cannot assign Ford franchise to Toyota dealer)) or because delegation is prohibited by other default law (In re Catapult Entertainment, Inc., 165 F.3d 747 (9th Cir. 1999) (patents nondelegable by federal law)). In truth, section 365(c) is not commonly, easily applied to leases of real estate.

On the other hand, leases commonly include a limitation or restriction on use of the property. Such a restriction is generally effective against any assignee because (1) assumption and assignment of a lease entails acceptance by the assignee of the burdens as well as the benefits of the lease and (2) nothing in section 365 explicitly invalidates a use restriction in a typical commercial real estate lease.

As a result, a use restriction can limit the assignability of a lease even in bankruptcy. In re Ames Dept. Stores, Inc., 316 B.R. 772 (Bankr. S.D.N.Y. 2004) (lease could not be assigned in violation of use restriction contained in deed that protected adjoining land owner). Indeed, a use restriction could work, in the extreme, as a de facto way of prohibiting assignment. For this reason, the courts scrutinize use restrictions in leases and will invalidate such a restriction that serves no substantial purpose or good other than limiting assignment. Matter of U.L. Radio Corp., 19 B.R. 537 (Bankr. S.D.N.Y. 1982). The courts will decide whether or not the clause is "material and economically significant" to the landlord by balancing the concerns of "preventing substantial economic detriment to the nondebtor contracting party and permitting the bankruptcy estate's realization of the intrinsic value of its assets." In re Fleming Companies, Inc., 499 F.3d 300, 305-06 (3d Cir. 2007).

BANKRUPTCY ESSAY EXAM #6 [CHAPTER 11 (PART 2)]

QUESTION #1

Getting MMW's Plan Confirmed

Identify the key steps and requirements in getting the Chapter 11 plan confirmed.

1. The debtor files the plan when she files the petition commencing the case or at any time thereafter, 11 U.S.C. §1121(a), and only the debtor can propose a plan until after 120 days after the date of the order for relief under this chapter. *Id.* §1121(b). This 120 days is referred to as the "exclusivity period."

2. The plan must comply with section 1123, which sets out certain requirements of a plan and elements that are permissible. *Id.* §§1123(a) & (b). Principally, the plan *shall*:
   - designate classes of claims and classes of interests;
   - specify any class of claims or interests that is not impaired under the plan;
   - specify the treatment of any class of claims or interests that is impaired under the plan;
   - provide the same treatment for each claim or interest of a particular class, unless the holder of a particular claim or interest agrees to a less favorable treatment of such particular claim or interest; and
   - provide adequate means for the plan's implementation.

   The plan *may*:
   - impair or leave unimpaired any class of claims, secured or unsecured, or of interests;
   - subject to section 365, provide for the assumption, rejection, or assignment of any executory contract or unexpired lease of the debtor not previously rejected under such section;
   - provide for —
     — the settlement or adjustment of any claim or interest belonging to the debtor or to the estate; or
     — the retention and enforcement by the debtor, by the trustee, or by a representative of the estate appointed for such purpose, of any such claim or interest;
   - provide for the sale of all or substantially all of the property of the estate, and the distribution of the proceeds of such sale among holders of claims or interests;
   - modify the rights of holders of secured claims, other than a claim secured only by a security interest in real property that is the debtor's

principal residence, or of holders of unsecured claims, or leave unaffected the rights of holders of any class of claims; and

- include any other appropriate provision not inconsistent with the applicable provisions of this title.

3. The debtor must transmit the plan or a summary of the plan to the holders of claims and interests and also a written disclosure statement approved, after notice and a hearing, by the court as containing adequate information. *Id.* §1125(b).

   a. A class of claims has accepted a plan if accepted by creditors that hold at least two-thirds in amount and more than one-half in number of the allowed claims of the class held by creditors that have accepted or rejected such plan. *Id.* §1126(c).

   b. A class of interests has accepted a plan if accepted by holders of such interests that hold at least two-thirds in amount of the allowed interests of the class held by holders of such interests that have accepted or rejected such plan. *Id.* §1126(d).

4. Depending on how the voting goes and for any other reason, the debtor can modify the plan at any time before confirmation. *Id.* §1127(a).

5. In due course, the court holds a hearing to decide whether or not to confirm a plan, and at this hearing hears objections to the plan by any party in interest. *Id.* §1128.

6. The court must confirm a plan under section 1129(a) if certain requirements are satisfied, principally:

   a. The plan and its proponent comply with the applicable provisions of this title. *Id.* §1129(a)(1).

   b. The plan has been proposed in good faith and not by any means forbidden by law. *Id.* §1129(a)(2) & (3).

   c. With respect to each impaired class of claims or interests, each holder of a claim or interest of such class—

      i. has accepted the plan; or

      ii. will receive or retain under the plan—on account of such claim or interest—property of a value, as of the effective date of the plan, that is not less than the amount that such holder would so receive or retain if the debtor were liquidated under Chapter 7 of this title on such date (which is known as the "best interest of the creditors" test). *Id.* §1129(a)(7).

         - A secured creditor would have received, in a Chapter 7 case, the full amount of the secured claim.

         - An unsecured creditor, on the other hand, would have received considerably less than the full amount of the unsecured claim.

            — Rather, in a Chapter 7 case, an unsecured creditor would have received only the creditor's pro rata share of the net bankruptcy estate, which includes only equity above liens and which is diluted by the payment of priority claims before the payment of general, unsecured claims.

— For example, Ms. Jack, in Essay Exam #4, may have a discrimination claim against MMW, which is unsecured. If such a claim were filed and allowed, MMW's reorganization plan would have to provide paying Ms. Jack only the present value of the amount she would have received on such a claim had the debtor liquidated under Chapter 7, which would likely be only pennies on the dollar.

d. Each class of claims or interests has accepted the plan or is not impaired under the plan. *Id.* §1129(a)(8).

e. Priority claims are appropriately provided for. *Id.* §1129(a)(9).

f. If a class of claims is impaired under the plan, at least one class of claims that is impaired under the plan has accepted the plan, determined without including any acceptance of the plan by any insider. *Id.* §1129(a)(10).

g. Confirmation of the plan is not likely to be followed by the liquidation, or the need for further financial reorganization, of the debtor or any successor to the debtor under the plan, unless such liquidation or reorganization is proposed in the plan. *Id.* §1129(a)(11).

7. If any impaired class of claims or interest fails to accept the plan as section 1129(a)(8) requires, the court can still confirm ("cram down") the plan under section 1129(b) if:

a. All of the other requirements of section 1129(a) are satisfied, *id.* §1129(b)(1), and

b. The plan does not discriminate unfairly, and is fair and equitable, with respect to each class of claims or interests that is impaired under, and has not accepted, the plan, *id.*, which principally means:

   i. The plan provides that the holders of secured claims retain the liens securing such claims, and each holder of a secured claim receive on account of such claim deferred cash payments totaling at least the allowed amount of such claim, of a value, as of the effective date of the plan, of at least the value of such holder's interest in the estate's interest in such property. *Id.* §1129(b)(2)(A).

   ii. The plan also provides that all unsecured claims are paid in full or, if not, that the holder of any claim or interest that is junior to the unsecured claims will not receive or retain any property under the plan on account of such junior claim or interest (which is known as the "absolute priority" rule). *Id.* §1129(b)(2)(B).

      • If unsecured claims are not fully paid, the effect is to give ownership of the company to them.

      • Existing equity, which would receive nothing in a liquidation proceeding if creditors weren't fully paid, cannot retain or receive anything under the plan, not even their ownership of the company.

8. Ordinarily, if the plan is not confirmed, another plan proposed by the debtor or another party in interest may be proposed or considered; the case will be converted to Chapter 7; or the case will be dismissed.

9. If a plan is confirmed, the principal effects are:
   a. The provisions of a confirmed plan bind the debtor, any entity issuing securities under the plan, any entity acquiring property under the plan, and any creditor, equity security holder, or general partner in the debtor, whether or not the claim or interest of such creditor, equity security holder, or general partner is impaired under the plan and whether or not such creditor, equity security holder, or general partner has accepted the plan, 11 U.S.C. §1141(a);
   b. All of the property of the estate vests in the debtor, id. §1141(b);
   c. The property dealt with by the plan is free and clear of all claims and interests of creditors, equity security holders, and of general partners in the debtor, id. §1141(c); and,
   d. The debtor is discharged from any debt that arose before the date of confirmation. Id. §1141(d).

10. Finally, the plan is carried out by the debtor and any entity organized or to be organized for the purpose of carrying out the plan. Id. §1142.

11. If a person does not receive what the plan promises, the remedy is often to complain to an appropriate nonbankruptcy court for damages for breach of the confirmed plan, although the bankruptcy court does retain or can re-establish post-confirmation jurisdiction for some purposes.

12. However, the time for asking the court to revoke an order of confirmation is limited to 180 days after confirmation and the only reason is that the order was procured by fraud. Id. §1144.

QUESTION #2

Displacing the Debtor in Possession

a) Explain the grounds for the Committee asking the court to replace the DIP with a trustee. Ordinarily, a trustee is not appointed in a Chapter 11 case. The debtor in possession remains in control as the debtor, and the DIP enjoys all of the rights, powers, and duties of a trustee, including the rights to continue operating the business and exclusively control, in the beginning, formation of a plan of reorganization. The DIP is essentially the firm's management, and this management is typically populated by the same people who controlled the firm before bankruptcy.

This control of a firm in bankruptcy by the DIP has never been complete or completely assured. The Bankruptcy Code has always provided for the displacement of the DIP in a Chapter 11 case and the appointment of a trustee to operate the debtor's business and manage the bankruptcy, including proposing a plan of reorganization. At least until 2005, a trustee was rarely appointed but the courts would do so for mismanagement and the like by the DIP. Another reason was acrimony between the DIP and creditors, usually because the former's interests conflicted so completely with the latter's interests that appointing a trustee was the only effective way to pursue reorganization.

In 2005, the Bankruptcy Code was amended to make easier (and perhaps more likely) the appointment of a trustee. The amended Code greatly expands the list of grounds on the basis of which a creditor can move for dismissing or converting a case or, alternatively, having a trustee appointed. The reasons for the court appointing a trustee are:

(1) for cause, including fraud, dishonesty, incompetence, or gross mismanagement of the affairs of the debtor by current management, either before or after the commencement of the case, or similar cause, but not including the number of holders of securities of the debtor or the amount of assets or liabilities of the debtor;

(2) if such appointment is in the interests of creditors, any equity security holders, and other interests of the estate, without regard to the number of holders of securities of the debtor or the amount of assets or liabilities of the debtor; or

(3) if grounds exist to convert or dismiss the case under section 1112, but the court determines that the appointment of a trustee or an examiner is in the best interests of creditors and the estate.

11 U.S.C. §1104(a). Also, the procedural burden for convincing the court to appoint a trustee may have slightly shifted and thus lightened. The movant is required to establish grounds, and the procedural requirements for doing so are challenging under some existing case law. However, if grounds are established, the 2005 amendment shifts the burden in the sense that the court must ordinarily grant the relief absent a specific finding of "unusual circumstances . . . that the requested [relief] is not in the best interests of creditors and the estate . . . ." 11 U.S.C.A. §1112(b)(1); see also 11 U.S.C.A. §1104(a)(3).

If the court decides that a trustee should be appointed, the United States trustee then decides which person to appoint, subject to the court's approval, unless the creditors act to select the trustee themselves. Additionally, the United States trustee is explicitly directed to move for the appointment of a trustee in any case in which the debtor's chief officers and directors participated in "dishonesty" in the management of the firm, *id.* §1104(e), which is potentially a very broad basis for appointing a trustee.

b) What is different about an examiner? If a trustee is not appointed, the court can order the appointment of an "examiner." Again, the court decides whether or not to appoint and the United States trustee decides which person to appoint, with the court's approval. The reasons for appointing an examiner are:

> to conduct such an investigation of the debtor as is appropriate, including an investigation of any allegations of fraud, dishonesty, incompetence, misconduct, mismanagement, or irregularity in the management of the affairs of the debtor of or by current or former management of the debtor, if . . . such appointment is in the interests of creditors, any equity security holders, and other interests of the estate. . . .

11 U.S.C. §1104(c).

In theory, the role of an examiner is different from that of a trustee. An examiner does not run the debtor's business or run the debtor's Chapter 11 case. An examiner merely examines: she investigates the competency and honesty of the debtor or other matters and files a report of the investigation with the court. *Id.* §§1104(b), 1106(b). In practice, the line between the roles of an examiner and the roles of a trustee is sometimes blurred.

QUESTION #3

Avoidance Action and Other Extraordinary Litigation by the Committee

a) Does an individual creditor or the Committee have standing to pursue an avoidance action with respect to the debtor's prepetition repayment of the loan to RFB? Bankruptcy principally aims to give the debtor a fresh financial start while allowing creditors to share equally, to a fair and equitable extent, in the debtor's accumulated assets that form the bankruptcy estate. This broad objective and its constituent goals are undermined by pre- and postbankruptcy transfers of property that unfairly or discriminatorily withhold or rob property from the estate to the prejudice of the debtor or her creditors.

To remedy this theft, the Bankruptcy Code condemns and provides for the *avoidance*, i.e., the undoing and recovery, of some prebankruptcy transfers of the debtor's property and most postbankruptcy transfers of estate property. The major provisions for avoidance are collected in Chapter 5 of the Bankruptcy Code and are referred to collectively as the trustee's *avoiding* or *avoidance powers*. The principal avoidance powers aimed at prepetition transfers are:

- 544 — trustee as hypothetical lien creditor and bona fide purchaser and as successor to actual creditors (principally permit the trustee to avoid unperfected or unrecorded conveyances and also to rely on state fraudulent transfer law);
- 547 — preferences; and
- 548 — fraudulent transfers and obligations.

Transfers condemned through the avoiding powers are not automatically avoided in a bankruptcy case. Avoidance does not occur by operation of law. Rather, a person whom the Code empowers to avoid transfers must bring an action or proceeding to do so, and the bankruptcy court then determines the matter.

As a broad, general rule, the bankruptcy trustee wields the avoiding powers. The statutes that describe the Code's principal avoiding powers explicitly give them only to the trustee. They repeatedly declare that the "trustee" is the person who "may avoid," which actually means that only she is authorized to bring an action or proceeding asking the court to order avoidance. The basic reason is that avoidance is designed to enlarge the estate for the benefit of creditors; and, for conceptual and practical reasons, representation of the estate, and authority to act for creditors collectively, are centered in the single person of the trustee. The trustee is not required, however, to request avoidance of a transfer; rather, she is the person empowered to do so if, in her discretion, avoidance is appropriate. This general rule, that only the trustee avoids, applies broadly in every kind of bankruptcy except a Chapter 9 case.

Usually, however, a trustee is not appointed in a Chapter 11 case. In place of a trustee is the debtor in possession who, by express statutory authorization, exercises all of the functions and duties of a trustee. Thus, in a typical Chapter 11 case, the avoiding powers are enforced by the debtor in possession.

Individual creditors generally are not empowered to use the trustee's avoiding powers in any kind of case either for their own benefit or for the benefit of the estate, not even to attack transfers the creditors could have avoided under state law because of harm to them personally. Creditors most often try to pursue avoidance actions in Chapter 11 cases when they believe that avoiding transfers for the benefit of creditors is against the interests of the debtor in possession who thus refuses to act. The courts are sensitive to this conflict-of-interest argument, but not to the extent of conferring the avoiding powers on creditors carte blanche.

Instead, the courts have outlined and endorsed more limited "powers" that frustrated creditors can assert to overcome and remedy indirectly the inaction of self-interested debtors-in-possession. For instance, in Nebraska State Bank v. Jones, 846 F.2d 477 (8th Cir. 1988), the Eighth Circuit suggested that a disgruntled individual creditor can alternatively:

- move to dismiss the Chapter 11 case;
- seek to convert the case to Chapter 7;
- move to replace the debtor in possession with a Chapter 11 trustee;
- petition the court to compel the debtor in possession to act; or,
- petition the court to allow the creditor herself to institute an avoidance action.

The last option, getting the bankruptcy court's permission for the creditor to act herself, really involves the creditor bringing an avoidance action in the form of a derivative suit for the estate's benefit. Other courts have endorsed this option of derivative standing as a means for creditors to overcome inaction by DIPs and even by trustees in Chapter 11 and other cases; but authority to so proceed, though presumably available to any appropriately interested creditor in any case, is most often actually given to *creditors' committees* in Chapter 11 cases. Moreover, most courts have held that the authority generally exists only on a case-by-case basis, when specifically approved beforehand by the court, and only upon a showing of good cause.

The authority for bankruptcy courts to authorize creditors, in appropriate instances, to bring claims on behalf of the bankruptcy estate is the courts' "equitable power" and is contemplated by "other provisions of the Bankruptcy Code, as well as pre-Code practice." In re Trailer Source, Inc., 555 F.3d 231, 241 (6th Cir. 2009).

> [I]n 11 U.S.C. §503(b)(3)(B) Congress has expressly provided that creditors may be compensated on a priority basis for their efforts in recovering property for the benefit of the estate. Specifically, §503(b)(3)(B) provides for the priority payment of the expenses of "a creditor that recovers, after the court's approval, for the benefit of the estate any property transferred or concealed by the debtor." 11 U.S.C. §503(b)(3)(B). An avoidance action pursuant to §544(b) . . . falls within the scope of §503(b)(3)(B) as an action to recover "property transferred . . . by the debtor." Based upon the text and statutory history of §503(b)(3)(B), we believe that the only explanation for this provision is that it approves the practice of permitting creditors, with court authorization, to pursue claims on behalf of bankrupt debtors. . . .
>
> We further believe that §503(b)(3)(B) would be meaningless if the Code did not also contemplate the practice of derivative standing. . . .
>
> The Supreme Court has long recognized that bankruptcy courts are courts of equity with the power to apply flexible equitable remedies in bankruptcy proceedings. . . . We agree . . . that "the ability to confer derivative standing . . . is a straightforward application of bankruptcy courts' equitable powers."

Id. at 241–42.

When the trustee or debtor in possession opposes the creditor's derivative action, good cause usually requires showing that there is a colorable claim for avoidance; the estate will benefit from avoidance; the creditor asked the trustee or debtor in possession to pursue the avoidance action; the request was refused; and the refusal to act is unjustifiable or an abuse of discretion. If the trustee or debtor in possession consents to the creditor's action or does not oppose it, the creditor still needs the court's approval to pursue the action, which requires the court to find "'that suit by [the creditor] is (a) in the *best interest* of the bankruptcy estate, and (b) *is necessary and beneficial* to the fair and efficient resolution of the bankruptcy proceedings.'"

b) Is the repayment of the loan avoidable?   The repayment may have effected a preference, which section 547(b) describes as:

- Any transfer of an interest of the debtor in property;
- To or for the benefit of a creditor;
- For or on account of an antecedent debt owed by the debtor before such transfer was made;
- Made while the debtor was insolvent;
- Made on or within 90 days before the date of the filing of the petition, or within one year of the filing if the creditor is an insider; and,
- That enables the creditor to receive more than she would receive in a Chapter 7 distribution of the bankruptcy estate had the transfer not been made.

11 U.S.C. §547(b). The creditor's subjective innocence is no defense. "Congress considered equality of distribution so important that it specifically eliminated consideration of creditors' good faith or knowledge from preference actions. . . ." In re

Southern Indus. Banking Corp., 92 B.R. 297, 301 (Bankr. E.D. Tenn. 1988). Similarly, the debtor's motive and intent are irrelevant. "All that is required for an avoidable preference is the actual transfer being made within the preferential period, in addition to establishing the other elements of §547(b)." In re Service Bolt & Nut Co., Inc., 98 B.R. 759, 761 (Bankr. N.D. Ohio 1989). Moreover, "[a]ny wrong-doing on the part of the debtor is not imputed to the Trustee so as to avoid his avoidance powers [with respect to preferences]." In re Lendvest Mortg., Inc., 123 B.R. 623, 624 (Bankr. N.D. Cal. 1991).

MMW's repayment of the loan to RFB seems to satisfy all of the requirements for preference. The only doubt concerns the timing of the repayment: did it fall within the reach-back period, which is 90 days or one year? RFB was repaid more than 90 days before bankruptcy but within one year of the filing. The one-year reach-back period applies when the transfer is to or for the benefit of a creditor who is an insider. When the debtor is a corporation, as is MMW, the meaning of insider includes:

- director of the debtor;
- officer of the debtor;
- person in control of the debtor;
- partnership in which the debtor is a general partner;
- general partner of the debtor;
- relative of a general partner, director, officer, or person in control of the debtor; or
- affiliate, or insider of an affiliate as if such affiliate were the debtor.

RFB is not an insider, but AVI, the surety, is arguably an insider. And, though the transfer (i.e., the repayment) was made *to* RFB, it was *for the benefit of AVI.*

Because section 547 is alternatively satisfied by a transfer of the debtor's property either "to" a creditor *or* "for the benefit of a creditor," a transfer of the debtor's property can be a preference to a creditor who is not a transferee of the property if the transfer nevertheless reduces the liability of the non-transferee creditor. In the case of the loan repayment to RFB:

- MMW is obligated to RFB on a unsecured debt to RFB of $2.5 million.
- AVI is surety for this debt and, as surety, is contingently liable to RFB.
- Significantly, AVI — as surety — is entitled to reimbursement from MMW if AVI pays the debt.
- AVI thus has a contingent claim against MMW and therefore MMW, like RFB, is a creditor of MMW.

As it happens, MMW paid the debt, and MMW's payment to RFB is obviously a transfer of the debtor's property to a creditor, RFB.

The payment is also for the benefit of AVI, a creditor, because the payment reduces AVI's contingent liability as a surety. If the other elements of 547(b) are satisfied, the payment is thus a preference for the benefit of AVI, a creditor, even though the debtor's property was actually transferred to RFB.

The follow-up question is how to remedy the preference. Section 550(a) assigns personal liability with respect to transfers that the trustee avoids by using her bankruptcy avoiding powers:

> Except as otherwise provided in this section, to the extent that a transfer is avoided . . . , the trustee may recover, for the benefit of the estate, the property transferred, or, if the court so orders, the value of such property, from
> > (1) the initial transferee of such transfer *or* the entity for whose benefit such transfer was made; *or*
> > (2) any immediate or mediate transferee of such initial transferee.

11 U.S.C. §550(a) (emphasis added). Therefore, according to this language, the trustee can recover from either AVI or the initial transferee, RFB. However, there is also section 550(c), which provides:

> If a transfer made between 90 days and one year before the filing of the petition —
> > (1) is avoided under section 547(b) of this title; and
> > (2) was made for the benefit of a creditor that at the time of such transfer was an insider;
> the trustee may not recover under subsection (a) from a transferee that is not an insider.

11 U.S.C. §550(c). Applied to these facts, section 550(a) imposes liability on RFB, but section 550(c) shields the bank. The remedy for this preference is therefore limited to recovering the amount of the repayment from AVI, even though the MMW paid the loan directly to RFB.

   c) What possible liability worries the officers, directors, banks, accountants, and lawyers?   To begin with, a debtor's officers and directors worry about being sued for the debtor's financial collapse based on claims of breaching fiduciary duties owed the debtor.

   Management's fiduciary duties are generally owed to the firm. Breaches of these duties create causes of action that belong to the firm and, outside of bankruptcy, are pursued by the firm or by shareholders on behalf of the firm in derivative actions. If the firm files bankruptcy, these causes of action become property of the bankruptcy estate. Generally, in any kind of bankruptcy case, only the trustee or a DIP, as representative of the estate, can assert causes of action of any kind that belong to the bankruptcy estate, including actions against management in a Chapter 11 case for prepetition breaches of fiduciary duties to the firm.

   Of course, the DIP suing themselves as DIP is not likely. In appropriate circumstances, however, the court in any kind of bankruptcy case can authorize other persons, including creditors' committees, to prosecute causes of action that belong to the estate and that ordinarily would be pursued by the trustee or a DIP, as when the court authorizes a creditors' committee to pursue avoidance actions on behalf of the estate. As summarized by the court in In re Industrial Commercial Electrical, Inc., 319 B.R. 35 (D. Mass. 2005), the "Bankruptcy Code . . . allows other parties in interest to act on the estate's behalf" in Chapter 11 cases on these grounds:

> Under 11 U.S.C. §1109(b), any party in interest in a Chapter 11 case may raise and may appear and be heard on any issue in the case. Section 1103(c) gives a

creditors' committee broad powers to consult with the trustee or debtor in possession regarding case administration, to investigate the debtor's business and conduct, to participate in plan formation, and to take other appropriate actions with respect to the case. Moreover, the Bankruptcy Code clearly contemplates that creditors may sometimes take legal action on behalf of the estate, subject to the Bankruptcy Court's approval. If a debtor in possession in bad faith refused to bring an action that would obviously benefit the estate, a creditors' committee could bring the action itself, although there may be some question as to whether it would need the Bankruptcy Court's authorization to do so.

Id. at 53. Thus, Congress clearly envisioned a system where a creditors' committee may cooperate with the trustee or debtor in possession on behalf of the estate, or may even bring suit itself when such suit is consistent with the purposes of the Bankruptcy Code. Therefore, the bankruptcy court can authorize prosecution of these actions — on behalf of the estate — by committees and even by individual creditors, especially actions against management for breaches of fiduciary duties owed to the firm.

Officers and directors also worry about being sued by individual creditors for breaching duties the officers and directors owe these creditors, personally and directly. It has been argued that when a company gets into financial trouble, i.e., when the company enters the "zone of insolvency," even before and apart from bankruptcy, the fiduciary duties of officers and directors expand and are owed to creditors. Banks, accountants, lawyers, and other professionals working with officers and directors are implicated on theories akin to aiding and abetting breach of fiduciary duty.

The principle and reasoning are as follows: "Typically, creditors may not allege fiduciary duty claims against corporate directors. It is presumed that creditors are capable of protecting themselves through the contractual agreements that govern their relationships . . . with firms." Production Resources Group, L.L.C. v. NCT Group, Inc., 863 A.2d 772, 787 (Del. Ch. 2004). However, when

a firm has reached the point of insolvency, . . . the firm's directors are said to owe fiduciary duties to the company's creditors. This is an uncontroversial proposition and does not completely turn on its head the equitable obligations of the directors to the firm itself. The directors continue to have the task of attempting to maximize the economic value of the firm. That much of their job does not change. But the fact of insolvency does necessarily affect the constituency on whose behalf the directors are pursuing that end. By definition, the fact of insolvency places the creditors in the shoes normally occupied by the shareholders — that of residual risk-bearers. Where the assets of the company are insufficient to pay its debts, and the remaining equity is underwater, whatever remains of the company's assets will be used to pay creditors, usually either by seniority of debt or on a pro rata basis among debtors of equal priority.

Id. at 790-91. Think about it. In insolvency, creditors, as residual claimants to a definitionally inadequate pool of assets, become exposed to substantial risks as the entity goes forward; poor decisions by management may erode the value of the remaining assets, leaving the corporation with even less capital to satisfy its debts in an ultimate dissolution. The elimination of the stockholders' interest in the firm upon liquidation under state law or by proceedings in bankruptcy and the increased risk to creditors is said to justify imposing fiduciary obligations on officers and directors toward the company's creditors. Compounding this expansion of management's fiduciary duties to creditors upon the firm's insolvency, the standard of conduct thus required by the firm toward creditors is, arguably, unusually high, and management's "deepening" of a firm's insolvency or related wrongs can amount, in itself, to a breach of fiduciary duty owed to creditors and the firm itself.

Much more solid claims based on more certain and specific torts can be pursued against officers, directors, and professionals working with them. With respect to MMW, remember the events before bankruptcy described in Essay Exam #5. Look closely at the facts, which report that despite the company's financial decline:

> MMW remained publicly optimistic. Together with FNB, MMW announced a "partnership for profitability," which was really a marketing campaign to reassure investors, suppliers, and workers. The company and the bank committed themselves to work more closely together and unselfishly to save MMW, make the company profitable again. The marketing materials proclaimed the birth of:
>
>> an innovative, strategic alliance with all shareholders — the community, labor, and vendors — so that everyone participates equally in rebuilding the company and participating in future prosperity for the common good.
>
> The mood among workers improved. Productivity surged. Suppliers noticed the change. They increased credit sales and extended payment terms. . . . FNB, however, did not extend more credit. Instead, pursuant to the comprehensive security arrangement between the bank and MMW, which gave FNB a perfected security interest in all of MMW's property present and after-acquired, the stream of the company's gross revenue flowing to FNB was enlarged.
>
> MMW also disproportionately paid accounts of certain critical suppliers who would be most important to the success of any reorganization plan should the company file Chapter 11 bankruptcy. The loan from RFB was also repaid (which was very good for the bank and also the surety, AVI, because MMW would end up filing bankruptcy a little more than three months later).
>
> Behind the scenes, the Hewes & Shayes lawyers have crafted a plan of reorganization. . . .

These facts combine to imply a tortious conspiracy of assorted wrongs to increase unsecured credit based on false and misleading statements about MMW's financial condition and prospects.

These kinds of claims belong to the creditors themselves. The creditors pursue the claims against the defendants, personally and directly, not against the debtor or the estate. The DIP lacks standing to stop these claims or the authority to take them over for the benefit of the estate or on behalf of the injured creditors.

This personal liability can extend to the banks and professionals working for the debtor who, along with officers and directors, directly or complicitly committed wrongs against the creditors. The debtor's lawyers are not immune. Whether or not the lawyers' professional responsibilities extended to creditors who were not clients, and whether or not the lawyers have liability for aiding any breach of fiduciary duties by officers and directors to creditors, a lawyer's accountability for other wrongs (beyond malpractice) may directly extend to third parties, including the client's creditors, as for common law fraud.

QUESTION #4

Third-Party Releases of Officers, Directors, and Professionals

Will the Committee likely win or lose in its attack against the provision in the plan releasing officers and directors and the company's banks, accountants, and lawyers from liability to creditors? It is not uncommon for a debtor's Chapter 11 plan to include a provision that aims to give management and other third parties limited or complete immunity to liability to just about everybody for just about anything they could have done to injure the debtor or parties in interest. Such a provision is commonly called a "third-party release" whereby

> insiders . . . seek to limit or eliminate the risk of liability that they may incur while employed by the debtor. The debtor may request that the bankruptcy court issue an order releasing or otherwise barring all claims and enjoining all suits against insiders relating to their employment with the debtor either temporarily or permanently. These are generally termed "third party releases." Alternatively, the debtor may ask the bankruptcy court to issue an order—a "channeling" injunction—directing all or part of the litigation against the debtor or insiders toward a single fund or group of assets. Not unusually, the provisions typically provide shelter from liability to the debtor, its insiders, and members of the insolvency community involved in the case.

George W. Kuney, *Hijacking Chapter 11*, 21 Emory Bankr. Dev. J. 19, 90-91 (2004). The courts have disagreed "on whether bankruptcy courts have the equitable authority to approve plans of reorganization containing releases and permanent injunctions in favor of third-parties, including directors. . . ." Myron M. Sheinfeld & Judy Harris Pippitt, *Fiduciary Duties of Directors of a Corporation in the Vicinity of Insolvency and After Initiation of a Bankruptcy Case*, 60 Bus. Law. 79, 98 (2004). After all, releasing non-debtors from liability seems contrary to the accepted notion that the bankruptcy discharge is limited to discharge of the debtor, not other persons. And the statute flatly provides that "discharge of a debt of the debtor does not affect the liability of any other entity on, or the property of any other entity for, such debt." 11 U.S.C. §524(e).

An important decision on third-party releases is In re Metromedia Fiber Network, Inc., 416 F.3d 136 (2d Cir. 2005). The Second Circuit, which has allowed third-party releases, strongly emphasized the limits of this allowance and the limited enforceability of these releases. The Second Circuit had said more than a decade earlier that in "bankruptcy cases, a court may enjoin a creditor from suing a third party, provided the injunction plays an important part in the debtor's reorganization plan." In re Drexel Burnham Lambert Group, Inc., 960 F.2d 285, 293 (2d Cir. 1992). The court had not explained, however, when a nondebtor or third-party release is sufficiently "important" for a bankruptcy court to approve it. In *Metromedia*, the

Second Circuit clarified and arguably tightened the requirements for approving such a release, saying that "such a release is proper only in rare cases," requires a "finding of circumstances that may be characterized as unique," and, absent affected creditors' consent, usually requires somehow otherwise compensating enjoined claims. In re Metromedia Fiber Network, 416 F.3d at 141-42.

Two reasons justify these stringent requirements. First, the Code does not explicitly authorize third-party releases. "Second, a nondebtor release is a device that lends itself to abuse. By it, a nondebtor can shield itself from liability to third parties. In form, it is a release; in effect, it may operate as a bankruptcy discharge arranged without a filing and without the safeguards of the Code." *Id.* at 142.

In the *Metromedia* case, the bankruptcy court had approved a third-party release that protected "numerous third parties" from "any claims relating to the debtor, 'whether for tort, fraud, contract, violations of federal or state securities laws, or otherwise, whether known or unknown, foreseen or unforeseen, liquidated or unliquidated, fixed or contingent, matured or unmatured.' " *Id.* at 142-43. The debtor in possession defended the release on the basis that the creditors were allocated a plan distribution, thus received consideration, and therefore were estopped from complaining about the release. The Second Circuit rejected this argument and concluded that the "bankruptcy court's findings were insufficient. A nondebtor release in a plan of reorganization should not be approved absent the finding that truly unusual circumstances render the release terms important to the success of the plan. . . ." *Id.* at 143.

The Seventh Circuit has agreed, saying "[a] nondebtor release should only be approved in 'rare cases,' " In re Ingersoll, Inc., 562 F.3d 856, 865 (7th Cir. 2009), and only when the release is:

- narrow and essential to the reorganization plan as a whole,
- does not provide blanket immunity for all times, all transgressions, and all omissions [and applies] only to claims arising out of or in connection with the reorganization itself and not [claims for] willful misconduct, and
- was the fruit of long-term negotiations and achieved by the exchange of good and valuable consideration . . . that will enable unsecured creditors to realize distribution in the case.

Id. at 864-65. Even a release that is limited to negligence arising out of the reorganization may be deemed too broad. In re Pacific Lumber Co., 584 F.3d 229, 252 (5th Cir. 2009).

Similar, "truly unusual" and extraordinary circumstances are not reflected in the facts of MMW's bankruptcy. The third-party release in MMW's plan of reorganization is very broad, and the record does not show why any release — even a much narrower, tailored release — is essential to the bankruptcy. It is therefore very likely that the Committee's attack on the release will prevail, and the release will fall out of the plan.

Interestingly, a release of members of a creditors' committee, which is not part of MMW's plan but is not uncommon in other cases, is more likely to stand up. In listing the powers of a creditors' committee, the Bankruptcy Code implies that committee members have qualified immunity for actions within the scope of their duties. See 11 U.S.C. §1103(c). And, compared to the group the MMW plan would release from liability, "[t]he Creditors' Committee and its members are the only disinterested volunteers . . ." *id.*, and giving them some immunity for their service is an incentive for them to serve.

QUESTION #5

Challenging Claims of the Family and FNB

a) Explain the meaning and significance of subordinating the family's claims and FNB's secured claim.   The facts of Essay Exam #5 report that MMW's "founding family, the Richardson clan, which collectively remains a principal owner, poured in $3.5 million to keep operations going. Much of the money, about $2.5 million, was in the form of an unsecured loan from Regional Finance Bank (RFB) guaranteed by the Richardson's investment firm, Anna Vision, Inc. (AVI), which managed the family's personal assets and investments." Eventually, the loan from RFB was repaid, but the family apparently still holds an unsecured claim for $1 million and probably more.

Most of the debt owed FNB is presumably sold to RFB. But, FNB retained some secured claim.

The amount of money (i.e., the size of the plan distribution) MMW's plan must provide other creditors is affected by FNB's lien. The lien reduces the size of the estate for all creditors whose distributions under the plan are calculated on what they would have received had MMW filed a Chapter 7 case.

The family's unsecured claim also affects these creditors. Whatever the size of the estate, the distributions to unsecured creditors in Chapter 7 is a prorated portion of the estate. The more claims there are and the bigger these claims, the less each creditor would receive in a Chapter 7 case and the less each of them must be provided for in a Chapter 11 plan.

The Creditors' Committee therefore would love for the court to completely "subordinate" the secured and unsecured claims of FNB and the family below the claims of unsecured creditors. The result would be that all of the claims of other creditors are paid before the family and FNB received anything. In effect, if the family and FNB claims are subordinated, the size of the estate "pie" is bigger and less diluted for other creditors.

Section 510(c) allows the bankruptcy court, under equitable principles, to subordinate claims and interests:

> [A]fter notice and a hearing, the court may —
>
>   (1) under principles of equitable subordination, subordinate for purposes of distribution all or part of an allowed claim to all or part of another allowed claim or all or part of an allowed interest to all or part of another allowed interest; or
>
>   (2) order that any lien securing such a subordinated claim be transferred to the estate.

11 U.S.C.A. §510(c). Subordination under section 510(c) results from force of law for reasons of equity and fairness. The purpose is to " 'undo or offset any inequity in the claim position of a creditor that will produce injustice or unfairness to other creditors in terms of the bankruptcy results.' " In re EMB Associates, Inc., 92 B.R. 9, 15 (Bankr. D.R.I. 1988), further proceeding, 100 B.R. 629 (Bankr. D.R.I. 1989), aff'd in part, rev'd in part sub nom. Max Sugarman Funeral Home, Inc. v. A.D.B. Investors, 127 B.R. 508 (Bankr. D.R.I. 1989), vacated and remanded, 926 F.2d 1248 (1st Cir. 1991).

This purpose is achieved in theory not by *disallowance* of the creditor's claim; rather, paying the claim is *delayed* until the claims of injured creditors are satisfied. In practice, however, the delay has the same result as disallowance if the assets are fully consumed in satisfying other creditors.

When a secured claim is subordinated, the ultimate possible effect is "a court order invalidating the security interest . . . requiring the secured creditor to return [any] . . . proceeds of [the] collateral to the debtor, and reclassifying the claim as an unsecured claim subordinate to all other unsecured claims." Chaitman, *The Equitable Subordination of Bank Claims*, 39 Bus. Law. 1561 (1984). A lien that secures a claim subordinated under section 510(c) can be transferred to the estate, 11 U.S.C. §510(c)(2), just as happens when a lien is voided through the exercise of the trustee's avoiding power. 11 U.S.C. §551.

The complete outcome, however, is potentially even worse under section 510(c) than having the lien undone by the trustee's avoiding powers. When the avoiding powers are successfully exercised the creditor usually retains a claim that minimally ranks *equally* with other unsecured claims. Subordinating a secured claim can put it *behind* them in order of priority. Thus, equitable subordination is used not only as a kind of avoidance tool instead of the trustee's avoiding powers, it is sometimes used as a further remedy in addition to them.

Significantly, the right to pursue equitable subordination is not limited to the trustee or debtor in possession. Individual creditors and creditors' committees, who generally cannot assert the trustee's avoiding powers save in special circumstances, can nevertheless seek equitable subordination of other creditors' claims. Indeed, it is normally a creditor or creditors' committee rather than a debtor in possession or trustee who asks for subordination under section 510(c). Also, the bankruptcy court itself may consider equitable subordination *sua sponte* if a party in interest fails to do so.

The Code does not describe the principles that justify equitable subordination under section 510(c). Rather, they "are defined by case law," which long predates the Code and which normally subordinates a claim "only if its holder is guilty of misconduct." S. Rep. No. 989, 95th Cong., 2d Sess. 74, reprinted in 1978 U.S. Code Cong. & Admin. News, 5787, 5860.

The main key to equitable subordination is usually *inequitable conduct*. It is the first and principal component of a three-pronged test for equitable subordination that is recited in almost every modern case in which a court considers section 510(c):

(1)   The claimant must have engaged in some type of inequitable conduct;
(2)   The misconduct must have resulted in injury to the creditors of the bankruptcy or conferred an unfair advantage on the claimant; and

(3)   Equitable subordination of the claim must not be inconsistent with the
      provisions of the Bankruptcy Act.

In re Winstar Communications, Inc., 554 F.3d 382, 411 (3d Cir. 2009), quoting
Benjamin v. Diamond (In re Mobile Steel Co.), 563 F.2d 692, 699-700 (5th
Cir.1977). Inequitable conduct toward the debtor or her other creditors "can
warrant subordination of a claim *irrespective of whether it was related to the acquisition
or assertion of that claim*," Benjamin v. Diamond (Matter of Mobile Steel), 563 F.2d
692, 700 (5th Cir. 1977) (emphasis added), and irrespective of "reliance or prudence"
of the other creditors. In re T. E. Mercer Trucking Co., 16 B.R. 176, 189 (Bankr.
N.D. Tex. 1981).

"Inequitable conduct" is, of course, a very slippery concept with little predictive value. In very general terms, inequitable conduct is "conduct of the claimant in
relation to other creditors [that] is or was . . . unjust or unfair. . . ." DeNatale &
Abram, *The Doctrine of Equitable Subordination as Applied to Nonmanagement Creditors*,
40 Bus. Law. 417, 419 (1985). Somewhat more specifically,

> [i]nequitable conduct is that conduct which may be lawful, yet shocks one's
> good conscience. It means, *inter alia*, a secret or open fraud; lack of good faith or
> guardianship by a fiduciary; an unjust enrichment, not enrichment by bon
> chance, astuteness or business acumen, but enrichment through another's loss
> brought about by one's own unconscionable, unjust, unfair, close, or double
> dealing or foul conduct.

In re Enron, 379 B.R. 425, 433 n.39 (S.D.N.Y. 2007), quoting In re Adelphia
Communications Corp., 365 B.R. 24, 67-69 (Bankr. S.D.N.Y. 2007) Unfortunately, these definitions simply substitute equally vague terms for the root concept.

Many courts have categorized the kinds of conduct that have justified equitable
subordination in past cases. A favorite listing of the courts is:

(1)   fraud, illegality, breach of fiduciary duties;
(2)   undercapitalization; and
(3)   claimant's use of the debtor as a mere instrumentality or alter ego.

In re Kreisler, 546 F.3d 863, 866 (7th Cir. 2008). A slightly different list is part of the
opinion in Matter of CTS Truss, Inc., 868 F.2d 146 (5th Cir.1989), in which the
court wrote:

> The courts have actually confined equitable subordination of claims to three
> general categories of cases: those in which a fiduciary of the debtor misuses his
> position to the disadvantage of other creditors; those in which a third party, in
> effect, controls the debtor to the disadvantage of others; and those in which a
> third-party defrauds other creditors.

Id. at 148-49. These and similar lists do not completely agree: the categories are broad
and non-exclusive, and they are often explained in terms that themselves need
further definition and explanation to prove reliably helpful.

The search for a firmer grip on section 510(c), and the usually necessary
"inequitable conduct," properly begins at the beginning: the two Supreme Court
cases that are the bedrock of equitable subordination in bankruptcy. They are
Taylor v. Standard Gas & Electric Co., 306 U.S. 307 (1938), and Pepper v. Litton,

308 U.S. 295 (1939). The Court in *Taylor* approved subordinating a parent corporation's claim against its subsidiary, the debtor, because the former had undercapitalized and mismanaged the latter to the detriment of preferred stockholders. In *Pepper*, the Court approved subordinating or altogether denying the claim of the corporate debtor's dominant and controlling stockholder, Litton, who used his "strategic position," i.e., his "dominant influence" over the debtor, "for his own preferment to the damage" of the debtor's creditors. Specifically,

> [Litton] used his power not to deal fairly with the creditors of [the debtor] . . . but to manipulate its affairs in such a manner that when one of its creditors came to collect her just debt the bulk of the [debtor's] assets had disappeared into another Litton company. [He] . . . was enabled . . . to acquire most of the assets of the bankrupt not for cash or other consideration of value to creditors but for bookkeeping entries representing at best merely Litton's appraisal of the worth of Litton's services over the years.

Id. at 311–12. Moreover, Litton so acted in deliberate and calculated reaction to the creditor's efforts to collect from the debtor.

Because section 510(c) is rooted in *Taylor* and *Pepper*, they teach much about "inequitable conduct" that still applies in most modern cases. Their most important lesson is that inequitable conduct is broader than unlawful conduct. The claimant in neither *Taylor* nor *Pepper* violated a statute, breached a contract, or committed a tort. While any of these wrongs is almost surely within the meaning of "inequitable conduct" and can justify subordination under section 510(c), none of them is required to subordinate a creditor's claim. Self-serving inattention, manipulation, or maneuvering that is legal but harmful to other creditors is sometimes sufficient.

Such lawful conduct is not always inequitable, however, despite being harmful. It was inequitable in *Taylor* and *Pepper* primarily because in each case the claimant was an insider who also controlled the debtor. A person who controls someone else must usually respect the other person's interests even if the other person is a corporation, and the person in control is expected to abide by the rules of fair play and good conscience in dealing with the corporation's stockholders and creditors.

> He cannot manipulate the affairs of his corporation to their detriment and in disregard of the standards of common decency and honesty. He cannot by the intervention of a corporate entity violate the ancient precept against serving two masters. He cannot by the use of the corporate device avail himself of privileges normally permitted outsiders in a race of creditors. He cannot utilize his insider information and his strategic position for his own preferment. He cannot violate rules of fair play by doing indirectly through the corporation what he could not do directly. He cannot use his power for his own personal advantage and to the detriment of the stockholders and creditors no matter how absolute in terms that power may be and no matter how meticulous he is to satisfy technical requirements. For that power is at all times subject to the equitable limitation that it may not be exercised for [his] . . . aggrandizement, preference, or advantage. . . . Where there is a violation of those principles, equity will undo the wrong or intervene to prevent its consummation.

Pepper v. Litton, 308 U.S. 295, 311 (1939).

Because section 510(c) is rooted in *Taylor* and *Pepper*, the statute is most comfortably and often applied to subordinate the claims of insiders. *Insider status is not, however, a sufficient basis in itself for equitable subordination under section 510(c).* The courts insist that, as in *Taylor* and *Pepper*, the insider must be guilty of "inequitable conduct." This requirement is satisfied if the insider acted unlawfully or committed the inequities condemned in *Taylor* and *Pepper*. Thus, in line with *Pepper*, an insider's claim will be subordinated under section 510(c) if she uses insider information and her strategic position for self-aggrandizement, preference, or advantage, or otherwise violates the rules of fair play by doing indirectly through the corporation what she could not do directly.

In MMW's case, Ms. Richardson (for herself and the family) — who is the ultimate, controlling insider — cooked up a "common good" campaign to puff up stakeholder confidence, which worked and added value to MMW. But, the whole thing was fundamentally just that — puffing — that hid from stakeholders the simultaneous secret meetings with lawyers to plan bankruptcy. Moreover, much of the resulting value from stakeholders was apparently siphoned off to pay down the debt to FNB and, in particular, to pay off the loan on which the family investment firm, AVI, was surety. Undoubtedly, part of the pay-off was funded indirectly by suppliers increasing unsecured credit on the promise of the "partnership for profitability."

This same unpaid, unsecured credit would then largely be written off in bankruptcy, better the debtor's financial condition, and increase the value the family hoped to capture by purchasing complete ownership of MMW through the bankruptcy process.

Does this pattern of activity by the Richardson family amount to inequitable conduct sufficient to subordinate the family's claim? Undoubtedly, the evidence is sufficient to defeat any motion summarily to dismiss the effort to subordinate.

Do the facts also support subordinating FNB's secured claim because of the bank's complicity? Although insiders are the usual targets of equitable subordination, it is not restricted to them. It can also affect the claims of non-insiders who are guilty of inequitable conduct, but subordinating their claims under section 510(c) is much tougher both procedurally and substantively.

With respect to procedure, the burden of proof is divided when an insider's claim is attacked but is borne entirely by the challenger when the claim belongs to a non-insider. As explained by the bankruptcy court in In re Sleepy Valley, Inc., 93 B.R. 925 (Bankr. W.D. Tex. 1988).

> A verified proof of claim establishes the claimant's prima facie case both for the validity of the claim and for the purpose of meeting an equitable subordination challenge, as the latter is considered a "defense," of sorts, to a creditor's claim. Thus, the party seeking to subordinate the claim must come forward with sufficient proof to justify modifying the claim's priority. If the claimant is a non-insider, the burden remains on the objectant throughout. However, if the claimant is an insider, fiduciary or alter ego, the burden begins with the objectant, but shifts to the claimant to prove the integrity of the claim once there is a substantial factual showing of inequitable conduct.

Id. at 932 n.11.

With respect to the substance of the proof, the meaning of "inequitable conduct" is much broader for an insider. Generally speaking, because of *Taylor* and *Pepper* an insider's conduct is subject to exacting judicial scrutiny; and the conduct is inequitable if it lacks the earmarks of an arm's-length transaction and, in terms of those cases, is merely unfair or lacking in good faith or conscience. A non-insider's conduct is inequitable only if she is guilty of much "more egregious conduct," that is, intentional, gross misconduct proved with particularity.

The substantial difference in the treatment of insiders and non-insiders under section 510(c) is the range of lawful conduct that is considered inequitable. It is generally narrower for a non-insider who is ordinarily free of the legal and equitable duties that an insider owes the debtor and the debtor's creditors.

Most obviously, for example, a non-insider is usually free to use every available legal device and technical maneuver for collecting or protecting her claim. She is also free to maximize fully the protection of her claim. In doing so the non-insider can use any position of strength that comes from being a source of credit or having the power to foreclose or otherwise enforce her claim against the debtor. Moreover, the non-insider creditor is not obligated to safeguard other creditors from the effects of her own legitimate efforts to protect or collect her claim, and she is not required to police the debtor's treatment of them. In sum:

> "A creditor is under no fiduciary obligation to its debtor or to other creditors of the debtor in the collection of its claim. . . ." The permissible parameters of a creditor's efforts to seek collection from a debtor are generally those with respect to voidable preferences and fraudulent conveyances proscribed by the Bankruptcy Act; apart from these there is generally no objection to a creditor's using his bargaining position, including his ability to refuse to make further loans needed by the debtor, to improve the status of his existing claims.

In re W.T. Grant Co., 699 F.2d 599, 609-10 (2d Cir. 1983), cert. denied, 464 U.S. 822 (1983). Finally, if a creditor enjoys a secured claim to the debtor's property that leaves other creditors with little or nothing, her enviable priority status in relation to their pitifully poor position is not sufficient cause to readjust the claims under section 510(c).

The range of acceptable lawful conduct for a non-insider narrows, however, when she strong-arms her way into actual control of the debtor, or by agreement with the debtor or otherwise positions herself so that she controls the debtor. In this event, which is actually very rare, the creditor becomes a real or de facto insider. She must therefore honor the principles of *Taylor* and *Pepper* and respect the debtor's interests, sometimes ahead of her own. Failing to do so is inequitable conduct justifying subordination of the creditor's claim even though the conduct is technically lawful.

The scope of acceptable conduct for a creditor who controls the debtor depends on the degree of the creditor's control. The least latitude is permitted in the rare case when the creditor effectively becomes the alter ego of the debtor who exists as a mere instrumentality. A close identity of interest, however, that fully satisfies the legally technical requirements of an alter ego relationship, is not essential to imposing on a controlling creditor the equitable duties and accountability of an insider under section 510(c).

Usually, the degree of control that is necessary to trigger insider-like treatment is rather large control. Some courts would say "*virtually* complete control." The probable explanation is that the creditor's accountability based on her control is ultimately based on the creditor having dictated the conduct as a real insider is able to do. Having this much power, so that the debtor is robbed of free and independent choice, ordinarily requires substantial control.

Remember, however, that it is not the existence of the creditor's contractual right or transactional power to influence the debtor's conduct that triggers insider-like equitable duties. They are triggered by the creditor's actual exercise of control in unilaterally directing the debtor's conduct that affects creditors. Yet, it is not this control that is inequitable. Indeed, "[e]ven total control of a debtor's affairs [by a real insider] does not necessarily lead to equitable subordination of claims. . . ." In re Featherworks Corp., 25 B.R. 634, 648 (Bankr. E.D.N.Y. 1982), order aff'd, 36 B.R. 460 (E.D.N.Y. 1984). It is rather exercising the control inequitably, as by the creditor violating the lessons of *Pepper* and using its position for its own selfish advantage.

The classic case is In re American Lumber Co., 5 B.R. 470 (D. Minn. 1980). In this case the debtor's major financer took over the management of the debtor and very deliberately kept the debtor in business solely for the purpose of advantaging the financer. It caused the debtor to generate receivables, in which the financer had a first priority, that were paid to the financer. Other creditors were paid little or nothing. The financer, using its position of power and its insider information, effectively shifted the debt from itself to the backs of unpaid inventory suppliers and trade creditors and in so doing acted inequitably within the meaning of *Pepper*.

American Lumber is remarkable and stands out not because of the holding, but because the case is a rare finding of insider-like status by a secured creditor. It is especially remarkable that the finding is rare considering that secured creditors are daily involved very deeply in the affairs of many thousands of debtors. This rarity, however, is right in terms of existing doctrine. By this law, the cases will be few in which an outsider creditor is deemed to have become as an insider and to have engaged in conduct that entitles the trustee to subordinate the creditor's claim. Specifically, when creditors intervene in the debtor's affairs to protect their own interests, it does not matter that they act aggressively and selfishly. Doing so, consistent with contract and law, is their right and is only natural. It matters only when they are unnaturally or unusually exploitative. Only then is there harm to other creditors that warrants subordination.

The harm in a case such as *American Lumber* is in continuing to extend credit to a debtor pursuant to a secret plan that provides no repayment to other creditors. These creditors are thus misled and essentially robbed of their property and services for the benefit of the controlling creditor who has exploited its unfair advantage.

In the case of MMW and its bankruptcy, FNB may have been complicit in the questionable conduct of Ms. Richardson and the family. In particular, FNB probably benefitted from suppliers' new unsecured credit extended to MMW: the proceeds were indirectly channeled to FNB. But, such things commonly happen in commercial financing whether by design or not. The key distinction here is that none of the suspect conduct happened because of any requirements imposed by FNB as a result of any extraordinary control of MMW. It's not likely that FNB's secured claim would be equitably subordinated.

b) Explain the meaning and the significance of recharacterizing the family's claims against the estate. Under state law and in bankruptcy, a creditor's claim against a debtor for debt trumps an investor's claim of an equity interest. Increasingly, bankruptcy courts are exercising their presumed equitable power to examine a creditor's claim of debt and, when appropriate, recharacterize the claim as an equity interest. The practical effect is to postpone paying a creditor's claim so that the creditor is entitled to nothing until all debt is paid, including unsecured debt, so that the claim of debt is treated as an equity interest.

As Professor Ken Klee has written, " '[r]echaracterization' refers to an equitable power exercised by bankruptcy courts to look beyond a given label and instead characterize a purported claim or transaction according to its true economic nature. The Bankruptcy Code does not expressly grant any such power, but many courts have nonetheless found an implied power to recharacterize based on their general powers as courts of equity." Kenneth N. Klee, Recharacterization in Bankruptcy, ALI-ABA Course of Study (June 2005) (available on Westlaw SK092 ALI-ABA 211). "Although the effect of recharacterizing a loan as equity is to subordinate it below debt creditors, it is a separate doctrine from equitable subordination, and courts may recharacterize debt as equity 'even if the other requirements of equitable subordination are not satisfied.' " In re Gluth Bros. Const., Inc., 424 B.R. 379, 395 (Bankr. N.D. Ill. 2009). "[T]he purpose of recharacterization is to determine the *existence* of a debt, not to decide whether the debt should be subordinated. If there is no debt, equitable subordination is not an issue, although de facto subordination is a consequence." In re Hoffinger Industries, Inc., 327 B.R. 389, 408 (Bankr. E.D. Ark. 2005).

When deciding whether or not to recharacterize a loan as debt or as equity capital, the ultimate issue is "whether 'the party infusing funds [did] so as a banker (the party expects to be repaid with interest no matter the borrower's fortunes; therefore, the funds are debt) or as an investor (the funds infused are repaid based on the borrower's fortunes; hence, they are equity).' " In re Gluth Bros. Const., Inc., 424 B.R. 379, 395 (Bankr. N.D. Ill. 2009). Unlike equitable subordination, which is based on inequitable conduct during the course of the relationship, recharacterization looks to the intent of the parties at the time the purported loan is made. This is a largely factual determination, and no single factor is controlling or decisive, but the list of factors the courts usually consider includes:

- the names given to the instruments, if any, evidencing the indebtedness;
- the presence or absence of a fixed maturity date and schedule of payments;
- the presence or absence of a fixed rate of interest and interest payments;
- the source of repayments;
- the adequacy or inadequacy of capitalization;
- the identity of interest between the [parties];
- the security, if any, for the advances;
- the corporation's ability to obtain financing from outside lending institutions;

- the extent to which the advances were subordinated to the claims of outside creditors;
- the extent to which the advances were used to acquire capital assets;
- the presence or absence of a sinking fund to provide repayments;
- the right to enforce payment of principal and interest;
- participation in management flowing as a result of the transaction; and
- the failure of the debtor to repay the obligation on the due date or to seek postponement.

In re Hoffinger Industries, Inc., 327 B.R. 389, 408 (Bankr. E.D. Ark. 2005). In sum, "[t]he more characteristics of an arm's length transaction that are present, the more likely the transaction would be treated as debt instead of an equity contribution." *Id.*

Although no single factor controls, recharacterization often involves unusual closeness between the creditor and the debtor that approaches the latter being the alter ego of the former. With this closeness, many of the other factors that trigger recharacterization more naturally follow.

The necessary markers are not obviously present in the case of MMW's debt to the family to justify recharacterizing the debt as equity. Insider status, already owning some equity, or even having a controlling position is not sufficient in itself. It is how these and other factors combine and operate to show the necessary intent to invest rather than to loan; and in this case, the suspicious factors just don't add up to the conclusion that the family was acting as an investor rather than a banker in loaning money to the debtor.

A non-insider's claim of debt usually cannot be recharacterized as an equity investment. The closeness, control, informality, and ambiguity that breed factors supporting recharacterization simply and naturally are rarely present when the lender is a non-insider. And, the presence of collateral for the loan and a history of payments on the loan argue strongly, in any case, against recharacterization. So, there is very little chance in this case that FNB's secured claim will be recharacterized as equity.

QUESTION #6

Cramming Down the Plan and Absolute Priority

Explain how the court is likely to rule on the Committee's argument that the plan cannot be confirmed because of the provision giving the Richardson family full ownership of the reorganized company. Ordinarily, confirmation of a plan requires that every impaired class of claims or interests has accepted the plan. Confirmation otherwise remains possible — it is said that the plan is "crammed down" on creditors — but only if:

- The plan provides that the holders of secured claims retain the liens securing such claims, and each holder of a secured claim receive on account of such claim deferred cash payments totaling at least the allowed amount of such claim, of a value, as of the effective date of the plan, of at least the value of such holder's interest in the estate's interest in such property. *Id.* §1129(b)(2)(A).
- The plan also provides that *all unsecured claims are paid in full* or, if not, that the holder of any claim or interest that is junior to the unsecured claims

will not receive or retain any property under the plan on account of such junior claim or interest (which is known as the "*absolute priority*" rule). *Id.* §1129(b)(2)(B).

MMW's plan does not provide for paying all unsecured claims. Yet, the plan provides for the Richardson family not only to keep their substantial equity interest but to expand their interest so that the family fully owns the reorganized company. The Committee argues that this provision violates the absolute priority rule because even though the family's equity interest is junior to unsecured claims, the family will retain and receive even more property (i.e., ownership) under the plan on account of their junior interest.

The plan proponents will argue that the provision avoids violating the absolute priority rule because the family will add "new value" under the plan that, in effect, compensates unsecured creditors for the interest the family will retain or receive. Therefore, the absolute priority rule is either not violated (because the family's equity in the reorganized company is received or retained on account of the new value, not on account of their existing junior interest) or is satisfied by an exception to the rule that applies when unsecured creditors are adequately compensated in some way.

Whether providing "new value," in one way or another avoids or satisfies the absolute priority rule is not absolutely certain. It is certain that even if there is a "new value" work-around, the MMW plan provision, whereby the Richardson family keeps and expands their ownership, fails to meet the stringent requirements for a new value exception that the Supreme Court would approve.

In Bank of America Nat. Tr. & Sav. Ass'n v. 203 North LaSalle St. Partnership, 526 U.S. 434 (1999), the single asset of the debtor partnership was an office building. Bank of America held a secured claim of about $55 million and an unsecured claim for about $39 million. The Chapter 11 plan proposed to satisfy the Bank's unsecured claim for 16 percent of its present value. And, some partners of the debtor would contribute $6.125 million in new capital over the course of five years in exchange for the partnership's entire ownership of the reorganized debtor. The partners were the only persons contributing the new capital. The Bank objected on the basis that the plan violated the absolute priority rule.

The bankruptcy court nevertheless approved the plan. The district court and court of appeals affirmed by interpreting the phrase "on account of" in the absolute priority rule as permitting a "new value" corollary. The corollary finds some support in the language of Case v. Los Angeles Lumber Products Co., 308 U.S. 106, 118 (1939), which says that that the objection of an impaired senior class does not bar junior claim holders from receiving or retaining property interests in the debtor after reorganization, if they contribute new capital in money or money's worth, reasonably equivalent to the property's value, and necessary for successful reorganization of the restructured enterprise. In *203 North LaSalle*, the Seventh Circuit majority held that the partnership's plan satisfied this new value principle and did not violate the absolute priority rule because:

> when an old equity holder retains an equity interest in the reorganized debtor by meeting the requirements of the new value corollary, he is not receiving or retaining that interest "on account of" his prior equitable ownership of the

debtor. Rather, he is allowed to participate in the reorganized entity "on account of" a new, substantial, necessary and fair infusion of capital.

In re 203 N. LaSalle Street Partnership, 126 F.3d 955, 964 (7th Cir. 1997), rev'd sub nom. In Bank of America Nat. Tr. & Sav. Ass'n v. 203 North LaSalle St. Partnership, 526 U.S. 434 (1999).

The Supreme Court reversed. The Court discussed the history of the absolute priority rule, the possible readings of the statute and statutory history, and different possible formulations of a new value corollary. In the end, however, the Court refused to decide the exact nature of any such exception because under any of the possible configurations, "the plan at issue in this case . . . is doomed . . . by its provision for vesting equity in the reorganized business in the Debtor's partners without extending an opportunity to anyone else either to compete for that equity or to propose a competing reorganization plan." Bank of America Nat. Tr. & Sav. Ass'n v. 203 North LaSalle St. Partnership, 526 U.S. 434, 454 (1999). The Court reasoned that even if "the Debtor's exclusive opportunity to propose a plan under §1121(b) is not itself 'property' within the meaning of subsection (b)(2)(B)(ii)," the partnership, i.e., its ownership, "has taken advantage of [their ownership interest and running the bankruptcy as DIP] by proposing a plan under which the benefit of equity ownership may be obtained by no one but old equity partners." *Id.* If the plan were approved,

> the partners were in the same position that they would have enjoyed had they exercised an exclusive option under the plan to buy the equity in the reorganized entity, or contracted to purchase it from a seller who had first agreed to deal with no one else. It is quite true that the escrow of the partners' proposed investment eliminated any formal need to set out an express option or exclusive dealing provision in the plan itself, since the court's approval that created the opportunity and the partners' action to obtain its advantage were simultaneous. But before the Debtor's plan was accepted no one else could propose an alternative one, and after its acceptance no one else could obtain equity in the reorganized entity. At the moment of the plan's approval the Debtor's partners necessarily enjoyed an exclusive opportunity that was in no economic sense distinguishable from the advantage of the exclusively entitled offeror or option holder. This opportunity should, first of all, be treated as an item of property in its own right.

Id. If there is a new value exception to absolute priority, there probably should be an auction or other, actual market test to determine the adequacy of the new value. On the other hand,

> Whether a market test would require an opportunity to offer competing plans or would be satisfied by a right to bid for the same interest sought by old equity, is a question we do not decide here. It is enough to say, assuming a new value corollary, that plans providing junior interest holders with exclusive opportunities free from competition and without benefit of market valuation fall within the prohibition of §1129(b)(2)(B)(ii).

Id. at 458.

The challenged provision of MMW's Chapter 11 plan allowing the Richardson family to buy ownership of the organized debtor for new value the family would contribute to the plan is essentially identical to the plan the Supreme Court rejected in the *LaSalle* case. The MMW plan gives the Richardson family the exclusive right to buy full ownership, and this right is property that they received under the plan because of their ownership of the debtor. It violates the absolute priority rule and is not saved by the Richardson family contributing any amount of new value when the exclusive opportunity to contribute the new value and buy ownership belongs exclusively to the family.

BANKRUPTCY
MULTIPLE CHOICE
100 QUESTIONS

ANSWER SHEET

Print or copy this answer sheet to all multiple choice questions.

1.	A B C D	26.	A B C D	51.	A B C D	76.	A B C D
2.	A B C D	27.	A B C D	52.	A B C D	77.	A B C D
3.	A B C D	28.	A B C D	53.	A B C D	78.	A B C D
4.	A B C D	29.	A B C D	54.	A B C D	79.	A B C D
5.	A B C D	30.	A B C D	55.	A B C D	80.	A B C D
6.	A B C D	31.	A B C D	56.	A B C D	81.	A B C D
7.	A B C D	32.	A B C D	57.	A B C D	82.	A B C D
8.	A B C D	33.	A B C D	58.	A B C D	83.	A B C D
9.	A B C D	34.	A B C D	59.	A B C D	84.	A B C D
10.	A B C D	35.	A B C D	60.	A B C D	85.	A B C D
11.	A B C D	36.	A B C D	61.	A B C D	86.	A B C D
12.	A B C D	37.	A B C D	62.	A B C D	87.	A B C D
13.	A B C D	38.	A B C D	63.	A B C D	88.	A B C D
14.	A B C D	39.	A B C D	64.	A B C D	89.	A B C D
15.	A B C D	40.	A B C D	65.	A B C D	90.	A B C D
16.	A B C D	41.	A B C D	66.	A B C D	91.	A B C D
17.	A B C D	42.	A B C D	67.	A B C D	92.	A B C D
18.	A B C D	43.	A B C D	68.	A B C D	93.	A B C D
19.	A B C D	44.	A B C D	69.	A B C D	94.	A B C D
20.	A B C D	45.	A B C D	70.	A B C D	95.	A B C D
21.	A B C D	46.	A B C D	71.	A B C D	96.	A B C D
22.	A B C D	47.	A B C D	72.	A B C D	97.	A B C D
23.	A B C D	48.	A B C D	73.	A B C D	98.	A B C D
24.	A B C D	49.	A B C D	74.	A B C D	99.	A B C D
25.	A B C D	50.	A B C D	75.	A B C D	100.	A B C D

BANKRUPTCY QUESTIONS

Who Can Be a Debtor

1. Which of these persons cannot be a debtor under Chapter 7?

   A) For-profit corporation

   B) Married couple

   C) Non-profit corporation

   D) Railroad

   E) Sole proprietor

2. Which of these persons cannot be a debtor under Chapter 13?

   A) Attorney who is a partner in a law firm

   B) Married couple

   C) Married individual

   D) Millionaire with millions of dollars of debt

   E) Sole proprietor

3. A debtor must satisfy which of these requirements to file Chapter 7?

   A) Have been domiciled in the state during the 180-day period preceding the date of filing the petition

   B) Insolvency

   C) Receive a credit counseling briefing

   D) Reside or be domiciled in the United States

   E) United States citizenship

4. Which of these persons is least likely to qualify for Chapter 13?

   A) Accountant

   B) Itinerate worker

   C) Part-time worker

   D) Self-employed person

   E) Trust-fund 20-year-old

5. Which of these persons cannot be a debtor under Chapter 11?

A) Individual with primarily consumer debts

B) Married couple

C) National bank

D) Railroad

E) Sole proprietor

6. An involuntary bankruptcy case can be commenced only under:

A) Chapter 7

B) Chapters 7 and 11

C) Chapters 7 and 13

D) Chapters 7, 11, 12, and 13

E) Chapters 7, 11, and 13

Jurisdiction and Venue

7. Which court or courts have original jurisdiction of bankruptcy cases?

A) All federal courts

B) Bankruptcy courts

C) Federal district courts

D) Federal district courts and bankruptcy courts

E) Federal district courts and, in extraordinary cases, circuit courts

8. Which of these proceedings is most likely beyond bankruptcy jurisdiction?

A) A dispute over whether or not a third party has a bankruptcy claim against the debtor based entirely on state law

B) A plaintiff's direct tort action against a surety of the debtor based on the surety's misrepresentation to plaintiff

C) A state-law tort action related to the bankruptcy case

D) A trustee suing to recover a fraudulent transfer under state law

E) An action based on a prepetition contract between the debtor and a third party

9. Debtor is a natural person. Her home is (and has long been) New York, but she travels extensively because of her job. Right now she is living in Texas where she moved last week. Before moving to Texas, Debtor lived five months in

South Dakota and, before that, six months in Virginia. She has decided to file Chapter 7 bankruptcy. Properly, she should file in the bankruptcy court of the federal district court in which state?

A) New York

B) Texas or South Dakota

C) Virginia

D) South Dakota or New York

E) New York or Virginia

10. Debtor is a company incorporated in Delaware; its chief business office is in Ohio where it operates several retail stores. Debtor also operates an equal number of retail stores in Indiana and Wisconsin, respectively. Where can debtor properly file Chapter 11?

A) Delaware

B) Delaware or Ohio

C) Delaware, Ohio, Indiana, or Wisconsin

D) Ohio

E) The state in which most of the debtor's assets are located

Commencement and Dismissal in General

11. When does a voluntary bankruptcy case commence?

A) After notice to creditors and an opportunity for a hearing

B) Once jurisdiction is established

C) Ten days after a petition is filed

D) The court approves and accepts the debtor's petition

E) Upon filing a bankruptcy petition with the bankruptcy court

12. Along with a bankruptcy petition, the debtor also files other documents but not a:

A) Certificate of birth or incorporation or comparable proof

B) List of creditors

C) Schedule of assets and liabilities

D) Schedule of current income and current expenditures

E) Statement of the debtor's financial affairs

13. A Chapter 7 bankruptcy case involving an individual debtor cannot be dismissed for this reason:

A) Abuse based on totality of circumstances

B) Debtor was discharged in another Chapter 7 case five years ago

C) Lack of good faith

D) Request of debtor

E) Sufficient income to pay unsecured creditors more than they would receive in a Chapter 7 liquidation

Automatic Stay

14. When does the automatic stay of bankruptcy arise?

A) After notice to creditors and an opportunity for a hearing

B) Once jurisdiction is established

C) Ten days after a petition is filed

D) The court approves and accepts the debtor's petition

E) Upon filing a proper bankruptcy petition with the bankruptcy court

15. The automatic stay of bankruptcy in a Chapter 7 case covers almost all creditor collection and enforcement efforts of every kind except:

A) Acts to create, perfect, or enforce any lien against property of the debtor

B) Acts to obtain possession of property of the estate or of property from the estate or to exercise control over property of the estate

C) Enforcement of a security interest in collateral that was repossessed before the debtor filed bankruptcy

D) Judicial, administrative, or other actions or proceedings against the debtor that was or could have been commenced before the commencement of the case

E) Self-help repossession of collateral securing a claim against the debtor that arose before the commencement of the case under this title

16. In a Chapter 7 case, the automatic stay of bankruptcy does not affect:

A) Creditors' actions to collect from people who guaranteed or otherwise insured the debtor's obligations

B) Creditors' conduct with respect to property of the debtor that is not also property of the estate

C) Enforcement of judgments against the debtor obtained and docketed before the bankruptcy case is commenced

D) Lawsuits against the debtor in state court

E) The legitimate rights to possession of a person who jointly owns property with the debtor

17. Typically, in a Chapter 7 case of an individual, the automatic stay ends when the:

A) Case is closed

B) Case is dismissed

C) Creditors' claims are paid or denied

D) Discharge is granted

E) Property is exempted by the debtor

18. Action taken in violation of the stay is always:

A) Accepted or rejected by the trustee

B) Compensative

C) Contemptible

D) Reviewable for harm

E) Void or voidable

19. To whom does the Bankruptcy Code explicitly give the right to recover damages for violation of the automatic stay?

A) Any party in interest harmed by the conduct

B) Debtor

C) Estate

D) Individual injured by willful violation

E) Person injured by willful or negligent violation

20. In a Chapter 13 case, the automatic stay is peculiarly different because the stay:

A) Applies only to postpetition debts and property

B) Applies only to property of the debtor used for any purpose other than work or professional activity that generates income to fund the Chapter 13 plan

C) Applies to the collection of a consumer debt from the debtor and also any individual liable on the debt with the debtor

D) Is limited to property of the estate used for personal, family, or household purposes

E) Protects members of the debtor's immediate family

21. Based on the supposed authority of 11 U.S.C. §105, a bankruptcy court will most likely enjoin a creditor's action to collect from a surety an obligation the debtor owes if:

A) Action against the surety will adversely affect the estate

B) Debtor agrees

C) Irreparable harm to the creditor will otherwise result

D) Surety is an officer of the debtor

E) Surety is a family member

22. In a Chapter 7 case, the bankruptcy court will lift the automatic stay and allow action against property affected by the stay when a party in interest requests such relief and the party in interest shows:

A) Irreparable harm to the party's interest in the property

B) Lien on the property that is enforceable under state law against all third parties with or without notice of the lien

C) Pending action against the property in state or federal court

D) Perfected security interest in the property in which the debtor has no equity

E) Property is subject to equitable distribution in a domestic dissolution proceeding

23. In a Chapter 11 case involving a manufacturing company, the court will lift the automatic stay with respect to equipment subject to a security interest when the secured party shows that its interest is perfected and:

A) Debtor lacks equity in the property

B) Property is not critically necessary for an effective reorganization

C) Property is depreciating in value

D) Property is necessary for reorganization but the security interest is not adequately perfected

E) Secured party will irreparably suffer opportunity costs resulting from the stay (i.e., losing, without compensation, present opportunity to dispose of collateral)

24. In a Chapter 11 case involving a corporate debtor, when will the bankruptcy court most likely lift the automatic stay with respect to property in which secured party, which is owed $500,000, has a perfected security interest:

A) Property is worth $500,000 and interest is rapidly accruing

B) Property is worth $500,000 and is slowly depreciating

C) Property is worth $500,000 or less and the economic cost of denying the secured party the right to foreclose is increasing daily

D) Property is worth $500,000 or less and value is stable for the foreseeable future

E) Property is worth $700,000 and is rapidly depreciating

Claims

25. A creditor's claim filed in a bankruptcy case is typically allowed when:

A) Bankruptcy judge approves the claim after notice and hearing

B) Claim has been reduced to judgment

C) Creditor submits authenticated proof of the claim and the amount of the claim

D) Nobody timely objects

E) Trustee formally approves the claim

26. The effect of an unsecured creditor not filing a claim in a Chapter 7 bankruptcy case is:

A) Claim is discharged

B) Claim is not discharged

C) Claim is paid last from the estate

D) Creditor cannot participate in distribution of the estate

E) None of these effects

27. The effect of a creditor not filing a secured claim in a Chapter 7 bankruptcy case is:

A) Interest is discharged

B) Claim is not discharged

C) Claim is paid last from the estate

D) Creditor cannot participate in distribution of the estate

E) None of these effects

28. The debtor is required to list and schedule all of her creditors when she files a bankruptcy case. 11 U.S.C. §521(a)(1). These creditors are notified of the bankruptcy and can file claims. What is the effect of the debtor omitting a creditor from the list?

A) Claim is discharged

B) Claim is not discharged

C) Claim is paid first from the estate

D) Creditor is paid from the estate on a pro rata basis

E) None of these effects

29. If a creditor's claim is $500,000 and is secured by collateral worth $300,000, the claim is administered in a bankruptcy case by:

A) Disallowing the claim to the extent of $200,000

B) Labeling and treating the claim (or the creditor's lien) for all purposes as "underwater"

C) Lifting the automatic stay to allow the creditor to enforce the claim

D) Providing adequate protection

E) Splitting or bifurcating the claim so that the creditor has a secured claim for $300,000 and an unsecured claim for $200,000

30. In a Chapter 11 case involving a corporation, if the debtor's equipment is subject to a perfected secured interest, the creditor's secured claim:

A) Always equals the amount of the secured debt

B) Is enforced because the stay is lifted

C) Is the lesser of the debt and the amount that is or would be received upon a foreclosure sale in the ordinary course

D) Never exceeds the value of the collateral

E) Takes into account accruing interest

Bankruptcy Estate

31. Debtor is the beneficiary of a spendthrift trust created for her by her grandparents. The principal or corpus of the trust is very large, and the terms of the trust provide for a monthly payment to Debtor. Under applicable state law, all of Debtor's rights to the trust are inalienable. When Debtor files Chapter 7 bankruptcy:

A) All payments made to and retained by Debtor before she filed bankruptcy become property of the estate.

B) Payments made to Debtor before and after she filed bankruptcy become property of the estate.

C) The principal becomes property of the estate.

D) The right to monthly payments becomes property of the estate.

E) None of the above

32. Debtor is the beneficiary of a spendthrift trust she created for herself. The principal or corpus of the trust is very large, and the terms of the trust provide for a monthly payment to Debtor. Nobody else benefits from the trust, and Debtor retains full powers with respect to the trust. When Debtor files Chapter 7 bankruptcy:

A) Payments made to Debtor before and after she filed bankruptcy become property of the estate.

B) The principal becomes property of the estate.

C) The right to monthly payments becomes property of the estate.

D) Nothing becomes part of the bankruptcy estate.

E) Everything becomes part of the bankruptcy estate.

33. Upon filing bankruptcy, all of the property an individual debtor owns automatically and immediately becomes part of the bankruptcy estate when the case is filed except:

A) Exempt property

B) Property in another person's possession and control

C) Property in another state

D) Property owned in common with a spouse

E) Tax-exempt retirement accounts

34. In a Chapter 7 case involving an individual debtor, property the debtor acquires after the bankruptcy petition is filed does not pass to the bankruptcy estate. However, there are exceptions for some property if all rights to the property are acquired within 180 days after the date of the filing of the petition. An example is:

A) Any cash gift exceeding $1000

B) Inheritance

C) Gold discovered while prospecting in Alaska

D) Lottery jackpot

E) Salary bonus other than ordinary salary increase

35. The following property, if acquired immediately after the debtor files Chapter 7, does not become part of the bankruptcy estate and the debtor is allowed to keep it for herself:

A) Check for last quarter stock dividends

B) Gold discovered while prospecting in Alaska

C) Jackpot from lottery ticket purchased the day before filing bankruptcy

D) Payment received on past-due account owed debtor

E) Salary for last pay period

36. In a Chapter 13 case, property of the estate:

A) Remains by default in the debtor's possession

B) Does not exist because no estate is created because the debtor's property will not be liquidated

C) Excludes most property acquired after the bankruptcy petition is filed

D) Cannot be used to pay prepetition debts because these debts will be paid under a Chapter 13 plan funded by the debtor's future income

E) Excludes property acquired before the bankruptcy petition is filed because the purpose of Chapter 13 is not liquidation

Exemptions

37. Basic exemptions in bankruptcy are always determined by:

A) Federal and/or applicable state law depending on state legislation

B) Federal law

C) State law of the last place where the debtor "resided" within 180 days before the bankruptcy filing

D) State law where the bankruptcy case is filed

E) State law where the debtor is "domiciled"

38. Debtor lived for more than 25 years in North Carolina, a state with very limited exemptions. Debtor then moved to Florida, a state with very generous exemptions, and lived there for a year. Debtor then moved back to North Carolina. Exactly 727 days after returning to North Carolina, Debtor filed a bankruptcy petition. Which state, North Carolina or Florida, is considered the Debtor's domicile for purposes of determining Debtor's exemptions?

A) Debtor elects one state or the other

B) Depends on where the majority of Debtor's assets are located

C) Florida

D) Neither state

E) North Carolina

39. Debtor purchased a parcel of undeveloped land in Nevada (the "Property") in May 1994, but he never improved or even lived on the Property until August 11, 2004. On this day, Debtor moved a mobile home onto the Property and began living there so that the place became his principal residence. On the same day, Debtor recorded a declaration of homestead with the County Recorder's Office covering the mobile home and the Property, which Nevada law requires to establish property as a homestead and benefit from the state homestead exemption. Sixteen days later, on August 27, 2004, Debtor filed a Chapter 7 bankruptcy petition. He claimed as exempt the mobile home and Property, which was worth $400,000, on the basis of Nevada law exempting a homestead to the extent of $350,000. A creditor timely filed an objection to Debtor's claim of a homestead exemption. Everybody agrees that Nevada exemptions apply, but they disagree about the value of the exemption the Debtor can claim. To what extent is Debtor's claim of homestead exemption valid?

A) $400,000

B) $350,000

C) Way less than $350,000 because of and pursuant to the limited cap on the amount of a homestead exemption imposed by federal law (§522(p))

D) Not at all because of the fraud in converting nonexempt property to exempt property on the eve of bankruptcy

E) Not at all because Debtor was not domiciled on the property for the greater part of the 180 days preceding the filing of the bankruptcy petition

40. Debtor owned her home where she had lived alone for five years. When she filed bankruptcy, she claimed the $350,000 state law homestead exemption. The home is valued at $350,000 and is unencumbered. During the last two years, Debtor paid $300,000 to fully satisfy the mortgage. To what extent can Debtor exempt the home?

A) $350,000

B) Less than $350,000 because of and pursuant to the limited cap on the amount of a homestead exemption imposed by federal law (§522(p))

C) Not at all because of the fraud in converting nonexempt property to exempt property on the eve of bankruptcy

D) Not at all because Debtor has no dependents living in the home

E) Not at all because Debtor has no family living in the home

41. Debtor owned a vehicle worth $20,000 subject to Bank's perfected security interest for $15,000 and a judicial lien for $5,000 obtained by a judgment creditor. Debtor filed Chapter 7 bankruptcy. Applicable state law provides a $20,000 vehicle exemption. To what extent can Debtor exempt the vehicle?

A) $20,000

B) $15,000

C) $5,000

D) Not at all unless the vehicle is used primarily for business purposes

E) Not at all unless the vehicle is used primarily for personal, family, household purposes

42. D borrowed money from F. The loan is secured by a perfected Article 9 security interest in certain of D's household goods. The collateral is worth $50,000. The amount of the loan is $60,000. State law exempts a debtor's interest in this property to the extent of $10,000. D files Chapter 7 bankruptcy. Under which of these circumstances can D exempt the property from the bankruptcy estate if state law is the prime source of D's bankruptcy exemptions?

A) D can exempt the property to the extent of $10,000 if the security interest is a purchase money security interest in consumer goods.

B) D can exempt the property to the extent of $10,000 if the security interest is a possessory, non-purchase money security interest in consumer goods.

C) D can exempt the property to the extent of $10,000 if the security interest is a nonpossessory, non-purchase money security interest in consumer goods.

D) D can exempt the property to the extent of $10,000 only if the security interest is a possessory, purchase money security interest in consumer goods.

E) D cannot exempt the property to any extent because state law protects a debtor's property from judicial liens, not consensual lien.

43. Two months before filing Chapter 7, Debtor sold several collections of stamps and baseball cards and used the money to buy property that is exempt from the claims of judicial creditors and the bankruptcy trustee. In the bankruptcy case, state-law exemptions control, and state law exempts all of the property Debtor acquired. In bankruptcy, can Debtor exempt the property considering it was acquired on the eve of bankruptcy?

A) Yes, because Debtor paid reasonably equivalent value

B) Yes, because exemptions are absolute

C) No, because the purchase of the property was a constructively fraudulent transfer

D) No, because the purchase had the effect of hindering creditors' collection efforts

E) Depends on whether or not Debtor acted with actual fraudulent intent

Discharge

44. Only this statement about the bankruptcy discharge is true:

A) A discharge does not extinguish the debt or otherwise make it go away.

B) A discharge relieves the debtor from personal liability for all debts.

C) Every person who is a debtor in any bankruptcy case receives a discharge.

D) Exceptions and objections to discharge have the same effect.

E) Only a natural person gets a discharge.

45. C financed D's purchase of a vehicle. D filed Chapter 7 bankruptcy, and the court granted a discharge. In which of these cases can C repossess the vehicle if D defaults?

A) The contract between C and D waives the bankruptcy discharge.

B) The contract between C and D provides for a consensual lien.

C) The purchase money debt is excepted from discharge under 11 U.S.C. §523.

D) The value of the vehicle is $20,000. The purchase money debt is equal to or less than $20,000.

E) The value of the vehicle is $20,000. The purchase money debt is more than $20,000.

46. When a creditor takes action that violates the discharge injunction, the effect is:

A) The creditor's claim is disallowed.

B) The creditor's claim is excepted from the discharge.

C) The creditor is liable for contempt.

D) The debtor has a cause of action for damages.

E) The creditor's claim is extinguished.

47. Ordinarily, the bankruptcy discharge does not affect the debts of any third-party nondebtor. So, the debtor's discharge does not protect third parties such as insiders, sureties, or insurers, who are also liable with respect to claims against the debtor. In a Chapter 11 case, however, the plan of reorganization can most legitimately provide for releasing such a third party from liability to creditors when:

A) The debt is excepted from discharge.

B) The debt is fully secured.

C) The third party is an officer of a corporate debtor.

D) The third party is the debtor's grandmother.

E) The third party's liability would adversely affect the debtor's bankruptcy estate.

48. D is a natural person. She filed bankruptcy. The bankruptcy court granted a discharge. It is unlawful, because of D's bankruptcy discharge, for:

A) A bank to refuse D a job

B) A church to deny D membership

C) A department store to deny D a credit card

D) A private university to deny D admission

E) A social club to deny D membership

49. D is a natural person who was fined for violating pollution laws and ordered to clean up the mess, which was estimated to cost $1 million. D filed Chapter 7 bankruptcy and won a discharge.

A) Only the fine is discharged.

B) Only the order is discharged.

C) The fine and order are discharged.

D) The fine is discharged only if payable as a criminal penalty.

E) The order is discharged if D is alternatively liable to pay the cost of someone else cleaning up.

50. Certain debts are excepted from discharge in Chapter 7, which means the debtor remains personally liable despite discharge and the end of the bankruptcy case. Excepted debts include:

A) All tax debts

B) Credit card debt

C) Criminal restitution

D) Domestic support obligations but not ordinary contract debts owed a former spouse

E) Liability for intentional torts

51. In a Chapter 7 case, the court can deny the debtor a discharge if:

A) Claim of exemptions exceeds what the applicable law allows

B) Debtor is a corporation

C) Filing the case was a substantial abuse of Chapter 7 in that the debtor could pay a significant amount of prepetition debt from future income

D) Lawyers' fees have not been paid

E) Waiver of discharge is given to any creditor for value and before the case was filed

Strong-Arm Clause (§544(a))

52. Soon before filing bankruptcy, D got a loan from Bank that was secured by an Article 9 security interest in the debtor's existing equipment. Can the trustee avoid the security interest under section 544(a) (11 U.S.C. §544(a))?

A) No

B) Yes, if Bank did not perfect its security interest before bankruptcy was filed

C) Yes, if Bank did not perfect its security interest before bankruptcy was filed or thereafter if within 20 days after the interest was created

D) Yes, if Bank did not perfect its security interest outside the 90-day period before bankruptcy was filed

E) Yes, if Bank is an "insider"

53. Soon before filing bankruptcy, D purchased equipment that was financed by Bank. The purchase price was secured by an Article 9 security interest in the new equipment. Can the trustee avoid the security interest under section 544(a) (11 U.S.C. §544(a))?

A) No

B) Yes, if Bank did not perfect its security interest before bankruptcy was filed

C) Yes, if Bank did not perfect its security interest before bankruptcy was filed or thereafter if within 20 days after the interest was created

D) Yes, if Bank did not perfect its security interest outside the 90-day period before bankruptcy was filed

E) Yes, if Bank is an "insider"

54. A month before filing Chapter 7 bankruptcy, D sold her vacation house at the beach to B for market value. Can the trustee avoid the conveyance?

A) Yes, if the deed was not properly recorded and the trustee lacked actual knowledge of the sale

B) Yes, if the deed was not properly recorded whether or not the trustee had actual knowledge of the sale

C) Yes, if B knew that D planned to file bankruptcy

D) No, because B paid market value

E) Not if B is a good faith purchaser for value

Fraudulent Transfers

55. A month before filing Chapter 7 bankruptcy, D gave another creditor, E, a perfected lien on D's property to secure a debt D's friend, F, owed E. D was insolvent when the lien was created but did so to help F. Can the trustee avoid the lien that D gave E?

A) Yes, because the creation of the lien was actually fraudulent

B) Yes, because creating the lien was constructively fraudulent

C) Yes, because the effect was to prefer E over C

D) No, because there was no transfer

E) Depends on whether or not the lien was recorded or otherwise perfected

56. A month before filing Chapter 7 bankruptcy, D sold and delivered a Picasso original (worth millions of dollars) to her Children for $100. There was a perfect writing, no public recording was required, and D was insolvent. Can the trustee avoid the sale of the painting?

A) Yes, because of actual fraud

B) Yes, because the transfer to the Children was constructively fraudulent

C) Yes, if D was insolvent at the time of the transfer or was rendered insolvent as a result of the transfer

D) Yes, even if not actually fraudulent

E) No

57. A month before filing Chapter 7 bankruptcy, D quietly deeded her vacation house at the beach to her Children as a gift. Can the trustee avoid the conveyance?

A) Yes, because of actual fraud

B) Yes, because the transfer to the Children was constructively fraudulent

C) Yes, if D was insolvent at the time of the transfer or was rendered insolvent as a result of the transfer

D) Yes, even if not actually fraudulent

E) No

58. A year before filing Chapter 7 bankruptcy, D quietly deeded her vacation house at the beach to her Children as a gift. The deed was recorded at the time of the conveyance. Can the trustee avoid the conveyance?

A) Yes, because of actual fraud

B) Yes, because the transfer to the Children was constructively fraudulent

C) Yes, if D was insolvent at the time of the transfer or was rendered insolvent as a result of the transfer

D) Yes, even if not fraudulent

E) No

59. A year before filing Chapter 7 bankruptcy, D quietly deeded her principal residence to her Children as a gift. Under state law, the home is fully exempt from the claims of judicial creditors. The deed was recorded at the time of the conveyance. Can the trustee avoid the conveyance?

A) Yes, because of actual fraud

B) Yes, because the transfer to the Children was constructively fraudulent

C) Yes, if D was insolvent at the time of the transfer or was rendered insolvent as a result of the transfer

D) Yes, even if not fraudulent

E) No

60. A year before filing Chapter 7 bankruptcy, D gave a creditor, E, a perfected lien on D's personal property to secure a long preexisting debt D owed E. D was insolvent when the lien was created. Can the trustee avoid the conveyance as a fraudulent transfer?

A) Yes, because of actual fraud

B) Yes, because the transfer to E was constructively fraudulent

C) Yes, if D was insolvent at the time of the transfer or was rendered insolvent as a result of the transfer

D) No, because fraudulent transfer law doesn't apply to liens

E) No, because there is no actual or constructive fraud

Preferences

61. A bankruptcy trustee can avoid a prepetition transfer under section 547(b) that is (1) a transfer of an interest of the debtor in property and (2) to or for the benefit of a creditor if all of these additional requirements, except one, are satisfied. The exception is:

A) The transfer was for or on account of an antecedent debt owed by the debtor before such transfer was made.

B) The transfer was made while the debtor was insolvent.

C) The transfer was made without good faith.

D) The transfer was made on or within the reach-back (i.e., preference) period (which is usually 90 days before the date of the filing of the petition).

E) The transfer caused a preferential effect.

62. There are some preferences that the trustee cannot avoid because special exceptions of section 547(c) protect them. Which of the following is not an exception?

A) Bona fide purchaser

B) Ordinary course of business or ordinary business terms

C) Purchase money

D) Subsequent new value

E) Substantially contemporaneous exchange

63. A year or so before filing bankruptcy, D borrowed money from C and secured the loan by giving C a consensual lien on property D owned. The lien was not perfected, however, until a few weeks before D filed bankruptcy.

A) The trustee has no remedy if the loan was made beyond a year before the filing.

B) There is no preference because the loan and lien were actually given more than 90 days before the filing.

C) The preference is excepted from avoidance because the loan and lien are purchase money.

D) There is no preference because the lien secures a preexisting debt that, under UCC Article 9, is "value."

E) The lien is a preference under section 547(b).

64. Which of the following transfers is a preference under section 547(b) in D's bankruptcy?

A) A few days before bankruptcy, D paid C a preexisting debt that was long and fully secured by a recorded mortgage on property D owned.

B) A few days before bankruptcy, D, who is an officer and director of Ace, Inc., paid C a preexisting debt that was long and fully secured by a recorded mortgage on property Ace owned.

C) Ace, Inc. paid D's preexisting debt to C within 90 days before D filed bankruptcy. D is an officer of Ace and on its board.

D) D paid C a preexisting debt 13 months before D filed bankruptcy.

E) Just days before filing bankruptcy, D defaulted on a debt owed C. The day before D filed bankruptcy, C collected the debt from S, a surety who had agreed to accommodate D on the obligation.

65. Six months before D filed bankruptcy, D abruptly repaid an unsecured loan from Bank on which S, D's Sister, was a surety.

A) The payment is a preference to Bank, and the trustee can recover alternatively from Bank or S.

B) The payment is a preference to Bank, but the trustee can recover only from Bank.

C) The payment is a preference to S, and the trustee can recover alternatively from Bank or S.

D) The payment is a preference to S, and the trustee can recover only from S.

E) The payment is not a preference to anyone.

66. Six months before D filed bankruptcy, D abruptly repaid an unsecured loan from Bank on which S was a surety.

A) The payment is a preference to Bank, and the trustee can recover alternatively from Bank or S.

B) The payment is a preference to Bank, but the trustee can recover only from Bank.

C) The payment is a preference to S, and the trustee can recover alternatively from Bank or S.

D) The payment is a preference to S, but the trustee can recover only from S.

E) The payment is not a preference to anyone.

Leases and Executory Contracts

67. T leased commercial real estate from L. By its terms, the lease terminates should T file bankruptcy. T filed Chapter 11 when five years remained on the term of the lease. What action can the debtor in possession take with respect to the lease?

A) Assign the lease

B) Assume the lease

C) Reject the lease

D) Reject, assume, and/or assign the lease in line with what section 365 allows

E) Do nothing with respect to the lease

68. T leased commercial real estate from L. T filed Chapter 11 when five years remained on the term of the lease. T, as debtor in possession, cannot:

A) Assign the lease

B) Assume the lease

C) Modify the lease

D) Reject the lease

E) Renegotiate the lease

69. The decision by a debtor in possession to reject or assume an executory contract or lease and the court's approval of the decision usually depend on:

A) Agreement of the counterparty

B) Business judgment rule

C) Market equivalency test

D) Reasonable person test

E) Sound financial basis

70. T leased commercial real estate from L. Five years remained on the lease term when T filed bankruptcy. Under what circumstances does the Bankruptcy Code prohibit T from assuming and assigning the lease?

A) State law excuses the lessor from accepting performance by any assignee of the lease.

B) State law prohibits alienation in any insolvency proceeding by or against the debtor.

C) The assignment would increase the economic risks to the lessor.

D) The lease contains a provision against alienation.

E) The lessor objects to the assignment.

71. T leased commercial real estate from L. Five years remained on the lease term when T filed Chapter 11 bankruptcy. The lease did not prohibit assignment generally but limited the use of the property by anybody to a particular purpose. In T's bankruptcy case, the debtor in possession proposes to assume and assign the lease to a third party who plans to use the property for a purpose not authorized by the lease terms. Can the court approve the assumption and assignment?

A) No

B) Yes, if local zoning laws permit the use intended by the assignee

C) Yes, if the assumption and assignment satisfy the business judgment rule

D) Yes, if the court determines that notwithstanding the use clause in the lease, there is really no harm to the lessor in allowing the unauthorized use

E) Yes, if the assignment includes an increase in rent

72. T leased commercial real estate from L. T filed Chapter 11. Five years remained on the lease term, and the rent is $50,000 per year. Unpaid rent at the time of the bankruptcy filing was $25,000. The court approved rejecting the lease.

A) L's claim cannot exceed approximately $75,000.

B) L has a claim for $250,000.

C) L has a claim for $25,000, which is the total of the prepetition debt.

D) L has a claim for $275,000.

E) L has a claim for $275,000 less the market value of the leasehold for the balance of the lease term.

73. A debtor in possession cannot assume an executory contract in a Chapter 11 case if:

A) It is a lease of personal property.

B) It is a commitment to loan money in a fixed amount of principal and interest.

C) Personal services are involved.

D) The contract includes a prohibition against assumption that is enforceable under applicable, nonbankruptcy law.

E) The remaining term is less than six months.

74. The lease of a commercial space in a shopping center:

A) Is assignable if two-thirds of the other tenants agree

B) Is assignable if one-half of the other tenants agree and the court finds the assignment reasonable

C) Is assignable consistent with contract or other law protecting the mix of tenants

D) Is never assignable because of the third-party interests of other tenants affected by the assignment

E) Is not assignable because the lease cannot be assumed

75. T leased commercial real estate from L. By its terms, the lease terminates should T file bankruptcy. T filed Chapter 11 with five years remaining on the term of the lease. The debtor in possession proposes to assume the lease, assign it to A, and disclaim further responsibility for the lease upon the court's approval of the assumption and assignment.

A) The court can approve the entire package without L's agreement and without providing L any recourse should A breach the lease.

B) The court will never approve because the lease terminated upon T's bankruptcy.

C) The court can approve the assumption and assignment but not the disclaimer of liability.

D) The court can approve the entire package if L is allowed a contingent claim against the estate.

E) The court can approve the assumption but not the assignment without L's agreement.

Some Issues Mainly Under Chapter 7

76. The court can dismiss a Chapter 7 case when, by statutory formula, the debtor has sufficient:

A) Actual income

B) Current monthly income

C) Disposable income

D) Median family income

E) Taxable income

77. The reasons a court can dismiss a Chapter 7 case do not include:

A) Abuse of Chapter 7

B) Debtor's failure to pay fees

C) Prejudicial delay by the debtor

D) Solvency of the debtor

E) Sufficient income to fund a Chapter 13 plan

78. A debtor can redeem collateral under Chapter 7 when the debtor is an individual and the collateral is:

A) Real or personal property

B) Consumer goods not subject to a purchase money security interest

C) Consumer goods exempted under section 522

D) Worth less than the secured debt

E) Worth more than the secured debt

79. The trustee's principal duty in a Chapter 7 case is to:

A) Assure the debtor's compliance with disclosure and procedure

B) Avoid prepetition transfers

C) Identify creditors

D) Liquidate the estate

E) Operate any business of the debtor

80. In a Chapter 7 case, property of the estate is distributed to pay claims against the estate in this order:

A) Administrative expenses, domestic support claims, general unsecured claims

B) Domestic support claims, administrative expenses, unsecured claims

C) Domestic support claims, other priority claims, general unsecured claims

D) Priority claims, secured claims, unsecured claims

E) Secured claims, priority claims, unsecured claims

81. If there is insufficient estate property in a Chapter 7 case to pay all claims against a debtor that is a general partnership:

A) The case is dismissed.

B) The creditors share the deficiency pro rata.

C) The deficiency is discharged without regard to proportionality of loss.

D) The stay is lifted so creditors can initiate consistent proceedings under state law.

E) The trustee can pursue claims against general partners.

Some Issues Mainly Under Chapter 13

82. The main difference between the automatic stay in Chapter 7 and 13 cases is:

A) Nothing material

B) Protection of certain sureties

C) Lasts longer in Chapter 13 cases because the discharge is long delayed

D) Protects postpetition property in Chapter 13 cases

E) Reasons for relief

83. In a Chapter 13 case, property of the estate:

A) Is not important because debts are paid from future income

B) Is non-existent because possession of the property remains with the debtor

C) Includes property of the debtor's spouse

D) Includes property of the debtor's spouse or anyone else contributing to household income

E) Remains in possession of the debtor

84. Who can file a Chapter 13 plan?

A) Any person the court appoints

B) Debtor

C) Debtor or trustee

D) Debtor, trustee, or any party in interest

E) United States trustee

85. "Applicable commitment period" means the term or length of a Chapter 13 plan and is typically how many years?

A) Either one or two

B) Either two or three

C) Either three or four

D) Either three or five

E) Either four or five

86. A Chapter 13 plan must always provide for paying in full which of these obligations:

A) Car loans

B) Credit card debt

C) Student loans

D) Taxes

E) Unsecured claims for domestic support obligations

87. If a Chapter 13 plan provides for paying a secured claim in installments over the full term of the plan, the plan must also provide (absent the secured creditor's agreement) for paying interest on the claim calculated according to this method:

A) Cost of funds

B) Presumptive contract

C) Prime-plus formula

D) Reasonable calculation considering all circumstances

E) Replacement value

88. In a Chapter 13 case, if the Debtor's vehicle is subject to a non-purchase money perfected secured interest and the secured obligation far exceeds (by any measure) the value of the collateral, the value of the creditor's secured claim is determined by:

A) Amount reasonable debtor would have paid for the vehicle

B) Book value of the vehicle

C) Contract amount of obligation the vehicle secures

D) Replacement value of the vehicle

E) Wholesale value of the vehicle

89. In a Chapter 13 case, if the Debtor's vehicle is subject to a purchase money perfected secured interest created within two years of filing the bankruptcy petition and the secured obligation far exceeds (by any measure) the value of the collateral, the amount of the creditor's secured claim for cramming down a Chapter 13 plan is the value of the collateral determined by:

A) Amount reasonable debtor would have paid for the vehicle

B) Book value of the vehicle

C) Contract amount of obligation the vehicle secures

D) Replacement value of the vehicle

E) Wholesale value of the vehicle

90. What percentage of creditors must accept a Chapter 13 plan as a condition of confirmation?

A) 0 percent

B) 33 percent

C) 50 percent

D) 66 percent

E) 75 percent

91. For confirmation, a Chapter 13 plan must provide for paying (at a minimum) unsecured creditors who object to the plan:

A) Amounts provided by the contracts with creditors

B) Amounts they would have received if debtor had liquidated under Chapter 7

C) Debtor's projected disposable income during term ("commitment period") of the Chapter 13 plan

D) Nothing if secured claims are fully provided for

E) Reasonably equivalent value

92. In calculating a debtor's disposable income for the purpose of confirming a Chapter 13 plan, does the court consider the historical, actual, or future finances of the debtor?

A) The court considers only the debtor's historical finances.

B) The court considers only the debtor's future finances.

C) The court considers both historical and future finances of the debtor.

D) The court considers the debtor's actual finances at the time the case was filed.

E) The courts have disagreed whether the proper approach is to look at the debtor's financial history before filing bankruptcy, i.e., an historical approach, or the debtor's likely financial situation at and after confirmation, i.e., a forward-looking approach.

Some Issues Mainly Under Chapter 11

93. When is a trustee appointed in a Chapter 11 case?

    A) Never. The debtor in possession exercises the trustee's powers.

    B) Always. The debtor in possession operates the business and represents the debtor's interests, and the trustee represents the interests of creditors.

    C) Upon request of a party in interest or the United States trustee when there is cause

    D) Upon request of the debtor in possession when there is cause

    E) *Sua sponte* by the court when there is cause

94. The "period of exclusivity" in a Chapter 11 case refers to:

    A) Creditors circulating their plan

    B) Creditors voting on the plan

    C) Debtor's right to file a plan

    D) Protection of equity owners' claims and governing rights

    E) Quiet time before voting on plan

95. The debtor in possession can use cash collateral:

    A) If the interest of the secured creditor is adequately protected

    B) If there is a reasonable likelihood of an "effective reorganization"

    C) In the ordinary course of business

    D) Never

    E) To pay critical vendors

96. A debtor in possession operating the debtor's business can freely, on its own, obtain credit if:

    A) The credit is unsecured.

    B) The credit is secured.

    C) The credit, whether secured or unsecured, is obtained in the ordinary course of business.

    D) The credit is secured and the creditor's interest is adequately protected.

    E) The credit is secured by lien on otherwise unencumbered property of the estate.

97. A class of claims is deemed to have accepted a plan if the plan is accepted by:

A) All of the creditors in the class

B) A majority of the creditors in the class

C) At least two-thirds in amount and more than one-half in number of the allowed claims of such class held by creditors

D) At least two-thirds in amount and more than two-thirds in number of the allowed claims of such class held by creditors

E) At least one-half in amount and more than two-thirds in number of the allowed claims of such class held by creditors

98. Confirmation of a plan other than by "cram down" requires that:

A) A simple majority of impaired classes has accepted the plan.

B) All holders of impaired claims have accepted the plan.

C) All impaired classes of creditors have accepted the plan.

D) An extraordinary majority of impaired classes has accepted the plan.

E) Two-thirds of all classes have accepted the plan.

99. If the plan provides for equity holders retaining their interests, confirmation of the plan by "cram down" requires that:

A) All secured claims are paid in full.

B) All unsecured claims are paid in full.

C) All unsecured claims are paid not less than the amount that such holder would receive or retain if the debtor were liquidated under Chapter 7.

D) Confirmation is necessary for an effective reorganization.

E) Confirmation serves the best interests of creditors.

100. The "new value exception" is a possible exception to:

A) "Best interests of the creditors" test

B) Absolute priority rule

C) Avoidance of fraudulent transfer by corporate debtor

D) Period of exclusivity

E) Section 1111(b) election

BANKRUPTCY
MULTIPLE CHOICE
100 ANSWERS & ANALYSIS

BANKRUPTCY ANSWERS AND ANALYSIS

1. Issue: Who can be a debtor under Chapter 7

The correct answer is **D**. Any person can be a debtor under Chapter 7 except:

- a railroad;
- a domestic insurance company, bank, savings bank, cooperative bank, savings and loan association, building and loan association, homestead association, a New Markets Venture Capital company as defined in section 351 of the Small Business Investment Act of 1958, a small business investment company licensed by the Small Business Administration under section 301 of the Small Business Investment Act of 1958, credit union, or industrial bank or similar institution which is an insured bank as defined in section 3(h) of the Federal Deposit Insurance Act, except that an uninsured State member bank, or a corporation organized under section 25A of the Federal Reserve Act, which operates, or operates as, a multilateral clearing organization pursuant to section 409 of the Federal Deposit Insurance Corporation Improvement Act of 1991 may be a debtor if a petition is filed at the direction of the Board of Governors of the Federal Reserve System; or
- a foreign insurance company, engaged in such business in the United States, or a foreign bank, savings bank, cooperative bank, savings and loan association, building and loan association, or credit union, that has a branch or agency [by] . . . the International Banking Act of 1978 in the United States.

11 U.S.C. §109(b).

2. Issue: Who can be a debtor under Chapter 13

The correct answer is **D**. Only an individual with regular income may be a debtor under Chapter 13 and only if the individual "owes, on the date of the filing of the petition, noncontingent, liquidated, unsecured debts of less than $250,000 and noncontingent, liquidated, secured debts of less than $750,000, or an individual with regular income and such individual's spouse, except a stockbroker or a commodity broker, that owe, on the date of the filing of the petition, noncontingent, liquidated, unsecured debts that aggregate less than $250,000 and noncontingent, liquidated, secured debts of less than $750,000. . . ." 11 U.S.C. §109(e).

3. Issue: Requirements to file Chapter 7

The correct answer is **D**. "[O]nly a person that resides or has a domicile, a place of business, or property in the United States, or a municipality, may be a debtor under this title." 11 U.S.C. §109(a). A credit counseling briefing is required of "individual" debtors, but not all debtors. *Id.* §109(h).

4. Issue: Individual with regular income

The correct answer is **B**. Chapter 13 is limited to individuals with a "regular income." The Code defines "individual with regular income" to mean: "individual whose income is sufficiently stable and regular to enable such individual to make payments under a plan under chapter 13 of this title, other than a stockbroker or a commodity broker." 11 U.S.C. §101(30). "[T]he Bankruptcy Code does not specifically exclude any source of funding from the regular income calculus; the Code does require that whatever source of income is claimed by a debtor, it must be regular and stable enough to fund a plan. The stable and regular focus of §101(30) has led several courts to state that 'the test for "regular income" is not the type or source of income, but rather its regularity and stability.' " In re Murphy, 226 B.R. 601, 604 (Bankr. M.D. Tenn. 1998).

5. Issue: Who can be a debtor under Chapter 11

The correct answer is **C**. "Any person that may be a debtor under chapter 7 of this title (except a stockbroker or a commodity broker) can also be a debtor under Chapter 11 and also a railroad and an uninsured State member bank, or a corporation organized under section 25A of the Federal Reserve Act, which operates, or operates as, a multilateral clearing organization pursuant to section 409 of the Federal Deposit Insurance Corporation Improvement Act of 1991." 11 U.S.C. §109(d).

6. Issue: Involuntary cases

The correct answer is **B**. "An involuntary case may be commenced only under chapter 7 or 11 of this title, and only against a person, except a farmer, family farmer, or a corporation that is not a moneyed, business, or commercial corporation, that may be a debtor under the chapter under which such case is commenced." 11 U.S.C. §303(a).

7. Issue: Original jurisdiction of bankruptcy cases

The correct answer is **C**. "[T]he [federal] district courts shall have original and exclusive jurisdiction of all cases under title 11 [i.e., the Bankruptcy Code]." 28 U.S.C. §1334(a). The district courts may, in turn, refer "any or all proceedings arising under title 11 or arising in or related to a case under title 11 . . . to the bankruptcy judges for the district." 28 U.S.C. §157(a).

8. Issue: Jurisdiction over proceedings in bankruptcy cases

The correct answer is **B**. All of the other disputes are beyond bankruptcy's jurisdiction of proceedings, which is limited to "civil proceedings *arising under* title 11, or *arising in* or *related to* cases under title 11." 28 U.S.C. §1334(b) (emphasis added). "The jurisdiction of the bankruptcy courts, like that of other federal courts, is grounded in, and limited by, statute. Title 28 U.S.C. §1334(b) provides that 'the district courts shall have original but not exclusive jurisdiction of all civil proceedings arising under title 11, or arising in or related to cases under title 11.' The district courts may, in turn, refer 'any or all proceedings arising under title 11 or arising in or related to a case under title 11 . . . to the bankruptcy judges for the district.' 28 U.S.C. §157(a)." Celotex Corp. v. Edwards, 514 U.S. 300, 307 (1995).

"A proceeding 'arises under' title 11 if a claim asserted is created by or based on a provision of the bankruptcy code. An action by a trustee under an avoiding power would be a proceeding arising under title 11, because the trustee would be acting based on a right conferred by the bankruptcy code. A proceeding 'arises in' a case under title 11 if it is not based on any right expressly created by the bankruptcy code but has no existence outside the bankruptcy case. Examples of 'arising in' would be allowance or disallowance of a claim, orders in respect to obtaining credit, confirmation of plans, and orders permitting the assumption or rejection of contracts. . . . [T]he test for determining whether a civil proceeding is 'related to' a case under title 11 is whether the outcome of that proceeding could conceivably have any effect on the estate being administered in bankruptcy. An action is related to bankruptcy if the outcome could alter the debtor's rights, liabilities, options, or freedom of action, and which in any way impacts upon the handling and administration of the bankruptcy estate." In re Grubbs Const. Co., 305 B.R. 476, 480 (Bankr. W.D. Ark. 2003).

"[T]he 'related to' language of §1334(b) must be read to give district courts (and bankruptcy courts . . .) jurisdiction over more than simple proceedings involving the property of the debtor or the estate, . . . [but] . . . a bankruptcy court's 'related to' jurisdiction cannot be limitless." Celotex Corp. v. Edwards, 514 U.S. 300, 308 (1995). "Proceedings 'related to' the bankruptcy include (1) causes of action owned by the debtor which become property of the estate pursuant to 11 U.S.C. §541, and (2) suits between third parties which have an effect on the bankruptcy estate. . . . 'The usual articulation of the test for determining whether a civil proceeding is related to bankruptcy is whether *the outcome of that proceeding could conceivably have any effect on the estate being administered in bankruptcy*. . . . Thus, the proceeding need not necessarily be against the debtor or against the debtor's property. An action is related to bankruptcy if the outcome could alter the debtor's rights, liabilities, options, or freedom of action (either positively or negatively) and which in any way impacts upon the handling and administration of the bankrupt estate.' " *Id.* at 308 nn.5-6 (emphasis in original), quoting Pacor, Inc. v. Higgins, 743 F.2d 984, 994 (3d Cir. 1984).

9. Issue: Venue of individual's bankruptcy case

The correct answer is **D**. A case under title 11 may be commenced in the district court for the district—

> (1) in which the domicile, residence, principal place of business in the United States, or principal assets in the United States, of the person or entity that is the subject of such case have been located for the one hundred and eighty days immediately preceding such commencement, or for a longer portion of such one-hundred-and-eighty-day period than

the domicile, residence, or principal place of business, in the United States, or principal assets in the United States, of such person were located in any other district; or

(2) in which there is pending a case under title 11 concerning such person's affiliate, general partner, or partnership.

28 U.S.C. §1408(1). D was domiciled in New York for the entire 180-day period but also resided in South Dakota for the longest portion of the period.

10. Issue: Venue of corporation's bankruptcy case

The correct answer is **C**. "Section 1408 provides that a district is a proper venue if [the debtor's domicile, residence, principal place of business] or principal assets of the debtor are located in that district. 28 U.S.C. §1408[(1)]. The . . . statute [does not] require[] that assets be concentrated in one district for principal assets to be located in that district. Instead, . . . a debtor's principal assets can be located in several different districts because '[t]he venue statute does not require that only the principal asset may support venue; rather, venue may be proper in a district where principal assets are located. Thus, a debtor may have more than one appropriate venue based upon more than one principal asset.'" In re Mid Atlantic Retail Group, Inc., 2008 WL 612287 *1, 3 (Bankr. M.D.N.C. 2008), and based also on the debtor's domicile, residence, or principal place of business.

11. Issue: Commencement of voluntary case

The correct answer is **E**. "A voluntary case under a chapter of this title is commenced by the filing with the bankruptcy court of a petition under such chapter by an entity that may be a debtor under such chapter." 11 U.S.C. §301(a).

12. Issue: What documents are filed

The correct answer is **A**. The other documents that a debtor files include:

- a list of creditors;
- a schedule of assets and liabilities;
- a schedule of current income and current expenditures;
- a statement of the debtor's financial affairs;
- copies of all payment advices or other evidence of payment received within 60 days before the date of the filing of the petition, by the debtor from any employer of the debtor;
- a statement of the amount of monthly net income, itemized to show how the amount is calculated; and
- a statement disclosing any reasonably anticipated increase in income or expenditures over the 12-month period following the date of the filing of the petition.

11 U.S.C. §521(a).

13. Issue: Dismissal under Chapter 7

The correct answer is **B**. The court cannot grant the debtor a discharge if the debtor was discharged in an earlier case commenced within eight years before the date of the filing of the petition in the present case. 11 U.S.C. §727(a)(8). However, the discharge in the earlier case is not the basis for dismissing the present case, though the benefits of the present case are reduced because a discharge is not possible.

14. Issue: When automatic stay arises

The correct answer is **E**. "[A] petition filed under [the Bankruptcy Code] operates as a stay. . . ." 11 U.S.C. §362(a).

15. Issue: Conduct against which the automatic stay operates

The correct answer is **A**. In a Chapter 7 case, the stay prevents creating, perfecting, or enforcing ANY LIEN against PROPERTY OF THE ESTATE, 11 U.S.C. §362(a)(4); but, with respect to PROPERTY OF THE DEBTOR, the stay prevents creating, perfecting, or enforcing only LIENS FOR PREPE-TITION DEBTS. 11 U.S.C. §362(a)(5). Property of the debtor is not protected against postpetition liens. Compare *id*. §§1115(a); 1306(a).

16. Issue: Whom the automatic stay protects in Chapter 7 cases

The correct answer is **A**. In a Chapter 7 case, the stay protects the debtor and the bankruptcy estate, not persons who are nondebtors. Sometimes, however, in the proper circumstances, a bankruptcy court in any case will separately issue an injunction to prevent creditors' actions to collect from people who guaranteed or otherwise insured the debtor's obligations. 11 U.S.C. §105(a). And, in Chapter 13 cases, the Bankruptcy Code explicitly extends the protection of the stay to certain sureties liable on the debtor on consumer debts. *Id*. §1301(a).

17. Issue: When the automatic stay ends

The correct answer is **D**. Except for the stay of an act against property of the estate, the stay of any other act continues until the earliest of—

> "(A) the time the case is closed;
> (B) the time the case is dismissed; or
> (C) if the case is a case under chapter 7 of this title concerning an individual or a case under chapter 9, 11, 12, or 13 of this title, the time a discharge is granted or denied."

11 U.S.C. §362(c)(2). In the typical individual Chapter 7 case, the case is not dismissed, the debtor gets a discharge, and then the case is closed. So, in such a case, the stay ends upon discharge.

18. Issue: Consequence of actions that violate the stay

The correct answer is **E**. The Bankruptcy Code does not say so, but the courts do. The courts disagree, however, whether an action that violates the stay is void or only voidable. Usually, it makes no real difference.

19. Issue: Damages for violation of the stay

The correct answer is **D**. "[A]n individual injured by any willful violation of a stay provided by this section shall recover actual damages, including costs and attorneys' fees, and, in appropriate circumstances, may recover punitive damages." 11 U.S.C. §362(k)(1).

20. Issue: Whom the stay protects in Chapter 13 cases

The correct answer is **C**. Section 362(a) applies in Chapter 13 cases, but in these cases section 1301 adds this further protection that is not part of section 362(a): "[A] creditor may not act, or commence or continue any civil action, to collect all or any part of a consumer debt of the debtor from any individual that is liable on such debt with the debtor, or that secured such debt, unless . . . such individual became liable on or secured such debt in the ordinary course of such individual's business. . . ." 11 U.S.C. §1301(a).

21. Issue: Injunction favoring nondebtors under section 105 (11 U.S.C. §105(a))

The correct answer is **A**. "Section 362 of the Bankruptcy Code embodies the automatic stay, which immediately applies when a debtor files a bankruptcy petition and is designed to preclude a variety of post-petition actions — both judicial and non-judicial — against the debtor or affecting property of the estate. The automatic stay is fundamental to bankruptcy law. It ensures that claims against the debtor will be brought in one place, the bankruptcy court. The stay protects the debtor by giving it room to breathe and, thereby, hopefully to reorganize. The stay also protects creditors as a group from any one creditor who might otherwise seek to obtain payment on its claims to the others' detriment.

"As a general rule, the automatic stay protects *only* the debtor, property of the debtor or property of the estate. The stay does not protect non-debtor parties or their property. . . . However, if the liability of the non-debtor party *were* to affect the property of the bankruptcy estate . . . it may be necessary for the plaintiff in such a case to proceed against the non-debtor party through [the] bankruptcy proceedings [and be stopped from proceeding in another court].

"Even then, the bankruptcy court would first need to [supplement] . . . the automatic stay under its equity jurisdiction. '[S]uch extensions, although referred to as extensions of the automatic stay, [are] in fact injunctions issued by the bankruptcy court after hearing and the establishment of unusual need to take this action to protect the administration of the bankruptcy estate.' See also 11 U.S.C. §105 (providing the bankruptcy court's power to "issue any order, process, or judgment that is necessary or appropriate to carry out the provisions of this title"). . . ." Boucher v. Shaw, 572 F.3d 1087, 1093 & n.3 (9th Cir. 2009).

22. Issue: Lift stay in Chapter 7 case

The correct answer is **D**. "On request of a party in interest and after notice and a hearing, the court shall grant relief from the stay provided under subsection (a) of this section, such as by terminating, annulling, modifying, or conditioning such stay . . . with respect to a stay of an act against property under subsection (a) of this section, if— . . . *the debtor does not have an equity in such property.* . . ." 11 U.S.C.A. §362(d)(2)(A) (emphasis added). The interest must be perfected or otherwise the trustee can and will avoid it. *Id.* §544.

23. Issue: Lift stay in Chapter 11 case

The correct answer is **D**. In this case, the debtor not having equity in the property is not a sufficient reason to lift stay if the property is necessary for a successful reorganization, 11 U.S.C. §362(d)(2), which it usually is. In this event, the only reason to lift stay is "cause," *Id.* §362(d)(1), such as the lack of adequate protection of the creditor's interest in the collateral. If the interest isn't adequately protected so that the value of the collateral will erode and thereby reduce the creditor's interest, the secured party is entitled to lift stay.

24. Issue: More on lift stay in Chapter 11 case

The correct answer is **B**. There is "cause" to lift stay because the creditor's interest, i.e., its secured claim, will shrink because of the decline in the value of the collateral. 11 U.S.C. §362(d)(2).

25. Issue: Allowing claims

The correct answer is **D**. "A claim or interest, proof of which is filed under section 501 of this title, is deemed allowed, unless a party in interest, including a creditor of a general partner in a partnership that is a debtor in a case under chapter 7 of this title, objects." 11 U.S.C. §502(a).

26. Issue: Unsecured creditor not filing claim

The correct answer is **D**. The general, unsecured claims that are paid from the estate are *allowed* claims. 11 U.S.C. §726(a). A claim is not allowed if not filed by the creditor or someone else whom the statute authorizes. *Id.* §§502(a); 501. Nevertheless, the claim is discharged unless otherwise excepted from discharge. "[A] discharge . . . discharges the debtor from all debts that arose before the date of the order for relief under this chapter, and any liability on a claim that is determined under section 502 of this title as if such claim had arisen before the commencement of the case, whether or not a proof of claim based on any such debt or liability is filed under section 501 of this title, and whether or not a claim based on any such debt or liability is allowed under section 502 of this title." 11 U.S.C. §727(b).

27. Issue: Secured creditor not filing claim

The correct answer is **E**. Discharge works against a debtor's personal liability to a creditor, not a secured creditor's interest in property. Generally, a creditor's lien or other interest that backs a secured claim is substantively unaffected by bankruptcy. And, secured claims are not paid from the estate. The creditor's interest rides through the bankruptcy unaffected and can be enforced after the automatic stay ends, unless the interest is avoided by the trustee asserting the avoiding powers of Chapter 5.

28. Issue: Debtor omitting creditor

The correct answer is **B**. The creditor's claim is excepted from the discharge. 11 U.S.C. §523(a)(3).

29. Issue: Undersecured claim

The correct answer is **E**. "An allowed claim of a creditor secured by a lien on property in which the estate has an interest . . . is a secured claim to the extent of the value of such creditor's interest in the estate's interest in such property . . . and is an unsecured claim to the extent that the value of such creditor's interest or the amount so subject to setoff is less than the amount of such allowed claim. . . ." 11 U.S.C. §506(a)(1).

30. Issue: Size of secured claim

The correct answer is **D**. A secured claim is limited to the amount of the debt or the value of the collateral, whichever is less. 11 U.S.C. §506(a)(1).

31. Issue: Spendthrift trust and bankruptcy estate

The correct answer is **A**. The Bankruptcy Code provides: "A restriction on the transfer of a beneficial interest of the debtor in a trust that is enforceable under applicable nonbankruptcy law is enforceable in a case under this title." 11 U.S.C. §541(c)(2). In this problem, none of the debtor's rights are alienable under state law. Thus, the debtor's rights cannot be alienated by transfer to the bankruptcy estate. So, the principal and right to payments are excluded from the estate. However, payments already distributed to the debtor are not excluded from the estate. They are included.

32. Issue: Self-settled trust and bankruptcy estate

The correct answer is **E**. The answer depends on whether the debtor's rights are alienable or inalienable under state law, but most states do not enforce and protect from creditors a trust the debtor creates for herself.

33. Issue: Property excluded from the bankruptcy estate

The correct answer is **E**. Typically, such a retirement account is completely inalienable under federal law. Therefore, the account does not become part of the bankruptcy estate because of section 541(c)(2), which provides that "a restriction on the transfer of a beneficial interest of the debtor in a trust that is enforceable under applicable nonbankruptcy law [including nonbankruptcy federal law] is enforceable in a case under this title." 11 U.S.C. §541(c)(2); Patterson v. Shumate, 504 U.S. 753 (1992).

34. Issue: Postpetition property and property of the Chapter 7 estate

The correct answer is **B**. The bankruptcy estate includes "[a]ny interest in property that would have been property of the estate if such interest had been an interest of the debtor on the date of the filing of the petition, and that the debtor acquires or becomes entitled to acquire within 180 days after such date . . . by bequest, devise, or inheritance. . . ." 11 U.S.C. §541(a)(5)(A).

35. Issue: Postpetition property again in a Chapter 7 case

The correct answer is **B**. All of the other property is "[p]roceeds, product, offspring, rents, or profits of or from property of the estate" and does become property of the estate even though the proceeds or profits were received after bankruptcy was filed. 11 U.S.C. §541(a)(6). The right to the dividends, right to the lottery jackpot, the right to the past-due account, and right to the last-period salary were prepetition property that became part of the estate. The proceeds or profits of the property are also included in the estate even though postpetition property.

36. Issue: Property of the estate in a Chapter 13 case

The correct answer is **A**. "Except as provided in a confirmed plan or order confirming a plan, the debtor shall remain in possession of all property of the estate." 11 U.S.C. §1306(b). The same is true in Chapter 11 cases. *Id.* §1115(b).

37. Issue: Source of exemption law

The correct answer is **A**. "[A]n individual debtor may exempt from property of the estate the property listed in either paragraph (2) [which is a set of federal bankruptcy exemptions] or, in the alternative, paragraph (3) of this subsection [which are exemptions provided by applicable, nonbankruptcy federal law and state law]," 11 U.S.C. §522(b)(1), "unless the State law that is applicable to the debtor . . . specifically does not so authorize." *Id.* §522(b)(2). So, basically, the debtor gets a choice between federal bankruptcy exemptions or state/non-bankruptcy federal law exemptions unless the state has enacted legislation providing that bankruptcy debtors cannot elect the federal bankruptcy exemptions, which is called "opting out." Most states have opted out.

38. Issue: Choice of state law

The correct answer is **C**. The state law that applies is the "state or local law that is applicable on the date of the filing of the petition at the place in which the debtor's domicile has been located for the 730 days immediately preceding the date of the filing of the petition or if the debtor's domicile has not been located at a single State for such 730-day period, the place in which the debtor's domicile was located for 180 days immediately preceding the 730-day period or for a longer portion of such 180-day period than in any other place. . . ." 11 U.S.C. §522(3)(A). The key to the problem is this language: "if the debtor's domicile has not been located at a single State for . . . [the] 730-day period [immediately preceding the date of the filing of the petition], the [state or local law that is applicable is the] place in which the debtor's domicile was located for 180 days immediately preceding the 730-day period or for a longer portion of such 180-day period than in any other place." Debtor did not live in a single state for the 730-day period. So, the governing law is the law of the state in which the debtor was domiciled for 180 days before the 730-day period, which is Florida.

39. Issue: Federal cap on homestead exemption

The correct answer is **B**. When the debtor's homestead exemption is based on state law, a federal limit or cap applies: "a debtor may not exempt any amount of interest [in a homestead] that was acquired by the debtor during the 1215-day period preceding the date of the filing of the petition that exceeds in the aggregate $125,000 in value. . . ." 11 U.S.C. §522(p). In the absence of this cap, the debtor's homestead exemption is $350,000. If the cap applies, the exemption is limited to $125,000. The debtor had owned the land before the beginning of the 1215-day period, but the property did not become a homestead until the debtor moved there, which was within the period. So, the issue is did the debtor acquire the interest in the homestead, for purposes of section 522(p), within the period or outside of it. "[T]he most plausible interpretation of Section 522(p)(1) is that the act of recording a homestead or moving onto the property to establish residency is not an 'amount of interest acquired' for purposes of applying the monetary cap in Section 522(p)." In re Green, 583 F.3d 614, 623 (9th Cir. 2009). Therefore, "Section 522(p) does not limit the homestead exemption that can be claimed under state law if the debtor owned the property before the 1215 day period. . . ." *Id.* at 621.

40. Issue: Federal cap on homestead exemption again

The correct answer is **A** (but the answer may change). Increasing equity by paying down a mortgage is not acquiring an interest for purposes of the federal homestead cap set by section 522(b) [11 U.S.C. §522(p)]. So, the cap is not applicable. "[O]ne does not actually 'acquire' equity in a home. One acquires title to a home. The Debtors acquired title and fee to their home . . . one and half years prior to the start of the 1215 day period applicable to their bankruptcy case. The 'interest' the Debtors acquired was the actual purchase of the home, which was completed well before the 1215-day period. Thus, the 'interest' held by the debtors in their homestead is outside the 1215-day period and not subject to the $125,000 cap." In re Blair, 334 B.R. 374, 376-77 (Bankr. N.D. Tex. 2005). "[T]he increase in the value of the equity in the debtors' homestead, which was acquired over 1215 days prior to the Petition Date, is not subject to the $125,000 cap in section 522(p)." *Id.* at 378. But see Parks v. Anderson, 406 B.R. 79, 95 (D. Kan. 2009) ("[T]he term 'interest,' as used within §522(p), refers to equity acquired by a debtor within the 1,215-day period prior to filing bankruptcy. As a result, a debtor may not exempt equity acquired in a homestead during the 1,215-day period prior to filing bankruptcy that exceeds in the aggregate $125,000.").

41. Issue: Avoiding judicial liens on exempt property

The correct answer is **C**. In many states, the debtor's interest in exempt property is shielded against judicial liens. Therefore, the lien in this problem would not have attached to the debtor's interest in the vehicle. However, where and when the lien does attach, the debtor "may avoid the fixing of a [judicial] lien on an interest of the debtor in property to the extent that such lien impairs an exemption to which the debtor would have been entitled. . . ." 11 U.S.C.

§522(f)(1)(A). Doing so would in the problem free the debtor's interest ($5,000) of the lien to the extent of the exemption, and the debtor could exempt the property. Security interests cannot be avoided under section 522(f), except a nonpossessory, non-purchase money interest in a few categories of goods. *Id.* §522(f)(1)(B).

42. Issue: Avoiding security interests in exempt property

The correct answer is **C**. Ordinarily, under nonbankruptcy law, exemptions are not effective against UCC Article 9 security interests or other consensual liens. However, the debtor may avoid the fixing of a lien on an interest of the debtor in property to the extent that such lien impairs an exemption to which the debtor would have been entitled if such lien is "a nonpossessory, non-purchase-money security interest in any —

- household furnishings, household goods, wearing apparel, appliances, books, animals, crops, musical instruments, or jewelry that are held primarily for the personal, family, or household use of the debtor or a dependent of the debtor;
- implements, professional books, or tools, of the trade of the debtor or the trade of a dependent of the debtor; or
- professionally prescribed health aids for the debtor or a dependent of the debtor."

11 U.S.C. §522(f)(1)(B).

43. Issue: Converting nonexempt property to exempt property

The correct answer is **E**. Generally speaking, "absent extrinsic evidence of fraud, mere conversion of non-exempt property to exempt property is not fraudulent as to creditors even if the motivation behind the conversion is to place those assets beyond the reach of creditors." In re Tveten, 848 F.2d 871, 874 (8th Cir. 1988). Actual fraud beyond the fact of the conversion itself must be proved.

44. Issue: Nature or effect of discharge

The correct answer is **A**. Mainly, a discharge "operates as an injunction against the commencement or continuation of an action, the employment of process, or an act, to collect, recover or offset any such debt as a personal liability of the debtor, whether or not discharge of such debt is waived. . . ." 11 U.S.C. §523(a)(2); see also *id.* §524(a)(2). It does not actually extinguish the liability. The other statements in the problem are incorrect.

45. Issue: Nature or effect of discharge again

The correct answer is **B**. The discharge enjoins action to collect personal liability, not conduct to enforce a third party's lien or other interest. However, the lien is enforceable only to the extent of the collateral's value. The creditor cannot take any action to collect any deficiency. Dewsnup v. Timm, 502 U.S. 410, 419 (1992) (as a rule, liens survive bankruptcy); Johnson v. Home State

Bank, 501 U.S. 78, 82-84 (1991) (unavoided liens survive bankruptcy, and lienholders may, pursuant to applicable state-law procedure, enforce them against the debtor's property after the bankruptcy case is closed).

46. Issue: Effect of violating discharge

The correct answer is **C**. The Bankruptcy Code "does not include an explicit enforcement mechanism [for violation of the discharge], but §105 of the Bankruptcy Code plainly provides the statutory authority, as the powers granted in that section authorize the courts to 'issue any order, process, or judgment that is necessary or appropriate to carry out the provisions of this title.'" 11 U.S.C. §105. "There is no serious question that a violation of the discharge . . . is punishable by contempt." In re Nassoko, 405 B.R. 515, 520 (Bankr. S.D.N.Y. 2009).

"Willful violation of the . . . [discharge] injunction warrants the finding of contempt. To find a creditor in civil contempt the court must find that the offending party knowingly violated a definite and specific court order. The burden . . . is on the Debtors to prove the violation by clear and convincing evidence. This Court can impose upon a creditor who violates the . . . injunction sanctions for civil contempt, which may consist of remedial and compensatory, but not punitive, sanctions.

"Other courts have long held that where a creditor has failed to comply with an order of discharge, civil contempt is a sanction to enforce compliance with an order of the court or to compensate for losses or damages sustained by reason of noncompliance. Civil contempt is therefore an appropriate sanction for a creditor's noncompliance with or violation of the Court's order of discharge.

"Knowledge of the discharge order and knowingly violating it are necessary requirements for contempt. A party's negligence or absence of intent to violate the discharge order is not a defense against a motion for contempt." In re Jarvar, 422 B.R. 242, 250 (Bankr. D. Mont. 2009).

47. Issue: Discharge and nondebtor parties

The correct answer is **E**. "[On] [t]he question whether a bankruptcy court can release a non-debtor from creditor liability over the objections of the creditor is one of first impression in this circuit. . . . [T]he [other] circuits . . . have set out a variety of approaches. Some have held that a non-consensual release of liability violates the bankruptcy code and is thus beyond the power of the bankruptcy court. Others permit the releases but have splintered on the governing standard.

"The nub of the circuits' disagreement concerns two interrelated questions. . . . The first is whether §524(e) of the bankruptcy code bars a bankruptcy court from releasing non-debtors from liability to a creditor without the creditor's consent. Section 524(e) provides that the 'discharge of a debt of the debtor does not affect the liability of another entity on, or the property of any other entity for, such debt.' 11 U.S.C. §524(e). The natural reading of this provision does not foreclose a third-party release from a creditor's claims. Section 524(e) is a saving clause; it limits the operation of other parts of the bankruptcy code and preserves rights that might otherwise be construed as lost after the reorganization. Thus, for example, because of §524, a creditor can still seek to collect a debt from a co-debtor who did not participate in the reorganization — even if that debt was discharged as to the debtor in the plan. Or a third party could proceed against the debtor's insurer or guarantor for liabilities incurred by the debtor even if the debtor cannot be held liable.

"In any event, §524(e) does not purport to limit the bankruptcy court's powers to release a non-debtor from a creditor's claims. If Congress meant to include such a limit, it would have used the mandatory terms 'shall' or 'will' rather than the definitional term 'does.' And it would have omitted the prepositional phrase 'on, or . . . for, such debt,' ensuring that the 'discharge of a debt of the debtor *shall* not affect the liability of another entity' — whether related to a debt or not. Also, where Congress has limited the powers of the bankruptcy court, it has done so clearly — for example, by expressly limiting the court's power. As a result, . . . §524(e) does not bar a non-consensual third-party release from liability.

"The second related question dividing the circuits is whether Congress affirmatively gave the bankruptcy court the power to release third parties from a creditor's claims without the creditor's consent, even if §524(e) does not expressly preclude the releases. A bankruptcy court 'appl[ies] the principles and rules of equity jurisprudence,' and its equitable powers are traditionally broad. Section 105(a) codifies this understanding of the bankruptcy court's powers by giving it the authority to effect any 'necessary or appropriate' order to carry out the provisions of the bankruptcy code. 11 U.S.C. §105(a). And a bankruptcy court is also able to exercise these broad equitable powers within the plans of reorganization themselves. Section 1123(b)(6) permits a court to 'include any other appropriate provision not inconsistent with the applicable provisions of this title.' 11 U.S.C. §1123(b)(6). In light of these provisions, we hold that this 'residual authority' permits the bankruptcy court to release third parties from liability to participating creditors if the release is 'appropriate' and not inconsistent with any provision of the bankruptcy code.

". . . Ultimately, whether a release is 'appropriate' for the reorganization is fact intensive and depends on the nature of the reorganization. [A release is appropriate when it is] . . . necessary for the reorganization and appropriately tailored [i.e.,] is narrow: it applies only to claims "arising out of or in connection with" the reorganization itself and does not include 'willful misconduct' [and] . . . is not 'blanket immunity' for all times, all transgressions, and all omissions. . . . [T]he immunity [does not] affect matters beyond the jurisdiction of the bankruptcy court or unrelated to the reorganization itself. . . . [And] the limitation is subject to the other provisions of the plan. . . ." In re Airadigm Communications, Inc., 519 F.3d 640, 65-57 (7th Cir. 2008).

"[But] [a] nondebtor release should only be approved in 'rare cases' . . . In most instances, releases . . . will not pass muster. . . ." In re Ingersoll, Inc., 562 F.3d 856, 865 (7th Cir. 2009).

The bottom line is that typically and usually, "a bankruptcy court only has jurisdiction to enjoin third-party non-debtor claims that directly affect the *res* of the bankruptcy estate." In re Johns-Manville Corp., 517 F.3d 52, 6 (2d Cir. 2008), rev'd on other grounds sub nom. Travelers Indem. Co. v. Bailey, 129 S. Ct. 2195 (2009).

48. Issue: Discharge and discrimination

The correct answer is **A**. "No private employer may terminate the *employment* of, or discriminate with respect to *employment* against, an individual who is or has been a debtor under this title, a debtor or bankrupt under the Bankruptcy Act, or an individual associated with such debtor or bankrupt, solely because such debtor or bankrupt — (1) is or has been a debtor under this title or a debtor or bankrupt under the Bankruptcy Act; (2) has been insolvent before the commencement of a case under this title or during the case but before the grant or denial of a discharge; or (3) has not paid a debt that is dischargeable in a case under this title or that was discharged under the Bankruptcy Act." 11 U.S.C. 525(b) (emphasis added).

49. Issue: Discharge of "debt" or "claim"

The correct answer is **E**. A Chapter 7 discharge "discharges the debtor from all *debts* that arose before the date of the order for relief. . . ." 11 U.S.C. §727(b) (emphasis added). "Debt" is "liability on a *claim*." *Id.* §101(12) (emphasis added). "Claim" is a . . . right to payment, whether or not such right is reduced to judgment, liquidated, unliquidated, fixed, contingent, matured, unmatured, disputed, undisputed, legal, equitable, secured, or unsecured; or . . . right to an equitable remedy for breach of performance if such breach gives rise to a right to payment. . . ." *Id.* §101(5). A court order personally directing a debtor to clean up is not a right to payment, is not a claim, is not a debt, and is not discharged, unless the order is converted into a personal obligation to pay money for the clean-up. Ohio v. Kovacs, 469 U.S. 274 (1985).

50. Issue: Debts excepted from discharge

The correct answer is **D**. Section 523 describes debts from which an individual is not discharged. None of the debts listed in this question, as such, is discharged except a "domestic support obligation." 11 U.S.C. §523(a)(5). Such an obligation means a debt in the nature of alimony, maintenance, or support (including assistance provided by a governmental unit) of such spouse, former spouse, or child of the debtor or such child's parent. 11 U.S.C. §101(14A).

51. Issue: Objection to discharge

The correct answer is **B**. Section 727 describes circumstances under which a debtor is completely denied a discharge in Chapter 7 cases, that is, none of her debts are discharged. 11 U.S.C. §727(a). These circumstances are called "objections" to discharge. None of the circumstances described in this question is the basis for an objection to discharge, except that "the debtor is not an individual." *Id.* §727(a)(1). "Individual" means natural person. In Chapter 11, however, corporate debtors are discharged.

52. Issue: Avoiding prepetition security interest under section 544

The correct answer is **B**. As of the commencement of the bankruptcy case, and without regard to any knowledge of the trustee or of any creditor, the trustee is deemed by federal law to have the rights and powers of, or may avoid any transfer of property of the debtor or any obligation incurred by the debtor that is voidable by—

- a creditor that extends credit to the debtor at the time of the commencement of the case, and that obtains, at such time and with respect to such credit, a judicial lien on all property on which a creditor on a simple contract could have obtained such a judicial lien, whether or not such a creditor exists;
- a creditor that extends credit to the debtor at the time of the commencement of the case, and obtains, at such time and with respect to such credit, an execution against the debtor that is returned unsatisfied at such time, whether or not such a creditor exists; or a bona fide purchaser of real property, other than fixtures, from the debtor, against whom applicable law permits such transfer to be perfected, that obtains the status of a bona fide purchaser and has perfected such transfer at the time of the commencement of the case, whether or not such a purchaser exists.

11 U.S.C. §544(a)(1)–(2). Under state law, an unperfected security interest is trumped by the rights of a person who becomes a lien creditor before the security interest is perfected. UCC §9-317(a)(2). A "lien creditor" is a person who acquires a lien by attachment, levy, or the like, as by judgment or execution. So, in this case, if the Bank's interest was not perfected before the debtor filed bankruptcy, the trustee as lien creditor would have priority under state law and could therefore fully avoid the security interest under section 544(a). In bankruptcy, it is not just that the trustee has priority to some extent. Rather, if a lien creditor would have priority to any extent under state law, the trustee completely eliminates the security interest under bankruptcy law. Moore v. Bay, 284 U.S. 4 (1931).

53. Issue: Avoiding prepetition purchase money security interest under section 544

The correct answer is **C** and is different from the answer to Question 52 because, in this case, the security interest is a purchase money security interest. Under state law, in the case of a purchase money security interest, if a secured party perfects by filing a financing statement with respect to the purchase money security interest before or within 20 days after the debtor receives delivery of the collateral, the security interest takes priority over the rights of a lien creditor which arise between the time the security interest attaches and the time of filing. UCC 9-317(e). The Bankruptcy Code recognizes this leeway by denying the trustee the right to avoid a purchase money security interest that is perfected after bankruptcy is filed by the secured party's compliance with section 9-317(e). 11 U.S.C. §546(b). In this case, perfecting after bankruptcy is filed does not violate the automatic stay, which provides an exception for "any act to perfect, or to maintain or continue the perfection of, an interest in property to the extent that the trustee's rights and powers are subject to such perfection under section 546(b) of this title or to the extent that such act is accomplished within the period provided under [the applicable nonbankruptcy law and] section 547(e)(2)(A). . . ." 11 U.S.C. §362(b)(3).

54. Issue: Avoiding prepetition sale of house under section 544

The correct answer is **B**. As of the commencement of the bankruptcy case, and without regard to any knowledge of the trustee or of any creditor, the trustee is deemed by federal law to have the rights and powers of, or may avoid any transfer of property of the debtor or any obligation incurred by the debtor that is voidable by, "a bona fide purchaser of real property, other than fixtures, from the debtor, against whom applicable law permits such transfer to be perfected, that obtains the status of a bona fide purchaser and has perfected such transfer at the time of the commencement of the case, whether or not such a purchaser exists." 11 U.S.C. §544(a)(3). Under state law, an unrecorded conveyance of real estate is void against a good faith purchaser of the property. So, relying on this state law and asserting the rights of such a purchaser, the trustee can rely on section 544(a)(3) to avoid the unrecorded conveyance of the vacation house to B, without regard to any knowledge of the trustee or anybody else.

55. Issue: Avoiding lien to secure third party's debt as fraudulent transfer

The correct answer is **B**. Section 548 empowers the trustee to avoid any voluntary or involuntary transfer of an interest of the debtor in property that was made or incurred on or within two years before the date of the filing of the petition, if the debtor received less than a reasonably equivalent value in exchange for such transfer or obligation and was insolvent on the date that such transfer was made or such obligation was incurred, or became insolvent as a result of such transfer or obligation. 11 U.S.C. §548(a)(1)(B). It is a type of constructive fraud without any requirement of actual fraud. State law typically allows a creditor to avoid such a transfer too, and the trustee can alternatively rely on such state law to avoid this constructively fraudulent transfer by the debtor. 11 U.S.C. §544(b). In this case, the lien was a transfer for which, on these facts, the debtor received no value whatever in exchange for the transfer, which means economic value to replace the value of the transfer.

56. Issue: Avoiding transfer for nominal consideration as fraudulent transfer

The correct answer is **D**. The explanation is the same as Question 55. Here, however, D did receive some value ($100) but not reasonably equivalent value, which is "ordinarily a meaning similar to fair market value." BFP v. Resolution Trust Corp., 511 U.S. 531, 544 (1994).

57. Issue: Avoiding unrecorded gift of vacation house even absent fraud

The correct answer is **D**. The transfer is constructively fraudulent. 11 U.S.C. §548(a)(1)(B). However, even if not, the trustee can avoid the transfer under section 544(a)(3) because, on these facts, the transfer was unrecorded. 11 U.S.C. §544(a)(3). See the analysis for Question 54.

58. Issue: Avoiding gift of vacation house as fraudulent transfer

The correct answer is **C**. The transfer cannot be avoided under section 544(a)(3) because the deed was recorded. The trustee can nevertheless avoid the transfer as constructively fraudulent **if the insolvency requirement is satisfied**. 11 U.S.C. §548(a)(1)(B). A trustee can avoid a transfer for actual fraud without regard to the debtor's insolvency before or after the transfer. Actual fraud can be proved by direct evidence or circumstantial evidence such as whether or not:

- the transfer or obligation was to an insider;
- the debtor retained possession or control of the property transferred after the transfer;
- the transfer or obligation was disclosed or concealed;
- before the transfer was made or obligation was incurred, the debtor had been sued or threatened with suit;
- the transfer was of substantially all the debtor's assets;
- the debtor absconded;
- the debtor removed or concealed assets;
- the value of the consideration received by the debtor was reasonably equivalent to the value of the asset transferred or the amount of the obligation incurred;
- the debtor was insolvent or became insolvent shortly after the transfer was made or the obligation was incurred;
- the transfer occurred shortly before or shortly after a substantial debt was incurred;
- the debtor transferred the essential assets of the business to a lien or who transferred the assets to an insider of the debtor;
- the debtor made the transfer or incurred the obligation without receiving a reasonably equivalent value in exchange for the transfer or obligation, and the debtor reasonably should have believed that the debtor would incur debts beyond the debtor's ability to pay as they became due; and
- the debtor transferred the assets in the course of legitimate estate or tax planning.

These circumstances are known as "badges of fraud." Gifting property is a badge of fraud, but in itself is not conclusive evidence of actual fraud.

59. Issue: Avoiding gift of exempt property as fraudulent transfer

The correct answer is **C**. Under state fraudulent transfer law, a transfer of property usually does not include a transfer of exempt property. So, transfers of exempt property cannot be avoided as fraudulent under state law. "[T]he [state-law] UFTA [Uniform Fraudulent Transfer Act] . . . applies to 'transfers,' which are defined as 'every mode, direct or indirect, . . . of disposing of or parting with an *asset* or an interest in an *asset* . . . .' Mich. Comp. Laws §566.31(l) (emphasis added). The definition of 'asset' in the UFTA expressly *excludes* '[p]roperty to the extent it is generally exempt under nonbankruptcy law' as well as '[a]n interest in property held in tenancy by the entireties to the extent it is not subject to process by a creditor holding a claim against only 1 tenant.' *Id.* at §566.31(b). Thus, the UFTA is consistent with the 'no harm, no foul' rule in that exempt property (including entireties property) cannot be subject to a claim of fraudulent transfer under the UFTA." Nino v. Moyer, 2009 WL 416295 ★7 (W.D. Mich. 2009). So, even though a trustee can assert state fraudulent transfer law to avoid transfers in a bankruptcy case, this state law will not allow avoiding a transfer of exempt property.

However, "[n]othing in [Bankruptcy Code] §548 indicates that a trustee must establish that a fraudulent conveyance actually harmed a creditor. Nor does §548 exclude from its scope transfers of exempt property. See 11 U.S.C. §548(a)(1)(A). Rather, section 548 states that '[t]he trustee may avoid *any* transfer of an interest of the debtor in property' if the transfer or obligation is entered into with the requisite intent. 11 U.S.C. §548(a)(1)(A) (emphasis added)." Tavenner v. Smoot, 257 F.3d 401, 407 (4th Cir. 2001). "[E]xempt property is fully subject to the fraudulent conveyance provisions of the Bankruptcy Code, and the fraudulent transfer of such property may be avoided by a trustee." In re Trujillo, 166 F.3d 1218 ★2 (9th Cir. 1998) (table); In re Alcon, 2010 WL 144408 ★3 (Bankr. N.D. Cal. 2010) (The law is clear that even the prepetition transfer of exempt property may qualify as a fraudulent transfer.).

60. Issue: Avoiding perfected security interest as fraudulent transfer

The correct answer is **E**. There is no constructive fraud because creating a lien to secure a valid, preexisting debt is not only reasonably equivalent value but is exact, dollar-for-dollar value. And, securing a debt is not in itself actually fraudulent.

61. Issue: Elements of a preference

The correct answer is **C**. The elements of an avoidable preference include transferring an interest of the debtor in property:

> (1) to or for the benefit of a creditor;
> (2) for or on account of an antecedent debt owed by the debtor before such transfer was made;
> (3) made while the debtor was insolvent;
> (4) made —
>> (A) on or within 90 days before the date of the filing of the petition; or
>> (B) between ninety days and one year before the date of the filing of the petition, if such creditor at the time of such transfer was an insider; and

(5) that enables such creditor to receive more than such creditor would receive if—

    (A) the case were a case under chapter 7 of this title;

    (B) the transfer had not been made; and

    (C) such creditor received payment of such debt to the extent provided by the provisions of this title.

11 U.S.C. §547(b). Lack of good faith is not required.

62. Issue: Exceptions to preference

The correct answer is **A**. Section 547(c) lists nine carefully limited, narrowly described preferences that are excepted from voidance under section 547(b) for a variety of policy reasons. Under subsection (c), the trustee may not avoid a transfer—

(1) to the extent that such transfer was—

    (A) intended by the debtor and the creditor to or for whose benefit such transfer was made to be a contemporaneous exchange for new value given to the debtor; and

    (B) in fact a substantially contemporaneous exchange;

(2) to the extent that such transfer was in payment of a debt incurred by the debtor in the ordinary course of business or financial affairs of the debtor and the transferee, and such transfer was—

    (A) made in the ordinary course of business or financial affairs of the debtor and the transferee; or

    (B) made according to ordinary business terms;

(3) that creates a security interest in property acquired by the debtor—

    (A) to the extent such security interest secures new value that was—

        (i) given at or after the signing of a security agreement that contains a description of such property as collateral;

        (ii) given by or on behalf of the secured party under such agreement;

        (iii) given to enable the debtor to acquire such property; and

        (iv) in fact used by the debtor to acquire such property; and

    (B) that is perfected on or before 30 days after the debtor receives possession of such property;

(4) to or for the benefit of a creditor, to the extent that, after such transfer, such creditor gave new value to or for the benefit of the debtor—

    (A) not secured by an otherwise unavoidable security interest; and

    (B) on account of which new value the debtor did not make an otherwise unavoidable transfer to or for the benefit of such creditor;

(5) that creates a perfected security interest in inventory or a receivable or the proceeds of either, except to the extent that the aggregate of all such transfers to the transferee caused a reduction, as of the date of the filing of the petition and to the prejudice of other creditors holding unsecured claims, of any amount by which the debt secured by such security interest exceeded the value of all security interests for such debt on the later of—

    (A)(i) with respect to a transfer to which subsection (b)(4)(A) of this section applies, 90 days before the date of the filing of the petition; or

(ii) with respect to a transfer to which subsection (b)(4)(B) of this section applies, one year before the date of the filing of the petition; or

(B) the date on which new value was first given under the security agreement creating such security interest;

(6) that is the fixing of a statutory lien that is not avoidable under section 545 of this title;

(7) to the extent such transfer was a bona fide payment of a debt for a domestic support obligation;

(8) if, in a case filed by an individual debtor whose debts are primarily consumer debts, the aggregate value of all property that constitutes or is affected by such transfer is less than $600; or

(9) if, in a case filed by a debtor whose debts are not primarily consumer debts, the aggregate value of all property that constitutes or is affected by such transfer is less than $5,850.

11 U.S.C. §547(c). There is no general, wide exception for preferences to a bona fide purchaser. And, that the transferee is not a bona fide purchaser is not a required element of preference under subsection (b).

63. Issue: When a transfer is deemed to have occurred

The correct answer is **E**. The lien was the transfer. The lien was created outside the preference period. However, for purposes of section 547(b), a transfer is not deemed to have occurred until the lien is perfected if perfection occurs more than 30 days after the lien is created. 11 U.S.C. §547(e). So, for purposes of this problem, the transfer of the lien to C was deemed to have occurred at the time of perfection, which was within a few weeks before bankruptcy and thus within the preference period. All of the other elements of preference are satisfied, 11 U.S.C. §547(b), and there is no applicable exception. *Id.* §547(c).

64. Issue: Paying secured debts and preferential effect

The correct answer is **B**. A preference requires that the transfer has a preferential effect, which means that the transfer enables the creditor to receive more than such creditor would receive if—

(A) the case were a case under chapter 7 of this title;

(B) the transfer had not been made; and

(C) such creditor received payment of such debt to the extent provided by the provisions of this title.

11 U.S.C. §547(a)(5). Paying a fully secured, fully perfected secured debt is generally not preferential because even if the payment had not been made, the secured debt would have been fully paid if the debtor had filed Chapter 7. Another way to look at the effect is that the payment was offset by the increase in the debtor's equity in the property. The estate is not diminished.

In this case, however, the debtor had no rights in the collateral. The property was owned by a third party, Ace. The debtor's estate was not compensated by the increase in Ace's equity in the property. The debtor's estate was diminished. Also, C is better off than C would have been had C not been paid and D had filed Chapter 7 in which C participated as an unsecured creditor in D's bankruptcy case.

Significantly, the transfer was to C (the initial transfer) and also benefitted Ace (the person for whose benefit the transfer was made). So, if all the other requirements of section 547(b) are met, there was a preference to C and an indirect preference to Ace. From whom the trustee can recover, however, is a different issue that is controlled in large part by section 550.

65. Issue: Indirect preference to an insider

The correct answer is **D**. The payment was made to Bank but outside the 90-day preference period. However, the payment reduced the suretyship liability of S and thereby benefitted her. So, there was an indirect preference to her. Because S is an insider, the reach-back period is one year, and the indirect preference to S is avoidable if all of the other requirements of section 547(b) are satisfied.

The language of section 550(a) allows the trustee, when a transfer is avoided, to recover from the initial transferee of such transfer or the entity for whose benefit such transfer was made, 11 U.S.C. §550(a)(1), which would include the Bank or S; but another provision limits the trustee to recovery only against S.

> If a transfer made between 90 days and one year before the filing of the petition —
> > (1) is avoided under section 547(b) of this title; and
> > (2) was made for the benefit of a creditor that at the time of such transfer was an insider;
> the trustee may not recover under subsection (a) from a transferee that is not an insider.

11 U.S.C. §550(c).

66. Issue: Indirect preference to a surety who is not an insider

The correct answer is **E**. In this problem, unlike Problem 65, S is not an insider. The 90-day reach-back period controls. The transfer was six months before bankruptcy and thus outside the 90-day period. There is no preference to anybody.

67. Issue: Affecting leases when the debtor is lessee

The correct answer is **D**. Section 365 generally allows the trustee to reject an unexpired lease or assume it and, after assumption, to assign the lease. 11 U.S.C. §365(a). The "lease" is composed of the rights and interests created (and limited) by the lease contract with the lessor, including the agreed term of the lease. If the lease has terminated by expiration or otherwise before or upon bankruptcy, there are no contractual lease rights (no unexpired lease) to affect under section 365. However, an ipso facto term in a lease, which ends the lease upon the lessee's bankruptcy, is ineffective. *Id.* §365(e).

68. Issue: Range of options respecting an unexpired lease or executory contract

The correct answer is **C**. The possibilities under section 365 are rejecting, assuming, or assuming and assigning the lease. Within the confines of the Bankruptcy Code, the trustee and lessor can renegotiate the lease, but the trustee cannot unilaterally, selectively modify the lease.

69. Issue: Legal standard for rejecting unexpired lease

The correct answer is **B**. "[A] bankruptcy court need engage in 'only a cursory review of a [debtor-in-possession]'s decision to reject the contract. Specifically, a bankruptcy court applies the business judgment rule to evaluate a [debtor-in-possession]'s rejection decision . . . .'

"We have never had the occasion to define the contours of the business judgment rule in the bankruptcy context. However, courts are no more equipped to make subjective business decisions for insolvent businesses than they are for solvent businesses, so we have no difficulty concluding that its formulation in corporate litigation is also appropriate here.

"Thus, in evaluating the rejection decision, the bankruptcy court should presume that the debtor-in-possession acted prudently, on an informed basis, in good faith, and in the honest belief that the action taken was in the best interests of the bankruptcy estate. It should approve the rejection of an executory contract [or unexpired lease] under §365(a) unless it finds that the debtor-in-possession's conclusion that rejection would be 'advantageous is so manifestly unreasonable that it could not be based on sound business judgment, but only on bad faith, or whim or caprice.' Such determinations, clearly, involve questions of fact, which we review for clear error." In re Pomona Valley Medical Group, Inc., 476 F.3d 665, 670 (9th Cir. 2007).

70. Issue: Limits on assuming and assigning unexpired lease

The correct answer is **A**. Generally speaking, "the trustee, subject to the court's approval, may assume or reject any executory contract or unexpired lease of the debtor." 11 U.S.C. §365(a). And, "notwithstanding a provision in an executory contract or unexpired lease of the debtor, or in applicable law, that prohibits, restricts, or conditions the assignment of such contract or lease, the trustee may assign such contract or lease" that is assumed. Id. §365(f). Agreements or laws against assignments in general are preempted. On the other hand, assignment by the trustee is not allowed if "applicable law excuses a party, other than the debtor, to such contract or lease from accepting performance from or rendering performance to the trustee or to an assignee of such contract or lease, whether or not such contract or lease prohibits or restricts assignment of rights or delegation of duties; and (ii) such party does not consent to such assumption or assignment. . . ." Id. §365(c)(1)(A). "The Court of Appeals for the Ninth Circuit has characterized the interaction between these two sections as, 'What §365(f)(1) appears to give, §365(c)(1)(A) seems to take away.' " Cinicola v. Scharffenberger, 248 F.3d 110, 121 n.11 (3d Cir. 2001) (citing In re Claremont Acquisition Corp., Inc., 113 F.3d 1029, 1032 (9th Cir. 1997)). "In order to determine whether a law is overridden by §365(f)(1) . . . , a court must ask *why* "applicable law" prohibits assignment. And only applicable anti-assignment law predicated on the rationale that the identity of the contracting party is material to the agreement resuscitated by §365(c)(1)." In re Sunterra Corp., 361 F.3d 257, 266-67 (4th Cir. 2004).

71. Issue: Effect of use clause on assignability

The correct answer is **D**. "Section 365 of the Bankruptcy Code generally permits the trustee to assume or reject any executory contract of the debtor. 11 U.S.C. §365(a). This allows 'the trustee to maximize the value of the debtor's estate by assuming executory contracts . . . that benefit the estate and rejecting those that do not.' Upon assuming an executory contract, the trustee is likewise authorized to assign the executory contract" if "*adequate assurance of future performance by the assignee* of such contract or lease is provided. . . ."

"The Bankruptcy Code expressly permits assignment of executory contracts even when contracts prohibit such assignment. 11 U.S.C. §365(f)(1). Section 365(f)(1) is not limited to explicit anti-assignment provisions. Provisions which are so restrictive that they constitute *de facto* anti-assignment provisions are also rendered unenforceable.

"[On the other hand,] [s]ection 365(f) requires a debtor to assume a contract subject to the benefits and burdens thereunder. 'The [debtor] . . . may not blow hot and cold. If he accepts the contract he accepts it *cum onere*. If he receives the benefits he must adopt the burdens. He cannot accept one and reject the other.' The *cum onere* rule 'prevents the [bankruptcy] estate from avoiding obligations that are an integral part of an assumed agreement.'" In re Fleming Companies, Inc., 499 F.3d 300, 304-08 (3d Cir. 2007).

With respect to the validity and enforceability of a use clause in bankruptcy, the issue is whether or not the use restriction operates as a de facto anti-assignment provision. And, "a fine line exists between reading a contractual term as a burdensome obligation [which bankruptcy nevertheless honors] or as a *de facto* restriction on assignment [which bankruptcy ignores]." *Id*. at 308.

Here's the bottom line: "Section 365 expresses a clear Congressional policy favoring assumption and assignment. Such a policy will insure that potential valuable assets will not be lost by a debtor who is reorganizing his affairs or liquidating assets for distribution to creditors. This policy parallels case law which disfavors forfeiture. See In re Huntington Limited, 654 F.2d 578, 584 n.7 (9th Cir. 1981); 2 Collier on Bankruptcy P 365.06 n.1 (15th ed. 1981). To prevent an assignment of an unexpired lease by demanding strict enforcement of a use clause, and thereby contradict clear Congressional policy, a landlord or lessor must show that actual and substantial detriment would be incurred by him if the deviation in use was permitted." Matter of U.L. Radio Corp., 19 B.R. 537, 544 (Bankr. S.D.N.Y. 1982).

72. Issue: Calculating landlord's claim for damages when lease rejected

The correct answer is **A**. Rejection of a lease gives the lessor a claim against the estate for damages for breach of the lease. 11 U.S.C. §365(g). These damages are in addition to accrued, unpaid rent and are calculated by whatever formula state law provides. In no event, however, can the landlord's claim exceed the amount bankruptcy law allows, which is "the rent reserved by such lease, without acceleration, for the greater of one year, or 15 percent, not to exceed three years, of the remaining term of such lease . . . plus any unpaid rent due under such lease, without acceleration, on the earlier of such dates. . . ." *Id.* §502(b)(6). In this problem, one year of rent, $50,000, is greater than 15 percent of the unaccrued rent for three years, which is $22,500. So, L's claim is somewhere around $50,000 plus unpaid, accrued rent of $25,000, which equals around $75,000.

73. Issue: Limits on assigning executory contracts

The correct answer is **B**. The general rule is that a trustee or debtor in possession can assume any executory contract, not just an unexpired lease. There are some restrictions, principally and explicitly:

- applicable law excuses a party, other than the debtor, to such contract or lease from accepting performance from or rendering performance to an entity other than the debtor or the debtor in possession, whether or not such contract or lease prohibits or restricts assignment of rights or delegation of duties; and (B) such party does not consent to such assumption or assignment; or
- *such contract is a contract to make a loan, or extend other debt financing or financial accommodations, to or for the benefit of the debtor, or to issue a security of the debtor;* or
- such lease is of nonresidential real property and has been terminated under applicable nonbankruptcy law prior to the order for relief.

11 U.S.C. §365(c) (emphasis added).

By the terms of the statute, these restrictions apply whenever a trustee wishes to "assume or assign any executory contract or unexpired lease. . . ." *Id.* A question is whether or not these restrictions apply when the trustee wishes only to assume without assigning. The answer is yes because §365(c) is drawn in the disjunctive and, by its plain language, prohibits Sunterra from "assuming *or* assigning," rather than from "assuming *and* assigning," the Agreement. And as a settled principle, "unless there is some ambiguity in the language of a statute, a court's analysis must end with the statute's plain language. . . ." In re Sunterra Corp., 361 F.3d 257 (4th Cir. 2004).

74. Issue: Assumption assignability of shopping center lease

The correct answer is **C**. Section 365(b)(3) contains special requirements for the debtor's assumption of a lease in a shopping center, mandating that the debtor demonstrate adequate assurance:

- of the source of rent and other consideration due under the lease;
- that any percentage rent due under the lease will not decline substantially;
- of compliance with all lease provisions, including those regarding radius, location, use and exclusivity, as well as compliance with such

provisions in other shopping center leases, financing agreements and master agreements relating to the shopping center; and
- of no disruption of tenant mix or balance in the shopping center.

11 U.S.C. §365(b)(3). So, the courts will generally enforce a carefully drafted shopping center lease provision that restricts a tenant's use of the property in order to protect the tenant mix throughout the center. However, if such a provision is so restrictive that it essentially acts as an additional anti-assignment clause, a bankruptcy court might invalidate that provision entirely.

Assignment under section 365(f)(2) requires assumption of the lease pursuant to section 365(a) and a showing of adequate assurance of future performance under the lease by the proposed assignee, even if there have been no defaults under the lease. Pursuant to section 365(l), the landlord may require a deposit or other security from the assignee comparable to what the landlord would have required upon the initial leasing to a similar tenant. The assignment of a lease, like the assumption of a lease, must be approved by bankruptcy court order. Just as the assumption of a shopping center lease is subject to special lessor-friendly provisions discussed above, the assignment of a shopping center lease is subject to additional requirements pursuant to section 365(b)(3) of the Bankruptcy Code, including a showing of adequate assurance that the financial condition and operating performance of the assignee (and its guarantors, if any) is similar to the financial condition and operating performance of the debtor (and its guarantors, if any) as of the time the debtor became the lessee under the lease.

75. Issue: Liability for post-assignment breaches of lease

The correct answer is **A**. The assignment of a real property lease pursuant to section 365(f) relieves the bankruptcy estate of all claims resulting from a subsequent breach of the lease. 11 U.S.C. §365(k) ("Assignment by the trustee to an entity of a contract or lease assumed under this section relieves the trustee and the estate from any liability for any breach of such contract or lease occurring after such assignment.").

76. Issue: Dismissing Chapter 7 case for reasons of income

The correct answer is **C**. "After notice and a hearing, the court, on its own motion or on a motion by the United States trustee, trustee (or bankruptcy administrator, if any), or any party in interest, may dismiss a case filed by an individual debtor under this chapter whose debts are primarily consumer debts, or, with the debtor's consent, convert such a case to a case under chapter 11 or 13 of this title, if it finds that the granting of relief would be an *abuse* of the provisions of this chapter." 11 U.S.C. §707(b)(1). "In considering . . . whether the granting of relief would be an abuse of the provisions of this chapter, the court shall presume abuse exists if the debtor's *current monthly income reduced by*" *certain allowed expenses* is equal to or greater than a statutory amount. *Id.* §707(b)(2)(A) (emphasis added). In Chapter 13 terms, this difference is called disposable income.

77. Issue: Reason court cannot dismiss a Chapter 7 case

The correct answer is **D**. All of these reasons justify dismissal, 11 U.S.C. §§707(a), (b)(2) & (3), except solvency of the debtor (at least solvency alone and by itself). Insolvency is not required to file bankruptcy. On the other hand, the debtor's solvency is a factor that the courts may consider in dismissing a case under the totality of circumstances standard or because the debtor filed the case in bad faith. 11 U.S.C. §707(b)(3). Similarly, increasing secured debt to avoid conversion to Chapter 13 is a factor that argues for dismissing a Chapter 7 case. (Remember: secured debt is among the deductions from current monthly income in calculating whether or not the debtor has sufficient disposable income to fund a Chapter 13 plan.) See In re Hageney, 422 B.R. 254 (Bankr. E.D. Wash. 2009); In re Oot, 368 B.R. 662 (Bankr. N.D. Ohio 2007); Ned W. Waxman & Justin H. Rucki, *Chapter 7 Bankruptcy Abuse: Means Testing Is Presumptive, but Totality Is Determinative*, 45 Hous. L. Rev. 901, 922-24 (2008); but see In re Jensen, 407 B.R. 378, 387-88 (Bankr. C.D. Cal. 2009) (Dismissing cases as abusive based on the debtor's high secured debt payments ignores that the Bankruptcy Code seeks to further policies other than making unsecured creditors whole, especially in situations where unsecured creditors can be made whole only at the expense of secured creditors. Chief among these policies is advancing the availability of secured credit. Also, refusing to permit debtors to retain secured-debt property reallocates the balance of risk between secured and unsecured creditors and is a zero-sum game.).

78. Issue: Redeeming collateral

The correct answer is **C**. "An *individual* debtor may, whether or not the debtor has waived the right to redeem under this section, redeem *tangible personal property* intended primarily for *personal, family, or household use*, from a lien securing a dischargeable *consumer debt*, if such property is *exempted* under section 522 of this title or has been abandoned under section 554 of this title, by paying the holder of such lien the amount of the allowed secured claim of such holder that is secured by such lien in full at the time of redemption." 11 U.S.C. §722 (emphasis added).

79. Issue: Trustee's duties in a Chapter 7 case

The correct answer is **D**. The trustee's several duties are detailed in section 704, but the principal duty is to "collect and reduce to money the property of the estate for which such trustee serves, and close such estate as expeditiously as is compatible with the best interests of parties in interest. . . ." 11 U.S.C. §704(a)(1). The other duties include:

- be accountable for all property received;
- ensure that the debtor shall perform his intention as specified in section 521(2)(B)of this title;
- investigate the financial affairs of the debtor;
- if a purpose would be served, examine proofs of claims and object to the allowance of any claim that is improper;

- if advisable, oppose the discharge of the debtor;
- unless the court orders otherwise, furnish such information concerning the estate and the estate's administration as is requested by a party in interest;
- if the business of the debtor is authorized to be operated, file with the court, with the United States trustee, and with any governmental unit charged with responsibility for collection or determination of any tax arising out of such operation, periodic reports and summaries of the operation of such business, including a statement of receipts and disbursements, and such other information as the United States trustee or the court requires;
- make a final report and file a final account of the administration of the estate with the court and with the United States trustee.

Id. §704(a)(2)–(9).

80. Issue: Distribution of property of the estate

The correct answer is **C**. Property of the estate is generally distributed in this order:

- claims of the kind specified in, and in the order specified in, section 507 of this title, which include:
  — first, allowed unsecured claims for domestic support obligations
  — second, administrative expenses, and
  — then certain other claims in the order listed in section 507(a).
- any allowed unsecured claim not entitled to priority under section 507 (a/k/a general, unsecured claims);
- any allowed claim, whether secured or unsecured, for any fine, penalty, or forfeiture, or for multiple, exemplary, or punitive damages, arising before the earlier of the order for relief or the appointment of a trustee, to the extent that such fine, penalty, forfeiture, or damages are not compensation for actual pecuniary loss suffered by the holder of such claim;
- interest at the legal rate from the date of the filing of the petition, on certain claims; and finally the balance
- to the debtor.

11 U.S.C. §726(a).

81. Issue: General partnership bankruptcy

The correct answer is **E**. "If there is a deficiency of property of the estate to pay in full all claims which are allowed in a case under this chapter concerning a partnership and with respect to which a general partner of the partnership is personally liable, the trustee shall have a claim against such general partner to the extent that under applicable nonbankruptcy law such general partner is personally liable for such deficiency." 11 U.S.C. §723(a). Under applicable, nonbankruptcy, general partnership law, all partners are jointly and severally liable for all debts and obligations of the partnership.

82. Issue: Automatic stay in Chapter 13 cases

The correct answer is **B**. The automatic stay of section 362 stops all collection efforts against the debtor or the debtor's property and property of the bankruptcy. It does not protect non-debtor third parties, not even a person who is liable with the debtor as a surety on a debt. In a Chapter 13 case, however, "a creditor may not act, or commence or continue any civil action, to collect all or any part of a consumer debt of the debtor from any individual that is liable on such debt with the debtor, or that secured such debt. . . ." 11 U.S.C. §1301(a).

83. Issue: Possession of property in a Chapter 13 case

The correct answer is **E**. The object of a Chapter 7 case is to liquidate the property of the estate and distribute the proceeds to creditors. Obviously, the debtor loses such property except exempt property. The objects of Chapter 13 are rehabilitation and paying creditors from future income. When the case is filed, the debtor's interest in property passes to the bankruptcy estate; but she nevertheless keeps the property, 11 U.S.C. §1306(b), which naturally aids her in generating income to pay creditors. The same is true in Chapter 11 cases. *Id.* §1115(b).

84. Issue: Who can file Chapter 13 plan

The correct answer is **B**. "The debtor shall file a plan," 11 U.S.C. §1321, and nobody else. "In fact, the Chapter 13 debtor has the exclusive right to file a plan. While the Chapter 13 trustee may advise the debtor on the preparation and performance under the plan, there is no authority for either a Chapter 13 trustee or a creditor under any circumstances to file a plan." In re Euler, 251 B.R. 740, 745 (Bankr. M.D. Fla. 2000).

The rule is different in Chapter 11. The debtor in possession has the exclusive right to file a plan for 120 days after the date of the order for relief under this chapter. 11 U.S.C. §1121(b). Other participants in the bankruptcy — any party in interest, a creditors' committee, an equity security holders' committee, a creditor, an equity security holder, or any indenture trustee — may file a plan if the debtor has not filed a plan before 120 days after the date of the order for relief under this chapter; or the debtor has not filed a plan that has been accepted, before 180 days after the date of the order for relief under this chapter, by each class of claims or interests that is impaired under the plan. *Id.* §1121(c).

85. Issue: Length of "applicable commitment period"

The correct answer is **D**. Typically, the period is five years if the current monthly income of the debtor and the debtor's spouse combined is equal to or greater than the median family income for a household of the same size. 11 U.S.C. §1322(d)(1). If the income is less than the median, the period is typically three years. *Id.* §1322(d)(2).

86. Issue: Debts fully paid through Chapter 13 plan

The correct answer is **E**. By the express terms of Chapter 13, the only debts that must be paid in full, though in deferred cash payments, are "all claims entitled to priority under section 507 of this title, unless the holder of a particular claim agrees to a different treatment of such claim. . . ." 11 U.S.C. §1322(a)(12). The number one priority claim under section 507 is any "allowed unsecured claims for domestic support obligations." *Id.* §507(a)(1).

The plan must also provide for paying fully a secured "claim" but not the secured debt or obligation. Any part of the debt that exceeds the value of the collateral is an unsecured claim, which typically will not be paid in full.

87. Issue: Interest rate on installment payments of secured claim

The correct answer is **C**. Section 1325 provides that unless the holder of a secured claim has accepted the plan, the plan must provide for paying the holder the present value of the secured claim. 11 U.S.C. §1325(a)(5). When a plan that provides for paying the claim in "installment payments over a period of years rather than a single payment . . . the amount of each installment must be calibrated to ensure that, over time, the creditor receives disbursements whose total present value equals or exceeds that of the allowed claim." Till v. SCS Credit Corp., 541 U.S. 465, 469 (2004). So, in effect, an installment plan must include interest. How is the interest rate calculated?

The Supreme Court decided this issue in the *Till* case, adopting a "prime-plus" formula approach:

> Taking its cue from ordinary lending practices, the approach begins by looking to the national prime rate, reported daily in the press, which reflects the financial market's estimate of the amount a commercial bank should charge a creditworthy commercial borrower to compensate for the opportunity costs of the loan, the risk of inflation, and the relatively slight risk of default. Because bankrupt debtors typically pose a greater risk of nonpayment than solvent commercial borrowers, the approach then requires a bankruptcy court to adjust the prime rate accordingly. The appropriate size of that risk adjustment depends, of course, on such factors as the circumstances of the estate, the nature of the security, and the duration and feasibility of the reorganization plan. The court must therefore hold a hearing at which the debtor and any creditors may present evidence about the appropriate risk adjustment. Some of this evidence will be included in the debtor's bankruptcy filings, however, so the debtor and creditors may not incur significant additional expense. Moreover, starting from a concededly low estimate and adjusting upward places the evidentiary burden squarely on the creditors, who are likely to have readier access to any information absent from the debtor's filing (such as evidence about the "liquidity of the collateral market," post, at 1973 (SCALIA, J., dissenting)). Finally, many of the factors relevant to the adjustment fall squarely within the bankruptcy court's area of expertise.
>
> Thus, . . . the formula approach entails a straightforward, familiar, and objective inquiry, and minimizes the need for potentially costly additional evidentiary proceedings. Moreover, the resulting "prime-plus" rate of interest depends only on the state of financial markets, the circumstances of the bankruptcy estate, and the characteristics of the loan, not on the creditor's circumstances or its prior interactions with the debtor. For these

reasons, the prime-plus or formula rate best comports with the purposes of the Bankruptcy Code.

Id. at 478-80.

The courts still are not certain that *Till* will control the determination of the appropriate interest rate in bankruptcy cases other than cases under Chapter 13. The Sixth Circuit thinks *Till* is limited.

> *Till*, however, was a Chapter 13 bankruptcy case. So even though the plurality is clear that the formula approach is the preferable method for Chapter 13 cases, the opinion is less clear about cases in the Chapter 11 context. On the one hand, the plurality noted that "the Bankruptcy Code includes numerous provisions that, like the [Chapter 13] cram down provision, require a court to 'discoun[t] . . . [a] stream of deferred payments back to the[ir] present dollar value' to ensure that a creditor receives at least the value of its claim." It further commented that "[w]e think it likely that Congress intended bankruptcy judges and trustees to follow essentially the same approach when choosing an appropriate interest rate under any of these provisions." Some commentators have taken this to mean that *Till*'s analysis of Chapter 13 cramdown interest rates might be applicable to Chapter 11 cramdowns as well.
>
> In a footnote, however, the plurality noted that "there is no readily apparent Chapter 13 'cram down market rate of interest.'" This follows from the fact that "[b]ecause every cram down loan is imposed by a court over the objection of the secured creditor, there is no free market of willing cram down lenders." But
>
>> [i]nterestingly, the same is not true in the Chapter 11 context, as numerous lenders advertise financing for Chapter 11 debtors in possession. Thus, when picking a cram down rate in a Chapter 11 case, it might make sense to ask what rate an efficient market would produce. In the Chapter 13 context, by contrast, the absence of any such market obligates courts to look to first principles and ask only what rate will fairly compensate a creditor for its exposure.
>
> This footnote suggests that a formula approach like the one adopted by the plurality is not required in the Chapter 11 context.
>
> At least one court that has examined cramdown interest rates post-*Till* has concluded that *Till* does not apply in a Chapter 11 context. . . . Several outside commentators, however, have argued that *Till*'s formula approach should apply to Chapter 11 cases as well as to Chapter 13 cases, noting that the two are not all that dissimilar. And at least one court has concluded that Till does apply in a Chapter 11 context.
>
> Taking all of this into account, we decline to blindly adopt *Till*'s endorsement of the formula approach for Chapter 13 cases in the Chapter 11 context. Rather, we opt to take our cue from Footnote 14 of the opinion, which offered the guiding principle that "when picking a cram down rate in a Chapter 11 case, it might make sense to ask what rate an efficient market would produce." This means that the market rate should be applied in Chapter 11 cases where there exists an efficient market. But

where no efficient market exists for a Chapter 11 debtor, then the bank-ruptcy court should employ the formula approach endorsed by the *Till* plurality. This nuanced approach should obviate the concern of commen-tators who argue that, even in the Chapter 11 context, there are instances where no efficient market exists.

In re American Homepatient, Inc., 420 F.3d 559, 566-67 (6th Cir. 2005).

88. Issue: Valuing collateral in Chapter 13 case

The correct answer is **D**. "If the debtor is an individual in a case under chapter 7 or 13, such value with respect to personal property securing an allowed claim shall be determined based on the *replacement value of such property as of the date of the filing of the petition* without deduction for costs of sale or marketing. With respect to property acquired for personal, family, or household purposes, replacement value shall mean the price a retail merchant would charge for property of that kind considering the age and condition of the property at the time value is determined." 11 U.S.C. §506(a)(2) (emphasis added).

89. Issue: Determining amount of secured claim in Chapter 13 case

The correct answer is **C**. The value of a secured claim for cramming down a Chapter 13 plan is usually limited by the value of the collateral. 11 U.S.C. §1325(a)(5). The value is not a higher amount equal to the debt. And, in most cases, as dictated by section 506, the value of the collateral in a Chapter 13 case is the replacement value of such property as of the date of the filing of the petition. 11 U.S.C. §506(a)(2). However, if the creditor has a claim (1) incurred within 910 days of the Chapter 13, (2) secured by a purchase money security interest in a motor vehicle, (3) acquired for the personal use of the debtor, section 506 does not apply. Rather, then section 506 does not apply to the claim. The reason is this paragraph "hanging" on or "dangling" from section 1325:

> [S]ection 506 shall not apply to a claim described in that paragraph if the creditor has a purchase money security interest securing the debt that is the subject of the claim, the debt was incurred within the 910-day preceding the date of the filing of the petition, and the collateral for that debt consists of a motor vehicle (as defined in section 30102 of title 49) acquired for the personal use of the debtor, or if collateral for that debt consists of any other thing of value, if the debt was incurred during the 1-year period preceding that filing.

11 U.S.C. §1325(a). Rather, when this dangling paragraph applies, the amount of the secured claim is the amount of the debt even if the value of the collateral is less.

90. Issue: Creditor approval of Chapter 13 plan

The correct answer is **A**. Confirmation of a plan in Chapter 11 requires certain creditor approval. 11 U.S.C. §§1129(a); 1126. Confirmation of a plan in Chapter 13 may be easier if creditors approve, but their approval is not necessary if the plan satisfies the requirements of confirmation.

91. Issue: Providing for unsecured creditors in Chapter 13 plan

The correct answer is **C**. "If the trustee or the holder of an allowed unsecured claim objects to the confirmation of the plan, then the court may not approve the plan unless, as of the effective date of the plan — the plan provides that all of the debtor's *projected disposable income to be received in the applicable commitment period* beginning on the date that the first payment is due under the plan will be applied to make payments to unsecured creditors under the plan." 11 U.S.C. §1125(b)(1)(B) (emphasis added).

92. Issue: Calculating disposable income

The correct answer is **E**. If a creditor or the trustee objects to the debtor's plan, "then the court may not approve the plan unless . . . the plan provides that all of the debtor's projected disposable income to be received in the applicable commitment period . . . will be applied to make payments to unsecured creditors under the plan." 11 U.S.C. §1125(b)(1)(B). The problem is the meaning of "projected disposable income." The Supreme Court has stated the issue as: "Whether, in calculating the debtor's 'projected disposable income' during the plan period, the bankruptcy court may consider evidence suggesting that the debtor's income or expenses during that period are likely to be different from her income or expenses during the pre-filing period." Hamilton v. Lanning, 130 S. Ct. 487 (2009), granting cert., In re Lanning, 545 F.3d 1269 (10th Cir. 2008).

The Code defines "disposable income" to mean "current monthly income received by the debtor . . . less amounts reasonably necessary to be expended . . ." 11 U.S.C. §1325(b)(1)-(2). The term "current monthly income" in section 1325(b)(2) is defined as the average monthly income of the debtor from all sources over the six-month period preceding the filing of the petition. 11 U.S.C. §101(10A)(A).

A few courts have held that the plain meaning of section 1325(b) dictates a "mechanical," "historical," backward-looking approach whereby "projected disposable income" is calculated simply by projecting the average prepetition "disposable income," as defined in subsection (b)(2), over "the applicable commitment period." See In re Kagenveama, 541 F.3d 868, 872 (9th Cir. 2008). The Ninth Circuit explained:

> The substitution of any data not covered by the §1325(b)(2) definition in the "projected disposable income" calculation would render as surplusage the definition of "disposable income" found in §1325(b)(2). There can be no reason for §1325(b)(2) to exist other than to define the term "disposable income" as used in §1325(b)(1)(B). "If 'disposable income' is not linked to 'projected disposable income' then it is just a floating definition with no apparent purpose."

Id. at 872-73.

By contrast, the majority of courts to have addressed the issue have held that "projected disposable income" should not be mechanically based on the historical "disposable income" calculation. Some courts adopting this "forward-looking" approach conclude that "projected disposable income" bears little or no relationship to the "disposable income" calculation, which is based on prepetition income and expenses. Other courts treat the mechanically determined "disposable income" as the presumptively correct calculation of "projected disposable income" but permit this presumption to be rebutted with evidence of a change in the debtor's circumstances that renders the historical figure an inaccurate predictor of disposable income during the pendency of the plan. See In re Lasowski, 575 F.3d 815 (8th Cir. 2009); In re Turner, 574 F.3d 349 (7th Cir. 2009); In the Matter of Nowlin, 576 F.3d 258 (5th Cir. 2009); In re Lanning, 545 F.3d 1269 (10th Cir. 2008), cert. granted, Hamilton v. Lanning, 130 S. Ct. 487 (2009).

93. Issue: Appointing a trustee in Chapter 11 cases

The correct answer is **C**. Typically and almost always, there is no Chapter 11 trustee. The debtor in possession runs the show and exercises the trustee's powers. Appointing a trustee in place of the debtor in possession is a possibility:

> At any time after the commencement of the case but before confirmation of a plan, on request of a party in interest or the United States trustee, and after notice and a hearing, the court shall order the appointment of a trustee—
>
>   (1) for cause, including fraud, dishonesty, incompetence, or gross mismanagement of the affairs of the debtor by current management, either before or after the commencement of the case, or similar cause, but not including the number of holders of securities of the debtor or the amount of assets or liabilities of the debtor;
>
>   (2) if such appointment is in the interests of creditors, any equity security holders, and other interests of the estate, without regard to the number of holders of securities of the debtor or the amount of assets or liabilities of the debtor; or
>
>   (3) if grounds exist to convert or dismiss the case . . . , but the court determines that the appointment of a trustee or an examiner is in the best interests of creditors and the estate.

11 U.S.C. §1104(a).

94. Issue: "Period of exclusivity" in a Chapter 11 case

The correct answer is **C**. Usually, only the debtor may file a plan until after 120 days after the date of the order for relief under this chapter. Thereafter, any party in interest, including the debtor, the trustee, a creditors' committee, an equity security holders' committee, a creditor, an equity security holder, or any indenture trustee, may file a plan. 11 U.S.C. §1121(a)-(b). The 120 days during which only the debtor can file a plan is called the "period of exclusivity."

95. Issue: Use of cash collateral

The correct answer is **A**. In the typical case, the debtor in possession may enter into transactions, including the sale or lease of property of the estate, in the ordinary course of business, without notice or a hearing, and may use property of the estate in the ordinary course of business without notice or a hearing. 11 U.S.C. §363(c)(1). However, the debtor in possession "may not use, sell, or lease cash collateral under paragraph (1) of this subsection unless — (A) each entity that has an interest in such cash collateral consents; or (B) the court, after notice and a hearing, authorizes such use, sale, or lease in accordance with the provisions of this section," *id.* 363(c)(2), and "this section" requires adequately protecting the interest of the secured creditor. *Id.* §363(e). Basically, the debtor in possession cannot use cash collateral without the consent of the secured creditor or without compensating the secured creditor for any loss in the value of the creditor's interest in the collateral.

96. Issue: Debtor in possession obtaining credit or incurring debt

The correct answer is **A**. The debtor in possession, acting alone, may obtain unsecured credit and incur unsecured debt in the ordinary course of business. 11 U.S.C. §364(a). Obtaining unsecured credit otherwise or obtaining secured credit generally requires court authorization after notice and a hearing.

97. Issue: Meaning of a class of claims "accepting" a plan

The correct answer is **C**. A class of claims has accepted a plan if such plan has been accepted by creditors that hold at least two-thirds in amount and more than one-half in number of the allowed claims of such class held by creditors, other than any entity designated under subsection (e) of this section, that have accepted or rejected such plan.

98. Issue: Holders of claims who must accept plan for confirmation

The correct answer is **B**. The court shall confirm a plan only if "[w]ith respect to each class of claims or interests — (A) such class has accepted the plan; or (B) such class is not impaired under the plan." 11 U.S.C. §1129(a)(8). Otherwise, the plan must be "crammed down," which means the plan must comply with the further requirements of section 1129(b). With respect to creditor acceptance, cram down requires only that at least one class of claims that is impaired under the plan has accepted the plan. *Id.* §§1129(b)(1); 1129(a)(10), compliance with which is not excused when a plan is crammed down.

99. Issue: Providing for unsecured claims when a Chapter 11 plan is "crammed down"

The correct answer is **B**. For a cram down, the plan must be "fair and equitable" with respect to secured and unsecured claims. With respect to unsecured claims, fair and equitable means:

> (i) the plan provides that each holder of a claim of such class receive or retain on account of such claim property of a value, as of the effective date of the plan, equal to the allowed amount of such claim; *or*
> (ii) the holder of any claim or interest that is junior to the claims of such class will not receive or retain under the plan on account of such junior claim or interest any property. . . .

11 U.S.C. §1129(b)(2)(B), which is known as the "absolute priority" rule. So, if equity holders retain their interests, all unsecured claims must be paid in full. If not, the plan must give nothing to equity holders and, basically, give ownership of the company to unsecured creditors.

100. Issue: "New value" exception to the "absolute priority rule"

The correct answer is **B**. The "absolute priority rule" requires that a Chapter 11 plan provide for paying unsecured claims in full if the plan provides anything for existing equity holders "on account of" their ownership of the debtor. The "new value exception" is a possible exception to the absolute priority rule. The exception allows holders of equity interests to retain property under the plan and provides for them giving "new value" to the debtor. In broad effect, they buy whatever interest they retain using their own fresh funds. The new value exception is only a "possible" exception because the Supreme Court has approved of the exception only under the most narrow, restrictive circumstances and only in dictum. See Bank of America Nat. Trust and Sav. Ass'n. v. 203 North LaSalle St. Partnership, 526 U.S. 434 (1999). Minimally, the "new value" exception prohibits vesting equity in the reorganized business in the debtor's existing equity holders "without extending an opportunity to anyone else either to compete for that equity or to propose a competing reorganization plan." And it is not sufficient that the plan calls for the court to determine the market value of the interest the equity holders are to retain but give them the exclusive right to acquire the interest for such value. There must be a true "market test" that requires "an opportunity to offer competing plans or would be satisfied by a right to bid for the same interest sought by old equity. . . . [A]ssuming [there is] a new value corollary, plans providing junior interest holders with exclusive opportunities free from competition and without benefit of market valuation" do not satisfy it. *Id.* at 458.